ONE DYKE'S THEATER

SELECTED PLAYS, 1975-2014

BY TERRY BAUM

SLIGHTLY WORLD-RENOWNED LESBIAN PLAYWRIGHT

One Dyke's Theater: Selected Plays, 1975-2014
by Terry Baum

Copyright © 2019
All rights reserved

Published by EXIT PRESS

Book Cover and Play Collages by Ingalls Design
Front Cover Photo by Liz Payne from *Waiting for the Podiatrist* (2003)
Book design by Richard Livingston

CAUTION: Professionals and amateurs are hereby warned that all plays represented in this book are subject to a royalty. They are fully protected under the copyright laws of the United States of America, and of all countries covered by the International Copyright Union (including the Dominion of Canada and the rest of the British Commonwealth), and of all countries with which the United States has reciprocal copyright relations. All rights, including professional, amateur, motion picture, recitation, lecturing, public reading, radio broadcasting, television, and the rights of translation into foreign languages, are strictly reserved.

All inquiries concerning rights for readings, productions, etc., should be addressed to:
    TERRY BAUM
    LILITH THEATER San Francisco
    terryjoanbaum@gmail.com
    547 Douglass Street
    San Francisco, CA 94114
    www.liliththeatersanfrancisco.com
    www.terrybaum.blogspot.com

ISBN: 978-1-941704-15-8

EXIT PRESS
156 Eddy Street
San Francisco, CA 94102-2708
mail@theexit.org

First Edition: 2019

Dedicated to Carolyn Myers

My crony, my editor, my collaborator, my co-writer, my director, my co-star, my improvisation partner, my upstairs neighbor, my best friend, my soul sister.

You are the great blessing of my life. What a joyful collaboration we have shared for 47 years.

Contents

PREFACE	I
ACKNOWLEDGEMENTS	V
INTRODUCTION	IX
DOS LESBOS	3
TWO MONOLOGUES	53
BISEXUAL CELIBATE—OR NOT	54
COMING-OUT STORY	60
IMMEDIATE FAMILY	69
ONE FOOL	91
TWO FOOLS	117
WAITING FOR THE PODIATRIST	167
BUBBIE & HER BUTCH	205
BRIDE OF LESBOSTEIN	223
HICK: A LOVE STORY	259
PLAYWRIGHT BIOGRAPHIES	303
COLLAGE DESIGN & PHOTO CREDITS	305

PREFACE

We all start out in theater. In every culture, children play games where they assume different roles: mother, cowgirl, bandit, baby. We pretend. I myself spent most of my childhood as a dog. I wasn't allowed to have one because of allergies. I will always be grateful to my mother for putting a bowl of water on the floor for my Doggie Self to lap up. At one point, a neighbor heard me barking and asked Mom if we'd gotten a puppy. I was so proud.

At a certain point, most of us stop pretending. But some of us never do. We love acting out stories, standing up in front of a crowd, collaboration. We are theater people.

In the first grade, my class was scheduled to perform the song *How Much Is That Doggie in the Window?* at the PTA extravaganza. If anyone vibrated with the desperate longing of those lyrics, it was me! Yet, the class voted for Marybeth, the cutest and most popular girl, to sing my song. I was devastated. The teacher consigned me to drag a gigantic paper mache goldfish across the stage on a leash as Marybeth sang that immortal lyric, "You can't take a goldfish for a walk."

And then it happened—the miracle that you've seen in so many Busby Berkeley movies: On the Big Night, five minutes before the first grade was scheduled to sing its song, Marybeth got stage fright, threw up and refused to go on! In a total panic, the teacher asked if any other students knew the Doggie Song by heart. Would you believe I was the only one? Believe. So, while Marybeth dragged that lousy goldfish for a walk, I belted out my passion for a puppy. My fate was sealed.

In junior high, I started writing plays. I was the go-to person when anyone needed a skit for an assembly. My crowning achievement was a full-length parody musical for the Journalism class—*My Fair Reporter*. Sadly, the manuscript has been lost. I can only remember the titles of two songs: "I Could Have Typed All Night" and "On the Beat Where I Slave."

When I reached high school, I realized that it was terribly embarrassing for a GIRL to write plays, so I stopped. Still committed to theater, I took the acting class. My greatest moment was playing Maurya, the mother in J.M. Synge's *Riders to the Sea*. There was no doubt in my mind that I captured an old Irish woman's grief at losing all her children to the voracious sea where they fished for a living. The fact that I was 16 and living a middle-class life in Los Angeles was no obstacle to my art. After all, I myself had lost a hamster. I understood. I would become an actress!

In college, I majored in Theater. But there was one niggling little problem: I almost never got cast in anything. My future as an actress seemed bleak. Then, in my senior year, I directed a one-act play. For the first time in my life, I got to tell people what to do! I loved being the boss, and I was damn good at it. I had found my place in theater, in life, in the world. I would not wait anxiously and endlessly to be chosen for a part. I would become a director and do the choosing!

I moved to New York City after graduation. My first off-off-Broadway directing project was for Circle Repertory Theater. Rehearsals were tense. The actors and I were not in sync. A week before opening, one actress showed up TWO hours late for rehearsal instead of her habitual one hour. When I blew up, she announced it was all my fault because—she had just discovered in therapy—I reminded her of her mother!

The rest of the cast rushed to comfort her. How dare I remind anyone of their mother?! They announced their intention to quit en masse. What could I do?

I found deep within myself my "The Show Must Go On!" speech. I have no memory of what I said. But I remember being brilliant, passionate.

"The show must go on!" But why? What could be LESS urgent than a bunch of people pretending to be someone else, acting out a story for a larger bunch of people? And yet, there is some primal need for this ancient form of storytelling that demands that, once the date is set, it must happen. "The show must go on!" has become part of our common language, a way to express stalwart commitment to any event. But it's ABOUT the theater.

And my show did go on at Circle Rep. I felt confirmed in my mission as a director.

Then, in 1971, I became a feminist. My understanding of the world, and myself in it, was transformed. But when I looked at my work in theater…

Oh my gosh! Every play I had directed or acted in was sexist! In fact, almost the entire dramatic canon was sexist! What's a newly-enlightened feminist director to do?!?

She's got to stop being just an interpreter and start a theater that creates its own plays. So I did. But I still wasn't a playwright. I was the artistic director of the collective, the producer. More often than not, the ideas were mine. But others wrote the scenes. Sometimes we would tape an improvisation, building a scene from the transcription.

Then came a moment when nobody understood my idea well

enough to write it or improvise it. Lilith Theater was creating/rehearsing *Moonlighting*, a play about women and work. (Isn't it strange now to think that was a startling concept in 1976?) My idea: A factory worker terrified of anything mechanical is forced by her co-workers to fix a broken toilet—the toilet being made up of three actresses manifesting all her fears. It was a short scene, a simple scene. It was the first scene I had written since *My Fair Reporter* in the ninth grade.

Shortly after that, I slept with a woman for the first time and came out as a lesbian. If there had been very little in theater that reflected my life as a woman, there was really NOTHING that reflected my life as a lesbian. At long last, I began to write the plays collected in this anthology.

To write a play is to create a world. It's like being God. That's what I felt when, for the first time, I saw a play of mine produced by others. It was *Dos Lesbos* in Portland in 1984. I know intimately how much work is involved in putting on a play. I was awed that my words had inspired other people to do that work.

Playwriting is understood to be the most difficult kind of writing, with the most restrictions. This writing, often done alone in a room, must eventually translate into something that is performed by and for actual people gathered together, within a strictly limited amount of time. I love the challenge of it. I am forever rewriting, much to the consternation of directors and actors. I know I will never perfect a play, but the pursuit of perfection is deeply satisfying. It's a great destiny to be a playwright.

ACKNOWLEDGEMENTS

It is impossible to acknowledge everyone who has supported me in creating 40 years of work. I am collaborative by nature, requiring the enthusiasm and criticism of others in order to face the blank page. Weekly meetings with other writers have been essential. Most recently, Paula Barish has lent her keen intellect and passion for theater to this project. Bobbi Ausubel, Calla Felicity and LauRose Felicity gave me writerly love for years and continue to do so. Currently, Carolyn and I are members of The Gang of Six, pioneers of women's theater and their partners, which has been a great source of support and long dinner parties. Along with Carolyn, Bobbi, and me, the Gang members are Martha Boesing (founder of At the Foot of the Mountain Theater in Minneapolis), Sandy Boucher, and Cecelia Wambach.

    The collaboration I've had with lyricist David Hyman and composer Scrumbly Koldewyn has been particularly delicious. I treasure the afternoons we spent around Scrumbly's piano, tossing ideas and words and melodies back and forth. David and I started working together in 1974. Whenever I have an idea for a song, I have the luxury of handing that idea to David. With his unfailing wit and voluminous vocabulary, he always finds the words. Gay men have been important in my life as friends, supporters and collaborators. The late Marty Selim, everyone's favorite dinner guest and Master of Muffins, was essential to my life. Like a giant elf, he always appeared to fill in the gaps—taking tickets, mopping stage floors, running errands.

    This book would not exist if Richard Livingston, publisher of Exit Press, had not said "Yes! People will be interested!" Nicole Gluckstern's perceptive input on publicity has been extremely helpful. Tom Ingalls, Christopher Jordan and Megan Lotter of Ingalls Design came up with the fabulous cover and collages.

    A great deal of my theater has been inspired and supported by my lovers. Sherry McVickar was the first woman who took the trouble to seduce me. If she hadn't, I might still be treating men badly. Alice Thompson lived *Dos Lesbos* with me. Our life together felt like theater. We were a comedy team let loose on the world. Why not write an actual play about us? Alice's powerful charisma was a big part of the play's success. Nobody forgets seeing Alice Thompson onstage. Margo Tufo was an upstanding citizen with a solid career until we fell in love and she ran away to join my circus. Her immense musical talent allowed me to live out my rock star fantasy when we toured the country as the Official

Lesbian Music and Comedy Act of the 1984 Olympics. Margo could do everything and did do everything—build the sets, design and hang the lights, create the sound cues, design the poster. She reminded me recently that for *Ego Trip*, she ran the light board and, at intermission, tore down the stairs to the lobby to sell refreshments. She gave 100% of her time and talent to *Ego Trip* and to *Immediate Family*. Greater love hath no dyke. Margo went on to fame as a blues singer in Portland, Oregon. She's like a butch Janis Joplin. Dorelies Kraakman was the reason I moved to Amsterdam. Our disastrous relationship inspired *One Fool*. I know she was not thrilled to end up as an evil coatrack in the play. Being involved with a playwright can be dangerous. Godelieve Smelt kept me coming back to Amsterdam and was the actual person who made love to me at the opera. That scene is part of *Two Fools*, a play that (except for the opera scene) was inspired by Diana Avila, a well-known Costa Rican poet. I've always felt a little guilty that I handed Godelieve's audacity to Diana's character. But one consolidates when one writes.

My parents, Suzanne and Macy Baum, gave me the financial support to continue in theater, despite their doubts about my path. They're gone now but their hard work, and reluctance to spend what they earned, allows me to keep writing and producing plays. I also inherited from them my love of the world and sense of humor.

Theater is the name of an art and also the name of a space. And without the space, the art doesn't happen. Joe Landini of SAFEhouse for the Arts has invited us year after year to fill his theater with our plays. Mary Alice Fry's Venue 9 birthed *Waiting for the Podiatrist*. So many venues, some of them long gone, needed to exist for my theater to happen: EXIT Theatre, Theatre Rhinoceros, Live Oak Theater, The Valencia Rose, Josie's, the Dark Room, W.O.W and Wings and Cornelia St. Café in New York, La Gozadera in Mexico City, the Melkweg and Stalhouderij in Amsterdam. To all of you who keep the doors open, the lights on, and the toilet paper dispenser full—I bow in eternal gratitude. I have never done what you do, and I couldn't do what I do without you.

Pam Higley, production stage manager for the openings of *Bubbie & Her Butch*, *Bride of Lesbostein* and *Hick: A Love Story*, was so responsible, so easygoing, so funny—a gem. And I cannot imagine the first production of *Two Fools* without Retts Scauzillo stage managing. Her first venture into theater, Retts was the proverbial duck in water. Both these women took care of everyone and everything and made the work fun.

Lesley Harter, my friend and booker, has kept me performing *Hick* around the country, which has allowed me to keep working on the script.

My general advisor and oldest friend, Dory Adams, helps me live without crashing on the shoals too often—as have my two Buddhist teachers, Tova Green and Susan O'Connell.

The Antioch College theater faculty gave me solid theater training from 1964–1969, which has served me in good stead. And I'm indebted to my old U.C. Santa Barbara professor, Dr. Reardon. He scolded me for not being "doctoral," told me that some people love theater too much to stay in school, and then invited me to leave the PhD program.

I am humbled by the courage of the great Henrik Ibsen, my role model. I am a moth flying toward the light of his moon.

The lesbian communities of the Bay Area and Amsterdam have been crucial supports over the years— sometimes less than I felt I needed and sometimes more than I could have dreamed. Knowing there is an audience out there who cares about my work has made all the difference. Without that, I'm not sure I would have written at all.

Most of all, I want to thank my crony, Carolyn Myers, for willing this book into being. She has been saying for years, "My greatest fear in life is that you'll die before me and I'll have to do an anthology of your plays by myself!" And, indeed, I cannot imagine one person carrying this burden alone. So yes, Crony, just in case I die before you, I'm so glad I didn't leave you this humongous task. And, if you die before me, I know I never would have gotten around to it on my own. With your great talent and your own dreams, you have chosen to devote yourself to my work these last few years. What an incredible gift to me.

INTRODUCTION

by Carolyn Myers

The Evolution of a Slightly World-Renowned Lesbian Playwright

Welcome to *One Dyke's Theater*, a collection of plays by Terry Baum, whose work inspired the first anthology of lesbian plays (*Places Please*, Aunt Lute Press, 1985), and once offended the Pope. Her plays have been translated into five languages and performed throughout the U.S. and Europe, and in Israel, Cuba, Mexico, Canada, and South Africa—often by Terry herself. The ten plays and monologues selected for this book reflect both Terry's personal journey and the concerns and celebrations of the lesbian community between 1975 and 2014. Her plays have created waves of laughter, spiked controversy, and provoked more than a few tears in audiences around the world.

 I have collaborated with Terry for more than 40 years—as director, producer, co-author, dramaturge, or consultant, and now as the editor of the first anthology of her work. In this introduction, I want to let you in on a bit of the wild ride Terry and I have shared, laboring over scripts in offices and kitchens and coffeehouses, and putting on plays in every type of rehearsal space and performance venue imaginable. The background of all of Terry's work is the Women's Movement, where thrill-seeking, outraged, civic-minded feminists such as ourselves continue to create community and plot to overthrow the patriarchy.

 Terry and I met in 1972 in Isla Vista, California, the student ghetto next to the University of California at Santa Barbara. She put a notice on a bulletin board calling for the creation of a community theater and I attended the first organizational meeting. That night we started the Isla Vista Community Theater (IVCT), a source of many productions, endless joyful work, no money, and great parties.

 One of the offshoots of the IVCT was The Isla Vista Feminist Theater, with a cast of both women and men. It was one of the very first feminist theaters in the country (1973). Unfortunately, no scripts created with this fabulous crew can be included in One Dyke's Theater, which focuses exclusively on Terry's plays that are about lesbians. During her time at the Isla Vista Community Theater, Terry was still living the life of a confused and ambivalent heterosexual woman, and astonishingly, regrettably, cluelessly, it never occurred to any company members to address lesbian issues in our feminist theater .

The two and a half years I spent immersed in the IVCT turned my life in a new direction. Although I had made theater a big part of my life since childhood, I had always squeezed it in between school and work responsibilities. Terry told me I was an artist and that my greatest responsibility was to share my unique voice with the world. Urged on by her, I would walk out of my respectable job at the Department of Motor Vehicles and let go of the "Real World" for a life in the theater.

Through my involvement with Terry's work, I have been privileged to boldly go to lesbian places where, perhaps, no straight woman has gone before. I invite you to time travel with me over the almost forty years of scripts selected for this anthology.

LILITH, WOMEN'S THEATER
and *Bisexual Celibate* from *LILITHEATER* 1975

In 1974, Terry deserted our Isla Vista Community Theater to move to Santa Cruz to help fellow theater graduates from Antioch College start a new company. She was the only woman in the Bear Republic Theater. Despite the fact that the men were, for the time, enlightened and sensitive and remain her friends to this day, she was not happy. Quite often, she disagreed with all of them. She felt strongly she was representing the woman's point of view, and they felt strongly she was a pain in the neck.

That summer, a bunch of us from Isla Vista crowded into my old VW and drove up the California coast to visit Terry. We went to The Amazon Music Festival, where there was great music and two hundred women dancing ecstatically, mostly shirtless. This was our first time in a women-only space. We were luxuriating in our new-found feeling of safety and sisterhood under the towering redwoods, when a group of tough-looking men on motorcycles roared up to the gate, hostile and aggressive, shouting, demanding to be let in. A few of us recognized that things could get bad quickly, and tried to reason with the five of them. We were followed by 195 angry women, including Terry, itching for a fight. Our ad hoc negotiating team pointed out to the men that they were outnumbered forty to one, and that even masculine superiority might not save them. Just before the point of conflagration, the bikers turned around, and roared off. That night, Terry told me, when she was part of the legion of women warriors, she had received a vision of a play about women's rage against men, created by an all-women theater troupe. She was going to move to San Francisco to realize her vision.

This is the mythological, yet true, creation story of Lilith Theater (named for the Bible's first uppity woman).

Lilith's first play in 1975, titled simply *Lilitheater*, brought a unique, irresistible combination of self-mocking humor and feminist politics to the Bay Area theater scene. Lilith was part of a community that was creating a new world. Women's liberation and the gay rights movement converged to upend social dynamics in even the most progressive political and cultural groups. As Terry described it later, "We were riding the wave, and we were creating the wave."

Lilitheater was a hit, with multiple runs in Berkeley and in San Francisco. As soon as I saw the show, I was hooked. I moved to the Bay Area and joined the company, working as the techie, and running lights. The structure of the show, made up of personal monologues, comedy sketches and song parodies, was the one we had developed for The Isla Vista Feminist Theater. Terry's personal monolog, *Bisexual Celibate*, was the showstopper of the play. She discussed sex in an upfront, humorous way, without the rose-tinted veil of romance, and she explored the subject of masturbation, a radical form of sexuality to investigate onstage in 1975. Even from the lighting booth at the back of the theater, I could feel the electric energy between Terry and the audience.

Terry served as the artistic director of Lilith for five years, and we both worked as actors, directors and playwrights. After our second show, the other actresses left, and Terry and I held auditions. Some actual lesbians joined Lilith and Terry fell in love with a woman for the first time. Lesbian material began to enter the scripts, although it was sometimes a struggle within the collective, whose members largely defined themselves as feminists but not as lesbians. Between 1975 and 1979, the company produced five plays, four of which we wrote ourselves. We toured the West Coast and Europe, and performed at international theater festivals. During the two months of the European tour of 1979, I met and bonded with Terry's second lover, Alice Thompson. I had my six-month-old daughter with me, and it took all three of us to meet the needs of one baby as we traveled on our Eurailpasses from Hamburg to Amsterdam to Rome, circling back through Austria and Switzerland to Sweden to Munich, performing everywhere we went.

DOS LESBOS 1981

In the summer of 1980, I went to visit Terry and Alice, who were living in bucolic splendor at a most remarkable estate. Tao House, the Danville home of Eugene O'Neill, the only American playwright to ever win the Nobel Prize in Literature, was about to become a National Historic Site. Alice had been hired as estate caretaker during the transition.

The gates of Tao House were locked that summer, closed to the public. Here, living in privacy in an apartment in the barn, were these two witty lesbian thespians, lovers of each other, theater, literature and the arts. They were engaged in constant dialogue about themselves, their stream of guests, and their experiences in the world. Terry recognized their conversations as stage-worthy and started scribbling them down. Alice called the two of them "dos lesbos." They began brainstorming a play of the same name.

I found it wonderful and confirming that they were creating a play about their lives at the very place where Eugene O'Neill had written his last three autobiographical plays, including *Long Day's Journey into Night*. When I came to visit, I stood alone in the study and gazed at an actual Nobel Prize, this one with gorgeous art deco design. It felt like fate to me, as if Terry and Alice had come to this place to begin the next Great American Play.

Terry had been a central writer on Lilith's original shows, but her creativity had always been channeled through the collective process. Now she had left Lilith behind and was free to write her own plays, focused on the lives of lesbians. Although I was heterosexual, Terry and Alice invited me to join them in creating *Dos Lesbos, a Play By, For, and About Perverts*. We brought in Judy Gottlieb and David Hyman, old theater buddies from Isla Vista, to write the songs. The five of us believed we had come together to do something important. In 1980, we knew of no plays about contemporary lesbians written from the perspective of an actual living, breathing lesbian. At that time, the existing plays with lesbian characters required that the lesbian die tragically, commit evil acts, be a vampire, or, at the very least, be consumed with self-loathing.

Indeed, we could not think of a single play, in the entire canon of Western Theater, and I'm talking 2,500 years here, where, for example, a daughter tells her mother that she is a lesbian. Could it be that a moment in family dynamics so fraught with tension, so needing of resolution, so full of "Drama," had been completely ignored by all playwrights since playwriting began?

We decided to correct this particularly egregious oversight by writing coming-out scenes in many theatrical styles, from Greek tragedy to American situation comedy. I remember dropping into a used bookstore to find a Restoration comedy. With no money in my pocket, I couldn't buy the book. So I stood in the aisle reading and rereading a scene to get its high-brow tone, its language of salacious innuendo. I walked home, commenting aloud on everything I saw with wit, cynicism, and licentiousness, trying to keep that Restoration style with me until I could sit down at my typewriter and start writing.

In the original version of *Dos Lesbos*, holding the songs, comic sketches, and intimate conversations together, was a plot about a lesbian bar belonging to Peg being attacked by homophobic vandals. Alice and Judy and I tried many methods for shattering glass backstage to create the sound effects of windows breaking, without sending dangerous shards flying everywhere.

Our last week of rehearsal was beset with problems. Terry had laryngitis. We still weren't sure exactly where to place the band onstage. We couldn't find cheap champagne for the opening night party. How lucky that our venue was in the dancehall-sized back room of a lesbian bar. After rehearsal, we could walk through a door, sit in a booth and relax with a beer. In early 1981 we opened *Dos Lesbos, A Play By, For and About Perverts* at Ollie's Bar in Oakland, California.

Opening night brought a huge lesbian audience. They laughed uproariously, focused intensely and, when the show ended, applauded ecstatically. We had a Q&A with the audience after the show. Onstage stood the five creators—two dykes, two straight women, and a gay man. We were unprepared for the tsunami of feedback that the lesbian community is always eager to supply. "Why didn't you have a lesbian write lyrics?" Alice: "We wanted to, but we couldn't find a lesbian with a sense of humor." "Why is Peg so butch and Gracie so femme? Playing roles is totally uncool." Terry: "Alice and I happen to be totally uncool and I find role-playing fascinating and very hot."

Most importantly, the audience loved Peg and Gracie's intimate conversations—and was unconvinced by the melodrama surrounding the threatened lesbian bar. Terry rewrote the play, bravely throwing out the original plot, and focusing entirely on the relationship between the eponymous "dos lesbos." The bar set was gone, and the apartment set took over the whole stage. We no longer had to worry about flying shards of glass!

This revision left the play with an open, loose structure similar to a variety show. There's a "girls band" onstage, accompanying the actors in comic songs. There's an audience sing-along. There's a feminist replication of a "99-pound weakling" bodybuilding advertisement. There's dramatic recitation of hyper-earnest poetry. And there are the assorted "Coming-Out Scenes," performed with exaggerated stylistic excess. These vaudevillian theatrics share the stage with realistic scenes between Peg and Gracie, a lesbian couple trying to figure out how to live well and with each other in a society prejudiced against both women and homosexuals.

The audiences grew and grew and clearly shared our belief that this play was something new under the sun. *Dos Lesbos* was holding up a mirror to the lesbian community. Joyce D., who reviewed a 1986 production in Oregon for *Herizons Newsletter*, described the experience: "The audience, a palpable entity which at times nearly silenced Peg and Gracie, was wildly responsive. I find it impossible to write a critique which adequately recreates more than a rudiment of the joy with which the audience accepted and absorbed the *Dos Lesbos* experience."

Yeah, the 1980s were like that.

Coming-Out Story from EGO TRIP 1982

The monologue *Coming-Out Story* was included in Terry's first solo show, *Ego Trip*. She was the writer, actor, and producer. At one performance she even announced, "Now, in a gesture of total omnipotence, I am going to run the lights!" She did this to give her techie and current lover, blues singer Margo Tufo, an opportunity to sing onstage.

As you can tell from its title, *Ego Trip* is a send-up of the self-important concept of solo theater. The subtitle, *I'm Getting My Shit Together and Dumping it All On You*," was a subversion of the title of a popular off-Broadway musical of the time, *I'm Getting My Act Together and Taking it On The Road*. This off-Broadway show was widely reviewed as a vehicle for healthy, positive, feel-good feminism. The playwrights, however, denied any political views. They said they were writing about relationships between men and women, not about changing women's roles in society.

In the early 1980s, in every interview, every panel discussion, every meeting, people would demand reassurance from feminists that they were no threat to the social order, and that they did not, in fact, hate men. At a national conference on women playwrights at Stanford University, Terry and I personally encountered this phenomenon. As two of seven local playwrights invited to read our work, we chose two scenes focused on lesbians. The other playwrights' work featured heterosexual women characters. As soon as the readings were finished, one of the other playwrights immediately disavowed any connection with Terry and me. She announced, nodding at Terry and me, "I just want to make it clear that I'm not like those two other playwrights. I don't hate men."

There had been no talk about hating men in our scenes, or in fact in any of the scenes presented. All seven scenes focused exclusively on relationships between women. But that did not prevent the other playwrights and the panel moderator from falling all over each other in their rush to declare to the audience that they, personally, did not, have not, and never would, hate men. They were married! They had boyfriends! They thought men were dandy! I desperately tried to figure out how to respond. I was afraid that if I claimed I was a straight woman proud to have written a scene about lesbians I would seem to be eagerly denying I was gay. I sat, agonized, in silence.

The women in the audience had no such qualms. They enthusiastically joined the chorus. It grew to an absolute frenzy of courageous women daring to declare their refusal to hate men! Only one member of the audience protested the insanity. The director of At The Foot of the Mountain, the largest women's theater in the country, Martha Boesing, stood, facing the audience. "Don't you see how ridiculous you are?" she said. "Do you think the men worry about what *we* think when *they* have a conference?" But Martha was ignored by the man-loving mob.

Suddenly, Terry stood up and shouted in a loud and clear voice, "I hate men! I hate men! I am what you are afraid of!" Everyone was stunned into silence. The only sound was Martha cackling in the back of the room. Terry's owning of the dreaded man-hater label defused its power.

That conference for women playwrights should have been a safe and welcoming space for plays about the lives of lesbians. But it wasn't. And this was in the 1980s! At Stanford!

For Terry, that day was like a red flag to a bull-dyke. She was determined to put her life, and the lives of other lesbians, onstage. In *Ego Trip*, she unapologetically presents her lesbian feminist viewpoint. In the final scene of the play, *Coming-Out Story*, Terry addresses the audience for the first time directly, speaking in the first person, sharing stories from her own tortured and at times hilarious, coming-out process. Then, in the very last moments of the monologue, Terry suddenly shifts perspective. She steps outside her personal story to declare a lesbian manifesto. (I had directed the play, but it wasn't until I saw it in performance while sitting with the audience that I felt the shock of the final confrontation.) Terry addresses the audience as "You straight people..." and directly challenges the heterosexuals in the house. We are jolted out of the comfort of listening to a fascinating personal story. We sit exposed, a bright unflattering light shone on us. Terry mocks our endless consumption of plays and movies and novels about ourselves. She states her manifesto: She is compelled to keep writing about lesbian lives, whether straight people want to listen or not. Then she leaves the stage.

Terry has lived up to that commitment. Lesbians aren't the only people she writes about, but they are the majority of characters in her work.

IMMEDIATE FAMILY 1983

Immediate Family centers on a single character, Virginia, visiting her longtime partner Rose, who lies comatose in a hospital. The play explores the crisis of medical ethics around death and dying, and criticizes laws that cruelly limited the definition of family to exclude gay people. Virginia is faced with an impossible decision. Her love for Rose demands that she turn off the ventilator which does all of Rose's breathing, because she knows that is what Rose would want. However, since she is not acknowledged as family, she has no say. To take action means breaking the law. Although the play ends with heartbreak, it feels triumphant. When Virginia pulls the plug and the ventilator stops its rhythmic mechanical hissing, we find in her brave final step the dignity of humanity's struggle against the degradation of rules, regulations, and machines. *Immediate Family* is a dramatic theatrical example of how the political becomes personal.

Immediate Family marked so many firsts for Terry as a playwright and performer: first full-length play written on her own; first time playing a main character not based on herself; and her first play that was not a comedy. When she opened the show at the National Women's Theater Festival in Santa Cruz in 1983, she worried the audience would find her seriousness pretentious. On opening night, she missed the continual laughter that always reassured her the audience was with her. Were they bored, just waiting to get out of the theater? Indeed, after the curtain call, when the usual throng of friends and fans failed to appear backstage, Terry feared *Immediate Family* had failed.

Then, magically, the radiant and fearless Z Budapest sailed into the tiny dressing room to congratulate Terry and bless her. There could be no better woman to bestow blessings on a nervous playwright and performer than Z, the founder of the Susan B. Anthony Coven, the first feminist, women-only, coven, and who, in 1975, became the last person to be tried and convicted as a witch in the U.S. Z informed Terry that she had received a standing ovation! Terry hadn't seen the audience because the stage lights had shown directly into her eyes. Now, she felt exultant, and blessed!

As to why no one else came backstage—Terry has learned, over the years of performing *Immediate Family,* that most audience members, even if friends, often leave the theater without talking to her after seeing the play. They want to keep their memory of the character of Virginia intact, and linger privately over the meaning and power of the play's final moments.

ONE FOOL 1986

One of the posters for a return engagement of *One Fool* reads: "*Don't miss the show that dazzled Europe with its Joie-de-vivre, Savoir-faire and Cul-de-sac!*"

That's got to be one of my favorite theatrical invitations ever, so joyously self-revealing in its pseudo-intellectual stance.

One Fool is a play whose subject matter emerged through several years of personal letters from Terry to myself. By 1985, our lives had diverged. I was firmly rooted in small town Ashland, Oregon, with my husband and children. Meanwhile, Terry was touring with *Immediate Family* throughout the U.S. and Europe, living the life of a vagabond performer, a lesbian-on-the-loose, falling in and out of love on two continents. Her letters to me recounted the most fabulous and the most heartbroken of times, a life that seemed almost ridiculously full and exciting. So, I was shocked when she wrote that her travelling days were over. She had fallen in love and was moving to Amsterdam permanently! My dear friend who had instilled in me the creed, "Never sleep with anyone who lives more than forty-five minutes away by public transportation," suddenly moved 6,000 miles for love. For the next nine years, Terry split her time between Amsterdam and San Francisco.

Terry premiered *One Fool* in Amsterdam. I didn't get to see it until 1988 when she performed the show at Theater Rhinoceros, San Francisco's renowned gay and lesbian theater. The opening of the show is my favorite opening of any show, anywhere. The Fool wanders through the audience, searching for The One, who she finds again and again, sequentially enamored of woman after woman, only to have her hopes for True Love dashed each time. Here were those long intense letters Terry had written me during her travels, brought to life in a series of increasingly zany three-minute relationships.

In condensing and acting out a speeded up version of relationships of her sexual past, Terry felt she was portraying the sex life of a modern 40-year-old woman. As she says, "I know that my secrets are everybody's secrets—and I'm liberating all of us by revealing them." And it's true; audience members of all sexual persuasions relate to The Fool's quest to find The One, even if they haven't acted on their impulses quite as often.

However, it's certainly safer to be a lesbian than to be a straight woman when it comes to seeking love in all the wrong places. If The Fool were a heterosexual woman approaching man after man in the audience, she would likely be seen as pathetic rather than funny. And some of The Fool's later actions, like throwing her dress over her head in a bar, would clearly put her at serious risk if the bar wasn't packed with other lesbians.

That The Fool is a lesbian makes it possible for *One Fool* to be a wild farce. No matter how bawdy or embarrassing she becomes, The Fool remains a plucky naïf, a survivor of battles of the heart in the streets, plazas, and lesbian bars of San Francisco and Amsterdam. Being a lesbian freed Terry to let The Fool be a fool to her heart's content.

TWO FOOLS 1996

Two Fools is billed as a romantic comedy. This time, the lesbian Odd Couple are the Costa Rican Luna, and the American Gracie.

Wait a minute! Could this be the Gracie of *Dos Lesbos*, who bears several striking similarities to The Fool of *One Fool*? Yes, and yes! *Dos Lesbos* and then *One Fool* and now *Two Fools*, even the titles suggest a personal journey for Terry's alter-ego, Gracie. *Two Fools* also continues Terry's exploration, which began in *Immediate Family*, of the suffering lesbians endure because of their lack of marriage rights, and resumes her lively investigation of sex onstage, introduced in *Bisexual Celibate* and ardently pursued in *One Fool*.

Romantic comedies are supposed to end with "happily ever after," but Terry subverts this familiar genre. *Two Fools* is both a witty romance between star-crossed, cross-cultural lesbian lovers, and also a serious play about immigration, racism and gay rights. And it doesn't end well. Luna and Gracie fall in love. They can't live without each other, but they can't legally live with each other either, as Luna has no legal right to stay in the United States. This time, the witty lovers end up permanently divided by the serious issues.

Two Fools explores politics within an intimate relationship. Sometimes, the politics are dominant, and the fraught subjects of racial, cultural and sexual identities are shown through the playwright's magnifying glass: "Look, this is how global politics play out in the bedroom." The audience winces at the small cruelties, whether accidental or intentional, that the lovers inflict on each other because of their cultural conditioning and expectations. At other times, the lovemaking is dominant, and Terry turns her lens so that it becomes a prism, refracting the light shown through it into rainbow hues: "Look, this is how lesbian lovers from different cultures add to the tapestry of couples in the world." Then, the audience glimpses the playfulness and passion of two women in love.

WAITING FOR THE PODIATRIST 2003

From the start, some of Terry's plays have been fictionalized versions of her own life. Before 2003, these plays focused on love relationships. Her parents had been offstage characters, their ongoing disapproval of her lifestyle always fodder for discussion. With *Waiting for the Podiatrist*, Mom and Dad (or "M and D" as they were referred to in in *Dos Lesbos*), finally appear center stage. Admittedly, they are not represented by human actors. Mom is an extremely vibrant puppet made from an oven mitt, wearing pearls and a stylish scarf; while Dad, a sock puppet, lies in a coma for most of the play.

I knew Terry's parents well. They had not only supported the work of the Isla Vista Community Theater, they even came to our shows. After staying overnight in our collective house, they had dubbed it "Motel 2," a tongue-in-cheek homage to the then cheap-and-cheesy Motel 6 chain. They had introduced me to Sunday mornings with lox and bagels and the Los Angeles Times. Since 1972, I had been privy to Terry's ever-evolving relationship with her parents. I was primed to appreciate her first "family" play, *Waiting for the Podiatrist*, a musical farce set in the nightmare funhouse that is any hospital's Intensive Care Unit.

Waiting for the Podiatrist and Terry's earlier play, *Immediate Family*, both explore Western medicine's determination to prolong life regardless of its quality; leaving the family with the heart-wrenching decision of whether or not to disconnect a loved one from life support machines. Whereas *Immediate Family* was created from Terry's imagination, before she had faced such a decision herself, *Waiting for the Podiatrist* tells a story about something that has actually happened to her. The imagined work is totally realistic, while this play written in 2003, drawn from complicated and painful experience, demands to be approached from the distance provided by farce, puppets and songs!

In *Waiting for the Podiatrist*, Terry plays three characters: Alexandra (her alter-ego) and both of Alexandra's parents—the Mom puppet on her left hand, the Dad puppet on her right. Suspension of disbelief is an important aspect of this play. The audience must perceive each of her hands as individual characters who are separate from Alexandra, even though Terry's lips move when the puppets speak. Fortunately, because Terry totally believes her hands are separate characters (and because the audience loves to suspend disbelief), it works.

Although the necessary suspension of disbelief is very pleasurable for the audience, it's not such a good frame of mind for a director. When I produced and directed *Podiatrist* in Ashland, I restaged the play to fit the venue. More than once, I delivered some inspired blocking suggestion that placed Alexandra on one side of the stage and Mom on the other. Terry would stay put and stare at me, until I realized, "Oh right, this staging can't happen because, in truth, Mom is a puppet attached to Terry's arm." Even I could forget that Terry alone was creating all the action, saying all the lines, singing all the songs (including duets and a finale written for all three), because it was so completely realized.

When *Podiatrist* first opened in 2003, Terry's parents were still alive. By 2016, when she revived the play for the San Francisco Fringe Festival, they had died. I was privileged to be with her for both of these goodbyes. I held Terry in my arms while she wept after finding out her dad had died. And I flew to Los Angeles to be her companion at her mother's funeral. I loved Terry's parents and I am so happy that other people get to experience them as Mother Puppet and Father Puppet.

THE CRACKPOT CRONES

Our next theatrical collaboration began late in the fall of 2007 when Terry was leafing through *Shewolf's Directory of Wimmin's Lands and Lesbian Communities*. She was inspired to go exploring and she invited me along. I was in rainy Oregon, teaching fulltime, ready to say "Yes" to a Winter Break vacation. I asked only that we go somewhere warm and that no work of any kind be required. Terry had found a listing for Casa Feminista, a women's lodge in the mountains of northern New Mexico, next to a hot springs resort. Ah yes, the promise of warmth!

When she called to reserve rooms, she discovered the lodge was run by Sonia Johnson and her partner Jade DeForest. Wait! Not *the* Sonia Johnson, the famous former housewife and mother who fled the Mormon Church, became a lesbian separatist visionary, campaigned for the ERA, and ran for President of the United States with the Citizen's Party?!? Yes, *that* Sonia Johnson! And, how could we *not* perform for

Sonia Johnson?

We arrived at the beautiful adobe casa in the snowy mountains of northern New Mexico, with old scripts and new ideas. We put together a New Year's Eve performance for the women of the tiny town of Ojo Caliente. We called ourselves The Crackpot Crones, a phrase I had just found in Mary Daly's *Wickedary*, a radical feminist dictionary, left like a Gideon's Bible on the nightstand in every room at Casa Feminista. We opened our show with the first scene of *One Fool* where Terry falls in love with various women in the audience. We did an audience sing-along of "the Twelve Days of Family Insults" from *Dos Lesbos*. We performed bawdy feminist improvisations based on suggestions from the audience. We also developed and premiered a scene Terry had sent me as a mere fragment in a letter years before. She had totally forgotten about this scene, but I had loved and carefully saved it: "Eve in Therapy," in which The First Woman visits the eminent psychiatrist Dr. Lilith in a desperate effort to get over feeling guilty about that apple. Our show was such a hit that word spread and we happily reprised it the next night.

During all our years in theater, we had never before performed together, just the two of us, onstage. We discovered our onstage magic chemistry, and had so much fun that we realized it was our destiny to perform feminist and lesbian sketch comedy and improvisation together for the rest of our lives. Instead of my requested restful vacation, we experienced the marvelous experience of working together. Once again, just like thirty-five years before, I gave up my job in "the real world," and moved to San Francisco. Terry and I began an intense creative work cycle that continues to this day.

For thirty years, we had allowed a silly geographic thing, like a separation of 350–6000 miles, to restrict our collaboration. Now we two Crones found ourselves still at the top of our game and in a frenzy of celebration to be working together full-time in the same city. During 2012 and 2013, we had especially productive seasons. We participated in the New York Fringe Festival, the Santa Cruz Fringe Festival, and the National Queer Arts Festival (twice). We also created The *"I Hate Valentine's Day" Show*; *Moms for Mother's Day*; *Bride of Lesbostein* for Halloween; and annual *Crones for the Holidays* shows in 2010, 2012, and 2013. (We skipped 2011 because Terry ran for Mayor of San Francisco!) And last but not least, we produced the first workshop production of *HICK: A Love Story*. Phew!

Each of the *Crones for the Holidays* shows was a collection of sketches, songs, personal stories, and improvisations. In 2012, we hired our Dream Team. Set designer Vola Ruben had worked with Lilith Theater in 1978. Lighting designer Stephanie Anne Johnson and Terry had created The *Black Jewish American Lesbian Show* in Amsterdam in 1985. To coordinate it all, production stage manager Pam Higley was recommended by a former director. These three women would work with us for two years, through *Hick: A Love Story*, bringing our production values up to match the level of our scripts and performance.

BUBBIE AND HER BUTCH from CRONES FOR THE HOLIDAYS 2012

In *Bubbie and her Butch*, with the romantic match-up of Frannie and Chris, we had a love affair of opposites: Jewish/non-Jewish; formerly straight/life-long lesbian; femme/butch; and grandmother/childless woman. The scene also provided us with a sketch about Chanukah and a lesbian home-for-the-holidays story, two important additions, since holiday shows tend to be overwhelmingly "heteronormative" and Christian.

I was eager for there to be a love story with women our own age (in their sixties) for the show, and Terry was happy to play a butch in love. Chris, the butch, is a well-realized character. She defines and defends her identity, her "people." But once we started rehearsals, I found Frannie, the femme, very difficult to portray. She defined herself only through her relationship to others, in this case as a Jewish grandmother, and as the thrilled new lover of a butch lesbian. She wanted everyone to be happy, to get along, and to love her. With those objectives, Frannie was manipulative and tense, even breaking into tears when she felt misunderstood or didn't get what she wanted. In discussions, Terry and I found her to be an inaccurate depiction of women we knew, much less "femmes" who must be strong in their determination to be recognized as lesbians. By daring to be publicly attracted to a butch woman, Frannie was announcing her own sexual difference and making her butch lover a known subject of desire. She was doing a brave thing. But, in trying to make sure the character read as "feminine," we had resorted to sexist stereotyping. Terry rewrote the part, giving Frannie more humor, more depth, more moxie, more reality.

Not to be defined solely through others, instead taking center stage in one's own life is the central feminist quest for women. As an actress, playing Frannie became a consciousness-raising journey of discovery for me. Because I acted the role before and after Terry gave the character a feminist rewrite, I had the opportunity to experience, in my own body, the shift from basing self-worth on how others see you, to basing it on internal focus and feelings. Once I recognized Frannie as an autonomous person, I loved her. I understood why she was pretty and desirable to Chris. I felt that way myself onstage, which has been rare for me and was great fun.

BRIDE OF LESBOSTEIN 2013

The Crackpot Crones were creating a tradition of holiday shows. It seemed only right and necessary that we write one for Halloween, that being the great holiday of Witches and Hags, with whom Crones closely identify.

Bride of Lesbostein was an idea that had been hanging in Terry's mental closet for years. To wit: Dr. Gertrude Lesbostein has never found a woman good enough for her. So she attempts to create the perfect wife by combining the DNA of her 34 ex-girlfriends, each of whom is perfect in some small way. If The Fool of *One Fool* and Dr. Frankenstein had a child, she would be Dr. Gertrude Lesbostein. She is aided in her fiendish designs by her slavishly adoring assistant, Igorina, whose job it is to sneak into bedrooms at night to collect DNA samples from slumbering exes.

I feel a deep kinship with Igorina and her dedication to the mad doctor's dream. I am certain that Terry wrote the part with me in mind. To my utter dismay, Terry denies this, or that the relationship between the two characters reflects our own relationship in any way! While acknowledging that there may be some slight similarities between Lesbostein and herself, she consistently maintains that Igorina is simply the logical adaptation of the stock character lab assistant of the Frankenstein movies of the 1930s. I remain unconvinced. We do agree on one thing: I was born to play Igorina. I experience complete fulfillment both as an actress and as Terry's collaborator when I am onstage helping that absurd egomaniac, Dr. Gertrude, bring The Bride to life.

I want to take a moment here to commemorate one of our long-time colleagues. In *Bride of Lesbostein* we worked for the final time with Joan Mankin, beloved actress, clown, teacher and director. In her long career, Joan was unique in continuing to work with theaters of every size in the Bay Area—from the smallest grassroots companies to the San Francisco Mime Troupe to the American Conservatory Theater, the biggest show in town. Joan performed with Lilith Theater in four plays, toured Europe with us in 1979, and directed *Crones for the Holidays 2012*. For Lesbostein, she played The Bride herself. Joan was ill, although we didn't know it at the time. The Bride, one of her last performances, proved to be a perfect vehicle for Joan's wild and skillful clowning.

HICK: A Love Story 2014

HICK: A Love Story is the only biographical play that Terry has written. It concerns the lesbian relationship between Eleanor Roosevelt and Lorena Hickok, a renowned journalist. They fell in love during FDR's first campaign for President in 1932. The love affair is documented in their letters to each other, particularly the 2,336 letters that Eleanor wrote to Hick.

By 2012, Terry and I had been performing as The Crackpot Crones for four years. When The Crones were invited back to the National Queer Arts Festival for the second time, we decided to make our performance a benefit for the Pat Bond Memorial Old Dyke Award, which Terry had founded in memory of her friend, who was one of the first women to tour nationally as an out lesbian. We wanted to do a scene from one of Pat's solo plays. I found *Eleanor Roosevelt and Lorena Hickok, A Love Story* by Pat Bond, in the archives of the Hormel Gay Center in the San Francisco Public Library. The manuscript, in a large manila folder, was actually a playwright's workbook of fragments of each scene, more the size of a city phone directory than of a standard script. I arranged the fragments in piles, trying to make sense of them. One pile, which I referred to as "The Silver Pearl Morning," was my favorite. It included many rewrites of a scene where Eleanor and Hick get off the FDR campaign train to stretch their legs and begin to fall in love. I knew Pat Bond must have imagined this part of the story, but I believed it utterly. I combined and edited "The Silver Pearl Morning" variations to create a fifteen-minute piece that would fit into the Crackpot Crones show.

The scene struck a powerful chord with the audience—and with Terry. She was perfect for Hick. Or should I say that Hick was perfect for her? She and I are in the habit of switching roles back and forth when we perform, but during rehearsal she told me I would only play this part over her dead body—although she swears she would never say something so crude to her beloved crony. We also knew from that first short performance, and from the audience's enthusiastic feedback, that Terry was destined to write and perform a full-length play about Lorena Hickok and that I was destined to direct it. Clearly, a new step in our creative partnership was afoot. We even reclaimed Lilith Theater as our company name, with its first production being *HICK: A Love Story*.

The romance between Eleanor Roosevelt and Lorena Hickok is a coming-out story of historical significance. During the first half of 2013, we happily immersed ourselves in research. I read Blanche Wiesen Cook's three-volume biography of Mrs. Roosevelt. Cook is the first contemporary historian to fully acknowledge the sexual nature of Eleanor's relationship with Hick. Terry visited the FDR Library to read original documents. In Hyde Park, she talked with people who actually knew Lorena Hickok. This project stretched our writing abilities, combining our love of history with our knowledge of dramatic structure, to find the best moments for a play. How to transform the mass of incidents, emotions, and characters that make up a relationship of thirty years into a story with an arc—and still reflect the truth of Lorena Hickok's love for Eleanor Roosevelt? Neither Terry nor I had attempted anything like this before. We worked together almost every day, Terry bringing in new writing for us to hash over. The script ended up with some scenes following very closely the letters from Eleanor to Hick, and some scenes that Terry invented, filling in the gaps.

Although Terry is very comfortable performing solo, she kept bringing up the possibility of hiring an actress to play Eleanor, expanding *HICK* to a two-person play. I felt this would be a mistake because Eleanor's presence onstage would become the audience's focus. We were writing a play about Lorena Hickok's life. Her famous lover must remain an offstage voice. Once Terry became convinced that *HICK* would remain solo, she asked actress Paula Barish, who had starred in one of Terry's short films, to record the voice of Eleanor reading her letters to Hick aloud. Paula's nuanced vocal performance brought the First Lady's presence onto the stage, and fully established the historical reality of the story.

HICK: A Love Story, The Romance of Lorena Hickok and Eleanor Roosevelt opened in San Francisco in the summer of 2014 and was a huge success. We filled the biggest theater we'd ever rented. I came to all the performances of that first run, sitting in the audience, among people who had chosen to step out of their bright, noisy, complicated worlds to sit quietly in the dark listening to a new story—laughing, gasping, and sometimes even crying together. It was also wonderful for me to watch Terry make small changes in her performance every night, the play never the exactly the same show as the night before, a moving, changing art form.

In Conclusion

Terry and I both recognize the oddity of a lesbian playwright having a heterosexual woman as her closest collaborator. But we have worked together joyfully from the beginning. Not that there haven't been difficult patches, but mostly there has been excitement, satisfaction and a whole lot of falling-off-the-chair laughing. As two feminist women working together, we know our artistic partnership, along with our work, is undervalued and misunderstood by the still-patriarchal art world at large. So it has been vital that we recognize and support each other. Terry and I have always easily shared our values and our vision. Often, when creating theater together, one of us thinks she has concluded what there is to say, and then the other picks up the thread and we improvise until a scene coalesces. I have finished this introduction. Now, to Terry's words! I invite you to read the plays themselves.

1981
DOS LESBOS

A PLAY BY, FOR & ABOUT PERVERTS

Dos Lesbos was written by Terry Baum and Carolyn Myers. The play was conceived by Terry Baum and Alice Thompson.

Premiere Information

Dos Lesbos was originally produced by Sharpened Spoons, opening on February 27, 1981 at Ollie's Bar in Oakland, California.

Directors .... Carolyn Myers and Alice Thompson
Musical Director .... Judy Gottlieb
Musical Arranger .... Nina Ruymaker
Set Design .... John Wullbrandt
Lighting Design .... Nancy Baum
House Manager .... Martin Selim

CAST

GRACIE .... Terry Baum
PEG .... Alice Thompson

Musical Numbers

I DON'T CARE .... Peg and Gracie
By Jean Lenox and Harry Sutton

JILL THE RIPPER ....Gracie
Music by Judy Gottlieb, lyrics by David Hyman

THE TWELVE DAYS ...... Peg, Gracie, The Band, The Audience
Lyrics by Terry Baum, Judy Gottlieb, David Hyman, Carolyn Myers & Alice Thompson

MISERY LOVES COMPANY ...... Peg
Music & lyrics by David Hyman

I DON'T CARE (reprise) ....Peg and Gracie
By Jean Lenox and Harry Sutton

PRODUCTION HISTORY

Although part of *Bisexual Celibate* was written earlier, *Dos Lesbos* comes first in this anthology because it is the beginning of my exploration of what it means to be a lesbian. *Dos Lesbos* ran for two years in the San Francisco Bay Area and was nominated for several awards. For many people in the audience, it was the first time they had seen a performance where the lives of lesbians were portrayed from a lesbian point of view. Kate McDermott saw the play in Santa Cruz and was so inspired that she created the first anthology of lesbian plays in the history of the universe—*Places, Please!* (1985). After being published, *Dos Lesbos* had many productions throughout the world and was translated into Swedish, Flemish, and French.

In 2000, an Italian production of the play was part of World Pride in Rome—the hometown of the patriarchy! The Pope and the neo-Fascists were doing everything they could to stop World Pride from happening. This epic struggle between Gay Liberation and the Pope was covered in all the newspapers. Of course, Carolyn, Alice and I had to fly to Rome to support our gay sisters and brothers—and to witness our play in Italian.

We would sit in the back row of the theater, to observe the audience's reactions. There were usually several older straight couples in the audience who we imagined were the parents of gay children, there to gain some understanding of their offspring. One night, one of the husbands stood up 10 minutes into the play and stomped noisily up the aisle to the exit. He stopped, looked around. His wife had not followed! He returned and gestured eloquently that she must also jump ship. She meekly got up and started to follow him. But then she sat down again to watch the play. He came back to get her *again*. He stood in the aisle glaring at her. She ignored him. He very reluctantly took a seat next to her. At the end of the show, we took great pleasure in watching him stand with the rest of the audience, applauding with great gusto.

The next day, the Pope, in his Sunday message from the balcony over St. Peter's Square, spoke bitterly of the gay pride events in his own city. Meanwhile, thousands and thousands of people marched by the Coliseum, that ancient symbol of human rights abuses, to celebrate how far we had come. Carolyn, Alice, and I marched too, proud that *Dos Lesbos* had been part of that voice of liberation.

CHARACTERS

PEG: A butch lesbian, mid-30s. She looks at the world with deadpan humor, and prefers to avoid conflict. She has been out as a lesbian a long time, and is comfortable in her butch identity. It never occurs to her that she is wrong about anything. She wears a "uniform" of her own choosing—a closet full of bowling shirts and chinos.

GRACIE: A femme-ish lesbian, mid-30s. She wishes she was a great poet. She is always on the look-out for the moments of heightened drama in her life. Peg is her first woman lover. It never occurs to Gracie that she is right about anything. She wears arty, color-saturated clothing, chosen to be noticed, and in unusual combinations.

THE GIRLS IN THE BAND: A keyboard player, a drummer, and a horn or flute player. Along with the music, they also provide sound effects.

TIME

The early 1980s. Ronald Reagan is President. The action takes place over four consecutive Friday evenings.

PLACE

The living room of Peg and Gracie's apartment, in a big, politically liberal city with an active gay community.

SETTING: The main portion of the stage is PEG and GRACIE's living room. These lesbians may be poor, but they show design sense within the mismatched thrift-store style of the early 1980's alternative scene. The central piece of furniture is a large overstuffed chair, very comfortable and solid. The chair is big enough to easily fit two people, if one of them sits on its arms or throws herself across the other person. Stage Right there is a writing desk for GRACIE, with a portable typewriter, a stack of journals, and a jar of assorted writing implements, including a quill. Stage Left there is a small table with two chairs, two mugs, newspapers, and meal accoutrements—napkin holder, salt and pepper shaker, sugar bowl. Upstage there is a coatrack and a bookcase, each more than full. On top of the bookcase there is a boombox, a shoe box overflowing with tape cassettes, and a basket of toys and props—including two ornate fans. The art on the walls shows an active engagement with their community—posters about gay rights, feminist and New Left politics; and paintings by friends. Everything reflects a lively and mischievous aesthetic.

The band is on a raised platform separate from the main set and designed to look like a nightclub. It is lighted only when the band plays. During the musical numbers, the actors join the band on the nightclub stage.

AT RISE: Lights up on THE GIRLS IN THE BAND, playing the

Pre-Show. Then PEG and GRACIE enter the nightclub stage and sing.

PEG and GRACIE:

Song: I DON'T CARE

They say I'm crazy, got no sense, but I don't care.
They may or may not take offense, but I don't care.
You see, I'm kind of independent, of a clever race descendant,
My star is on the ascendant,
That's why I don't care.

I don't care, I don't care
What people think of me.
I'm happy-go-lucky
They say I am plucky
So jolly and carefree.

I don't care, I don't care
If I do get the mean and stony stare.
If I'm never successful, it won't be distressful
'Cause I don't care.

Lights Fade To Black.

Scene 1
The Job

Early evening. Friday.

AT RISE: PEG is discovered at the table, drinking beer and reading the newspaper. GRACIE enters, kisses PEG.

GRACIE: Hi, Peg. How'd it go today, Hon?

PEG throws the newspaper down.

PEG: (*With mock frustation.*) I can't understand it. I did everything Ronald Reagan told me to do. I answered every single want ad in the paper, and I'm still unemployed. Maybe I should take up typing.

GRACIE: (*Very dramatically.*) Please don't speak to me about typing.

PEG: How was your day?

GRACIE: Don't ask. (*The drama intensifies.*) I don't want to talk about work. I don't want to think about work. Every day I have to go out on the streets and sell my fingers to the highest bidder. So just don't ask me about work.

PEG: Alright, I won't ask.

GRACIE: I had a very traumatic experience at the office today. I was a coward. Gracie Levy: The coward of Abromowitz, Rodriguez and Chan, attorneys at law…esquire. (*Furious with herself.*) It was disgusting. Why didn't I say something? Why didn't I do something?

> *PEG shrugs her shoulders.*

It just so happens I've written a poem about it.

PEG: Great.

GRACIE: Would you like to hear it?

PEG: Sure.

> *She gets a beer and settles down to listen. GRACIE rummages in her purse until she finds the poem.*

GRACIE: (*Reading.*) "In the Staff Room Before Work." (*Pause.*) No.

> *She writes down the new title. She reads:*

"In the Staff Room Before Work **Begins.**"

PEG: That's much better.

GRACIE: Yes, I think so. (*Begins reading again.*) "In the Staff Room Before Work Begins." (*Melodramatically.*)

> Precious moments of talk before chaining ourselves to the typewriter.
> Stolen moments of freedom before the slavery begins.
> We are all one, all one.
> All women, all women
> All groveling, all groveling
> To survive.
> But that happens at eight a.m.
> Now it is seven forty-five a.m. and we are HAPPY!
> We suckle the coffe urn.
> Mother Caffeine gives us our daily zap.
> Some call it gossip,
> These countless slender umbilical cords
> Through which we make connection.
> I am connected.
> > I float in the placenta of sisterhood under flourescent lights.

GRACIE uses a high whiny voice when she quotes Nancy Nice.

"I went to the wildest party last night," says Nancy Nice...

PEG: (*Interrupting.*) Nancy Nice?

GRACIE: There's Nancy Kaufman, Nancy Minor and Nancy Nice.

PEG: I think I'd kill myself if my last name was "Nice."

GRACIE: (*Gives up on the poem and decides to tell the story.*) Anyhow, so Nancy Nice goes to this wild party, right? And she sees some dirty movies there, right? "It was awful," she says. "But," she says, "At least it was a man and a woman, if you know what I mean." Everybody laughed.

PEG: Except you.

GRACIE: Except me. And then she said it again, just in case we all hadn't heard it the first time. "At least it was a man and a woman, if you know what I mean." I was furious. I wanted to say something. I wanted to do something. I thought of fifty things to say. I almost said one of them. But they would have thought I was a jerk—partly because I was a lesbian, but mainly because I got upset when they were having a good time. So I said nothing. (*Sarcastically.*) "At least it was a man and a woman."

PEG: If you know what I mean.

GRACIE: If you know what I mean.

PEG comforts GRACIE with a hug.

PEG: They're idiots. You know that. You shouldn't let them get to you.

GRACIE: I just didn't want to be a pill and ruin a good time. I just wanted to be one of the gang.

PEG: Don't be so hard on yourself. It takes a while to figure out what to do in situations like that.

GRACIE: But by the time I've figured it out, the situation is all over. Nancy Nice insulted me, and she doesn't even know it. Why didn't I say something?

PEG: You know what you need?

GRACIE: What?

PEG takes on the character of a quick-talking huckster.

PEG: You need the Charlene Atlas Course in Word-Lifting!

GRACIE: Word-lifting?

PEG: That's right! Through a series of gradual exercises, you train yourself to talk back, to lift those heavy, heavy words that have a tendency to get stuck at the back of your throat when you're offended.

GRACIE: Mine seem to stay down somewhere in my diaphragm.

PEG: In your diaphragm? That's serious.

GRACIE: Oh no!

PEG: But, not to worry! Charlene Atlas will teach you to bench press those courageous rejoinders, lifting them from deep down in your diaphragm, up to your esophagus, past your vocal chords—and actually say them to someone.

GRACIE: No kidding!

PEG: Are you tired of having insults kicked in your face at the office?

GRACIE: You bet.

PEG: Are you sick of having innuendos hurled at your head in the street?

GRACIE: I sure am.

PEG: Are you fed up with ignorant assholes trampling on your tenderest feelings?

GRACIE: You'd better believe it, sister.

PEG: Then Charlene Atlas has the answer for you! Her guaranteed, foolproof course in Word-Lifting!

GRACIE: When do I start?

PEG: Right now. First, close your eyes and say to yourself "I am a lesbian."

GRACIE: (*Closes and then opens her eyes.*) Okay. I did that.

PEG: Now, say it out loud, not to anyone in particular.

GRACIE: (*Looking around.*) I am a lesbian.

PEG: Now, look at me when you say it.

GRACIE: (*Looking lovingly at PEG.*) I am a lesbian.

PEG: Now…Imagine I'm Nancy Nice. (*Taunting.*) At least it was a man and a woman. At least it was a man and a woman.

GRACIE: You have to say, "If you know what I mean." That was the worst part.

PEG: Right, I forgot. (*Continues as "Nancy Nice."*) At least it was a man and a woman, if you know what I mean.

PEG, as "Nancy Nice," bears down on GRACIE, who backs away.

At least it was a man and a woman, if you know what I mean. If you know what I mean, if you know what I mean...

GRACIE: (*Disconcerted and mumbling.*) Nancy Nice, I'm a...

PEG, as "Nancy Nice," drives GRACIE into a corner.

PEG: A man and a woman, a man and a woman, if you know what I mean, if you know what I mean!

GRACIE pulls herself together and turns the tables.

GRACIE: Nancy Nice, what's wrong with a *woman* and a *woman*? Do you think it's disgusting, perverted? Do you think that we're all too nice here in this staff room to have ever done IT with a woman? You're wrong, Nancy Nice. You may be nice, but I'm not nice at all.

GRACIE caresses PEG as "Nancy Nice," who moans in horror.

I'm a bad girl, a nasty girl. I do IT with a woman all the time. Nancy Nice, I AM A LESBIAN!

"Nancy Nice" collapses.

And I don't like you making fun of it, if you know what I mean!

PEG transforms from the collapsed "Nancy Nice" back to the "The Huckster."

PEG: Congratulations! Here's your certificate of graduation.

PEG hands GRACIE the funnies from the paper she was reading.

GRACIE: (*Thrilled.*) I am a lesbian!

PEG: You are now qualified to bring up a host of unpleasant subjects in daily conversation, such as your own homosexuality...

GRACIE: (*Taking a bold stance.*) I am a lesbian!

PEG: ....A woman's right to choose...

GRACIE: (*Taking a heroic pose.*) I am a lesbian!

PEG: And various other topics that people would really rather not even think about!

GRACIE climbs on a chair to tell the world.

GRACIE: (*In a Presidential tone.*) My fellow Americans, I am a… LESBIAN!

Lights Fade To Black.

Scene 2
Coming Out To The Parents

Later the same evening.

AT RISE: PEG is straightening up, while GRACIE lounges in the armchair, deep in thought.

GRACIE: Maybe I should write my parents and tell them that I'm a lesbian.

PEG: (*Pause.*) That's an interesting idea.

GRACIE: Maybe I shouldn't write my parents and tell them that I'm a lesbian.

PEG: That's a less interesting but perhaps better idea.

GRACIE: What do you think I should do?

PEG: I think it's up to you.

GRACIE: What did your parents do when you came out to them?

PEG stops cleaning.

PEG: My mother cried and my father said I was dragging the family name through the mud. That was so hysterical. After all the crap that's gone on in my family, I'm the one to bring shame on them.

PEG starts to clean again, stops.

Oh yeah, and they disowned me.

GRACIE: That's very impressive.

PEG: It was kind of scary at the time.

GRACIE: What exactly does one have to do to disown one's daughter?

PEG: You say "I disown thee" three times and change your will. That way, if your parents die while you're disowned, you're up shit creek. No inheritance.

GRACIE: And all because you're queer.

PEG: They really make it very hard to be a lesbian, parents do.

GRACIE: How long were you disowned?

PEG: Two years. I didn't speak to them once. It was great. (*Extremely cheerful.*) You can't imagine how relaxing it is to be disowned. I didn't have to phone, didn't have to write, didn't have to go home for Thanksgiving or Christmas. Now that I'm part of the family again, I have endure my mother's endless critique of my life. Yes, the nightmare of Christmas has returned!

> *The lights dim on the main stage, rise on the band stage. PEG and GRACIE join THE BAND, who are all wearing elf and Santa hats. The song is sung by PEG, with GRACIE and THE BAND joining in as a chorus on this traditional holiday tune.*

> Song: TWELVE DAYS OF CHRISTMAS

On my first day home for Christmas, my mother said to me
"You have no good clothes to wear."
On my second day home for Christmas, my mother said to me,
"You've put on some weight.
You have no good clothes to wear."
Third day: "You should get a job."
Fourth day: "Visit your aunt Ruby."
Fifth day: "Still no boyfriend!?!"
Sixth day: "What's this in your suitcase?"
Seventh day: "Susan's getting married!"
Eighth day: "Esther has three kids now."
Ninth day: "Do I smell marijuana?"
Tenth day: "Are you still on foodstamps?"
Eleventh day: "Your life is a disaster."
Twelfth day: (*PEG sings.*) On the twelfth day home for Christmas…(*PEG pauses, then speaks.*)

I left! I couldn't take it anymore.

Refrain: (All sing slowly together.)

"You have no good clothes to wear!"

NOTE: For the final time through, change Sixth Day line: "What's this in your suitcase?" to "How do you use this thing, anyway?"

Lights down on THE BAND. PEG and GRACIE return to the living room.

PEG: Oh, those two years without Christmas. I really enjoyed being disowned.

GRACIE: Why did they repossess you?

PEG: They missed me.

GRACIE: They missed you, huh? So how long do you think it will take my parents to get over my coming out to them?

PEG: For you, a minimum of four years.

GRACIE: Four years! Come on, they're liberal Jews. They've got to be able to do it faster than that.

PEG: Oh no. No, no, no. Liberal Jews can be the worst. You're supposed to be better than everyone else because you're Jewish. Not worse than everyone else.

GRACIE: So what else did your parents say when you came out to them?

PEG: I remember my father using the word "slimy" many more times than was absolutely necessary. And my mother said her stomach hurt and she hoped she didn't get a bleeding ulcer from the whole ordeal. And my younger brother informed me that he'd like to smash my face in.

GRACIE: Wow!

PEG: Well, my younger brother's very melodramatic. Besides, he's been wanting to smash my face in since he was five years old. The fact that I'm a lesbian just gave him a good excuse.

GRACIE: (*Thoughtfully.*) It sounds like fun.

PEG: It most definitely is not fun. (*Sarcastically.*) Although maybe you'd enjoy it. It'd give you something to write about.

GRACIE: I could never tell them in person, though, like you did.

PEG: Of course not. You'd want a written document to show what you'd been through.

GRACIE: (*Decisively.*) I want to do it.

PEG: Why now?

GRACIE embraces PEG, then pulls back and looks her right in the eyes.

GRACIE: Our relationship is pretty serious, right?

PEG: (*That's obvious.*) Right.

GRACIE: And we're going to spend the rest of our lives together, right?

PEG: (*That's a bit less obvious. Pause.*) Right.

GRACIE: So my parents will have to find out sometime, right?

PEG: (*This is not obvious at all.*) Not necessarily...

GRACIE: (*Blithely.*) So it might as well be right now, right? Right!

GRACIE sits herself down at the typewriter.

PEG: (*While GRACIE is typing.*) Okay, but get ready for the fireworks.

GRACIE: Now, how does this sound? (*Reading what she's typed.*) Dear M and D—

PEG: M and D? It sounds like a tampon.

GRACIE: I really call them Mommy and Daddy. But I'm too old to say Mommy and Daddy anymore. So to get around it, I say M and D.

PEG: Get back to the letter.

GRACIE: (*Reading.*) Dear M and D, I have some good news and some bad news. (*Typing.*) The good news is...I have finally found the person I want to spend the rest of my life with. (*Types.*) The bad news is (*Pause.*) ...she's not Jewish! You see, I'm trying to disarm them with humor.

PEG: Now that they're rolling around on the floor in hysterics, what do you say next?

GRACIE: I don't know. On second thought, maybe a joke is the wrong approach. How about something simple but eloquent like... (*Types.*) Dear M and D, I am a lesbian, period.

PEG: And then?

GRACIE: Isn't that enough? That's the relevant information. What do you say after you say you're queer? I'm so tired of coming out. I'm so sick of figuring out how much to say and when to say it. I'm fed up with always thinking about when I can touch you and how much. I just wish that everyone in the entire world knew that I was a lesbian right now. Then I wouldn't have to come out anymore.

PEG: It's pretty tedious, this coming out business.

GRACIE: (*Types.*) Dear M and...

She pulls paper out of the typewriter and rips it up, throws herself in the big chair.

PEG: Why don't you tell M and D to their faces?

GRACIE: (*Embarrassed.*) I don't want to see their expressions.

PEG dances around GRACIE who still sits in the big chair.

PEG: How about sending them a Polaroid picture of you and me kissing? Skywriting? An anonymous phone call?

She adopts a foreign accent and pretends to talk on the phone.

Hello? M and D? Your daughter is a lesbian. Heh heh heh.

GRACIE: You're not taking this seriously. This is a serious problem and I don't know what to do about it.

PEG: Why don't you talk it over with your therapist?

GRACIE: She'd charge me $30.00 to act like my mother.

PEG: (*Taken aback.*) Thirty dollars? (*This is a lot of money in the 1980s.*)

GRACIE: Yep.

PEG: Hell, I'll do it for nothing. I can play your mother. I'll just do and say all the most disgusting things I can imagine doing and saying.

PEG dons an apron to play "The Mother." GRACIE takes the apron away from PEG, and puts it on herself. She will keep the apron on throughout all the following mother and daughter scenes.

GRACIE: No no no. You don't know my mother, but I do. So I get to play her.

PEG: But I do know you!

GRACIE: Precisely! So you can play me.

PEG: Okay. I'm going out there and come back as you, and announce to you, that's your mother, that I, that's you, am a lesbian—are a lesbian—whatever.

GRACIE: Got it.

PEG exits. GRACIE grabs a mixing bowl and a big colorful mixing spoon and mimes mixing. PEG re-enters.

PEG: (*Entering.*) Hi, Mom.

GRACIE: Hello, dear. (*A motherly kiss.*) How was your day?

PEG: Fine. I'm a lesbian. (*Silence.*) Well, say something.

GRACIE: I can't think of anything to say.

PEG: This is hopeless.

GRACIE: I don't like the way you played me. I would never just stomp in and say, "Hi Mom, I'm a lesbian." How tacky.

PEG: I was giving you a chance to role play.

GRACIE: I can't believe you would portray me as so totally lacking in finesse.

PEG: Look, let's start over.

GRACIE: I need to approach this situation gradually. I need to slowly immerse myself in the intense emotion, the stark drama, the tragic conflict of the generations…

PEG: What if we acted it out in the style of Greek tragedy?

GRACIE: Oh, you're so smart.

PEG: I am, aren't I?

> *PEG takes two shawls from the coatrack.*

GRACIE: What are you doing?

PEG: (*Handing a shawl to GRACIE with great ceremony.*) Your Greek robe, madam.

GRACIE: Yes!

> *There is a dramatic change in the lighting; it becomes stark with intense color. THE BAND plays discordant and melodramatic sounds of cymbals crashing, flute playing, drum rolling. GRACIE and PEG wrap the shawls around their heads and shoulders. They assume an erect bearing and use broad sweeeping gestures when they talk. They speak passionately, overclearly and sonorously, so that they sound ancient and Greeky.*

DAUGHTER: Mother, I must tell you of the love I bear for women, of the world I have found on the Isle of Lesbos. If only you could see the women there—how brave they are, how strong, how modest. Astonishing!

MOTHER: I have heard that they are drunk, hopelessly drunk on sexual desire. It revolts me to imagine them nestling like birds in thick leaves, locked in their lust.

DAUGHTER: (*With bitterness.*) You do not know how to listen.

MOTHER: I should have let your father guard you with bronze shields, kept you from going abroad, disgracing your family.

DAUGHTER: Bronze shields do not hold off women's hands.

MOTHER: The last time I saw you was the day you set sail with your brothers. Some inhuman power took my senses then, to let you go, and decided your fate for you. (*Cold, with hatred.*) And now I look at you and find I have no daughter.

DAUGHTER: (*Pleading, desperate.*) Mother, you need only choose between some false image you hold of a daughter of perfection, and me, your real, your living child.

She grabs her MOTHER's arm.

MOTHER: No! Do not touch me. (*She pulls her arm away.*) Do not pretend to be the daughter I have lost. My daughter lies dead…

DAUGHTER: (*In despair.*) Your sword edges near the heart. It stabs deep, bittersharp.

MOTHER: Get thee gone.

Arm outstretched, she points into the distance, away.

DAUGHTER: (*Straightening up, to herself.*) I will set my sail again. There is no place for me here. In my city, in my house, in my mother's arms, all despise me.

She turns to MOTHER, one last plea.

Will you give me your farewell?

MOTHER: Shall I say, "terrible but blest"? No mere mother can bless what the gods revile. When the gods despise someone, she goes outcast, forgotten. So go you from me.

> *Pointing once more, MOTHER silently indicates that DAUGHTER must leave. DAUGHTER walks away slowly, heartbroken. Cymbals crash, drums roll. Then, lights return to normal, as do PEG and GRACIE. They return their shawls to the coatrack.*

GRACIE: Bleagh!

PEG: Too heavy, too heavy.

GRACIE: I want something that reflects the absurdity of human relations. Some scene that's comic...

PEG: ...and fast-moving...

GRACIE: ...and witty...

PEG: ...and lascivious...

TOGETHER: Restoration comedy!

> *THE BAND plays Baroque music. The lighting is pink and amber and sparkling. PEG and GRACIE pirouette around the stage, picking up fans from the basket on the bookcase, dancing a minuet. MOTHER sits and fans herself prettily.*

MOTHER: Dearest daughter, at Mrs. Williperk's salon today, your name was mentioned gently and with praise by...Margaret Thatchery.

DAUGHTER: (*Aside.*) Margaret Thatchery! At the very name I swoon.

MOTHER: And I wondered how you two happed to meet.

DAUGHTER: (*Aside.*) She attempts to ferret me out. I must dissemble to protect my Margaret. (*To MOTHER.*) Margaret Thatcher? Do I remember her?

MOTHER: No, no no! Margaret Thatcher-*eee*, the parson's wife.

DAUGHTER: Nay! Do not define her so!

> *She stamps her little foot.*

Not as someone's wife!

> *She gets a grip on herself.*

Describe the lady's more personal qualities.

MOTHER: She has a tongue of power...for poetry, can read the Latin and the French...

DAUGHTER: (*Aside.*) Oh, the languages that tongue can speak!

MOTHER: She is well expressed. And when she speaks her ivory bosom heaves with all the passions of a...good mother, a wife, a neighbor.

DAUGHTER: (*Aside.*) And a lover.

MOTHER: Her fingers dance the dance of needles and of fire...over her lacework and embroidery.

> *PEG grabs the dishtowel she was using earlier to clean up, and, as DAUGHTER, smells it rapturously as though it were a perfumed lace handkerchief.*

DAUGHTER: I'faith, mother, say no more. I know the lady. And I love her.

MOTHER: As a friend, love?

DAUGHTER: (*Aside.*) I will be brave. (*To MOTHER.*) Nay, more than that.

MOTHER: As a mother, child?

DAUGHTER: (*Enough of this pussy-footing, so to speak.*) No, no, no! As a lover, mother. As a wife. Yea, as a mistress!

MOTHER: (*Completely, totally horrified.*) No!

> *DAUGHTER fondles the handkerchief.*

DAUGHTER: She has embroidered me this handkerchief as a token of her love.

> *MOTHER grabs handkerchief.*

MOTHER: Let me see that. Oh! I faint! I die!!

> *MOTHER collapses in the chair, and throws the handkerchief into the air. DAUGHTER catches the handkerchief. She fans MOTHER furiously.*

DAUGHTER: Oh, I have shocked you, Mother. But rest here and list a moment, I beg you. (*Rapturously.*) Ours is a true love, Mother. As true as that of yours and Father's.

MOTHER: (*Aside.*) Truer than that, I hope.

DAUGHTER: And though this love cannot be bandied about at garden parties or gossiped of at court, is't less for that?

MOTHER: (*GROAN.*)

DAUGHTER: Mother, dear Mother, please consider what a good woman is Margaret, what an honorable woman.

MOTHER: (*GROAN!!*)

DAUGHTER: And when you spoke of her tongue…

MOTHER: (*GROOAANN!!!*)

DAUGHTER: …Her ivory bosom…

MOTHER: (*GROOOAAANNN!!!!!!*)

DAUGHTER: …Her finger's work…

> *MOTHER rises from her prostrate position. She advances on DAUGHTER, poking at her with her closed fan.*

MOTHER: Daughter, stop. I can bear no more. This woman is a traitor, a harpie, a vixen!

DAUGHTER: (*Haughty, dismissive.*) You speak from shallow prejudice.

> *MOTHER grabs handkerchief.*

MOTHER: Even this handkerchief is counterfeit!

DAUGHTER: Now you go too far!!!

> *DAUGHTER dives for the handkerchief, but MOTHER whisks it out of her reach.*

MOTHER: Margaret Thatchery did not design this handkerchief. It was given t'her by another.

> *DAUGHTER successfully retrieves the handkerchief.*

DAUGHTER: Mother, I call you out. Lookkee here.

> *She points to the embroidery on the edge of the handkerchief.*

From M.T. to M.T. That is, from Margaret Thatchery to me, Millicent Teaselwop.

MOTHER: Or *to* Margaret Thatchery *from* me, Maria Teaselwop.

DAUGHTER: (*Pause. Dawning horror.*) What!??? Maria Teaselwop??!!

MOTHER: (*Bowing.*) The same. I embroidered this for Margaret Thatchery.

DAUGHTER: Methought this dainty smelled familiar.

MOTHER: Yes, my Daughter. I too have fallen under the spell of deceitful Margaret Thatchery.

DAUGHTER: But Mother, you are married!

MOTHER: So is Margaret Thatchery.

DAUGHTER: But you are married to Father!

MOTHER: (*Laughing at her naivete.*) Daughter, you have much to learn of the conjugal bed. Why, your Father doesn't know his…

DAUGHTER: Mother, I pray you, stop!

MOTHER: Very well, suffice it to say that your Father prefers his billiards, and on occassion, his young men's rumps…

DAUGHTER puts hands over ears.

DAUGHTER: La la la la la la! Mother, this is nothing my ears wish to hear from your lips…Ohhh, my heart is breaking.

DAUGHTER now collapses into the chair.

MOTHER: (*Quite astonished.*) I never knew you were so fond of Father.

DAUGHTER: Over Margaret Thatchery!

MOTHER: Oh, I'd forgotten about her. Your first love…

DAUGHTER leaps up, throws the handkerchief on the ground and stomps on it.

DAUGHTER: And my last! Pernicious womanhood!

MOTHER retrieves the handkerchief, folding it neatly, tucking it into her bosom.

MOTHER: Oh nonsense. There are plenty of ladies of fashion who prefer the gentler sex. Now, I know naught of your younger set, but among my friends…Mrs. Williperk…

DAUGHTER: (*Very surprised.*) You and Mrs. Williperk?

MOTHER: Mrs. Ashford…

DAUGHTER: (*Absolutley shocked.*) You and Mrs. Ashford?

MOTHER: And especially Miss Nusbern. You remember her.

DAUGHTER: (*Completely gobsmacked.*) My mother and my harpsichord teacher?!?!

MOTHER: (*Carried away with nostalgia.*) I remember well those sweet, golden drawing room afternoons, while you practiced your instrument in the locked room next door.

MOTHER and DAUGHTER regard each other. They fan

themselves. DAUGHTER laughs tentatively, MOTHER laughs generously. They laugh together, acknowledging the absurdity of their dalliances with Margaret. A merry minuet plays as they dance together, ending the scene.

Lights return to normal, as do PEG and GRACIE.

GRACIE: That one was fun! What's next?

PEG: Are you ready for a dose of modern American reality?

GRACIE: Not yet.

PEG: How about a little modern American unreality?

GRACIE: T.V.! A T.V. situation comedy!

THE BAND plays a generic theme from an imaginary sitcom. GRACIE gets the mixing bowl and wooden spoon and starts to vigorously mix. PEG gets a baseball cap, glove and ball from the coatrack. They again assume their daughter-mother roles. MOTHER is stirring cookie dough. DAUGHTER walks in wearing the baseball cap backwards, and smashing the ball into the mitt—a classic baby butch.

DAUGHTER: Hi, Mom!

MOTHER: Hello, sweetie pie!

MOTHER gives DAUGHTER a maternal kiss.

You know, the phone has been ringing off the hook all afternoon!

DAUGHTER: (*Excited.*) Did Jeannie call?

MOTHER: Three different boys!!

DAUGHTER: (*Disappointed.*) Oh.

She takes a fingerfull of cookie dough.

MOTHER: Huey, Dewey, and Louie. And if you ask me, I think they were all calling to ask you to the dance. At least, I know Huey was, because his mother told me…

DAUGHTER: (*Tries to say something through a mouthful of cookie dough.*)

MOTHER: Honeybun, you know I don't like you to talk with your mouth full.

DAUGHTER: (*Finally able to articulate.*) Mom, I heard two new words today, and I don't know what they mean.

MOTHER: What are the words, darling?

DAUGHTER: Well, somebody called…somebody a "dyke."

MOTHER: Oh! A dike is a big wall of earth to hold back the water.

DAUGHTER: Oh. And then somebody also called…this girl a "lesbian."

Long pause.

MOTHER: A les…A lesbi…(*She cannot bring herself to say the word.*) And the other one is a sick, unhappy woman whose father probably beat her and whose mother was a prostitute or worked full-time and didn't pay attention to protecting her little girl!

DAUGHTER: (*Mystified.*) And that's what a lesbian is?

MOTHER: You don't need to worry, princess. No les…no lesbi…No "one of those" ever came from a family like ours.

DAUGHTER: (*Still mystified.*) Oh.

MOTHER: Anyhow, I want to tell you all about your exciting phone calls. Huey's mother said…

DAUGHTER: (*Exploding.*) I hate Huey! He's a cootie, he's a jerk! Why can't he be more like his sister? (*With great longing.*) Jeannie's so nice. She's so funny and smart and beautiful. And she's the best shortstop, and she's such a good speller…

MOTHER: (*A bit manic.*) Well, dear, you know what they always say: "Boys will be boys!" And then, when they grow up, men will be men. There's just nothing you can do about it. But they're wonderful, because without men, we wouldn't have little babies!

DAUGHTER: Mom, would you be mad if I never had any little babies?

MOTHER: Oh, you just can't help it, sweetie pie. Once you get married, it just…sort of happens!

DAUGHTER: What if I don't get married?

MOTHER: Oh now, that's silly! Somebody will like you.

DAUGHTER: But somebody likes me now!

MOTHER: Oh! (*Happy.*)

DAUGHTER: (*With great joy.*) Jeannie likes me!

MOTHER: Oh. (*Not so happy.*)

DAUGHTER: And I like Jeannie too. (*Her dream unfolds.*) And we want to live together for ever and ever. We're gonna buy a big ranch and have horses. But I have to go into town to go to work, and she's gonna make a pie every day so when I come home…

MOTHER: (*Really manic.*) You had THREE phone calls today from three different boys. I'd say you're an "It" girl! When I was young, that's what we called the girls who were popular with the boys. We called them "It" girls, because they had "It." Get it?

DAUGHTER: Can't I be an "It" girl with the other girls?

MOTHER: (*Very direct and angry.*) No, dear, don't be silly. You can be an "It" girl for Huey, and that's IT. (*Returning to her perfect sitcom mother voice.*) I invited him over for dinner tonight.

DAUGHTER: (*Exploding.*) But I told you, I hate Huey!

MOTHER: I'm going to barbecue some hamburgers. And I made my famous macaroni salad…

DAUGHTER: But Mom! Jeannie's coming over to spend the night tonight. We've been planning this all week. I told you.

MOTHER: (*Pause.*) Jeannie's gone to visit her grandma…

DAUGHTER: (*Very confident.*) No, she's coming here tonight…

MOTHER: …For the whole summer.

DAUGHTER is devastated.

Jeannie's mom and I got together last night, and we decided that Jeannie needed to go to the country…right away.

DAUGHTER'S chin begins to quiver. She bows her head, crying.

Oh, baby doll, I know that you're upset now. But later on in your life, you'll thank us for worrying about you and loving you so much. And maybe, someday, after you and Jeannie are all grown up and have babies of your own, you'll get together and look back on this time and just laugh and laugh!

Doorbell.

Oops! There's the doorbell. That must be Huey!

THE BAND returns to the sit-com theme, as the scene ends with the DAUGHTER sobbing piteously.

The lights return to normal, as do PEG and GRACIE.

PEG: So far we've failed to capture the depth of revulsion your mother will feel...

GRACIE: ...the disgust, the terror...

PEG: ...the sense of overwhelming panic...

GRACIE: ...the feeling that the world is coming to an end...

TOGETHER: A horror movie!

The stage grows dark, there are flashes of lighting. Low, thrilling music and thunder are heard. GRACIE finds a long dark vest and a pair of tights on the coatrack. She pulls the tights over her head so that the legs hang down like some strange medieval headgear. PEG finds a tattered but beautiful dressing gown. She takes the quill from the pencil jar on GRACIE's desk.

DAUGHTER: (*Very ladylike.*) Mother dear, I intend to spend the evening in my study, quietly reading and writing. Pray, do not disturb me.

MOTHER: As you wish, daughter.

DAUGHTER sits down to write, a strong moonbeam pours down directly upon her.

DAUGHTER: My dearest darling Hubert, my great love for you fills me, as I sit here while the beautiful full moon pours its beams on me...

MOTHER exits, nodding and smiling. DAUGHTER begins to pant and heave, some strange power is taking over her body. She regains control of herself and returns to writing the letter.

Dear Huey, the moon...

The word "moon" becomes a howl. She stops herself and tries to write the letter again.

The moon...

Same problem.

That orb in the sky... beats down on me mercilessly. I like you... every once in awhile...

DAUGHTER begins to transform into a bulldyke, growling, panting. She discovers her own breasts, and takes quite a bit of pleasure in them. She emits lots of weird wolfy, sexual sounds.

She tears up the letter. She walks around room, feeling her strength. MOTHER enters with a mug of cocoa.

MOTHER: Daughter, would you like some cocoa?

She stops and stares in horror at DAUGHTER, who is now a full-fledged bulldagger. DAUGHTER turns to MOTHER and laughs maniacally. She approaches MOTHER. MOTHER cowers. There is a small tug-of-war over the mug of cocoa. DAUGHTER gets mug and quaffs it all in a few huge gulps, then hands it back to MOTHER, wiping her mouth on her sleeve, belching and laughing insanely. MOTHER cowers in fright at the monster her DAUGHTER has become. DAUGHTER returns to her letter writing.

DAUGHTER: Dear Hubert, you disgust me!

She tears off that sheet and tosses it off, laughing [as always] maniacally. She thinks a moment, then, with tender, crooning sounds, begins another letter.

My dearest Jeannie, as I sit here in the moonlight, I think of your beautiful breasts and I want to...

DAUGHTER howls like a wolf. MOTHER addresses the audience, piteously.

MOTHER: My daughter is a—my daughter is a—my daughter is a LESBIAN!

She is wracked with sobs. DAUGHTER addresses the audience.

DAUGHTER: It feels so good to come out to your mother!

Lights Fade To Black as DAUGHTER howls and MOTHER sobs.

Scene 3
Men

The next Friday. 5:30 p.m.
AT RISE: GRACIE sits at her desk, writing. She reads aloud what she has just written.

GRACIE: Dear M and D...

PEG enters from outside.

Hey, listen to this. I think I've finally...got ...it...

She realizes PEG is not listening. PEG is in a rage.

PEG: I just got off the bus, see? Not in a very good fucking mood from looking for fucking work all day. This creep starts following me down the street. "Hey baby, let's have some fun. You look like you need a real man to fuck you." You know, all the traditional pleasantries. I didn't say anything. Just kept walking, "Come on, baby. Suck my cock. You know you want to. You know you do." Finally, I turn around and I say, "Listen, man, I'm a lesbian. I'm not interested in men. So just leave me alone, Okay?" AND HE SPIT ON ME! I started screaming. I don't know what I said…"You bastard!"…"You stupid …!" I wanted to kill him! He took off down the street. I scared the shit out of him! I wanted to kill him! (*Pause.*) Those miserable little wienie brains! Why can't they leave us alone? Isn't it enough for them that most of the women in the world are straight? No, it drives them crazy that a few of us don't want to be fucked by them. Find a hole and stick it in. That's all they think about. They don't care if it's a woman, a man, a chicken, or a cantaloupe.

GRACIE: Gay men aren't so bad. At least they do it to each other instead of doing it to women.

PEG sits in the big chair.

PEG: Let them act out their bizarre fantasies with other men. I don't care.

GRACIE: Honey, what can I do to make you feel better? Fix you a drink? Give you a massage? How about some potato chips?

PEG: A massage sounds good.

GRACIE crosses over, stands behind PEG, massaging her neck.

Oh, and when you have some free time, you might kill all the men in the world. That would definitely make me feel better.

GRACIE: Actually, that's a very interesting idea. We could have an international plot to kill all the men! After all, what do Genghis Khan, Stalin, Hitler, and Idi Amin all have in common?

During the next few lines, her massage becomes much more intense, even violent.

Are they all white? No. Are they all capitalists? NO. Are they all heterosexual? Probably, although there's a little doubt about Hitler. But what do these people indisputably have in common, besides the fact that they screwed up the world? They're all men!

After a very strong karate chop to PEG's neck, PEG takes

GRACIE's hands in hers.

Now, if all the women kill all the men…

PEGS pulls GRACIE down onto her lap.

PEG: Then we would be a world of murderers.

GRACIE: A world of female murderers. Murderesses. (*Fervently.*) I'd rather live in that world than the one we are living in right now.

PEG: What about the faggots? Would you kill them?

GRACIE: I would miss the faggots. They are so charming and such good dancers.

PEG: They make excellent roommates.

GRACIE: And they do have a great sense of style.

PEG: They cut hair so well.

GRACIE: But they gossip too much.

TOGETHER: Let's kill them.

PEG: Actually, with AIDS, we don't have to worry about killing off the faggots, do we?

GRACIE: (*Pause.*) No, I guess not.

Silence. They hold each other, leaning into each other for comfort as they remember the friends they have lost. After a few moments, PEG breaks away.

PEG: How about your father? Would you kill your father?

GRACIE stands up. Crosses to desk.

GRACIE: My father…I have to think about that…I love him…I would feel great sorrow at his death…but…Yes! If it meant we could start all over in a world of women, I would do it. Would you kill Russell?

PEG stands up. Crosses to table.

PEG: Russell? He's my best friend. We grew up together. (*Pause.*) No, I couldn't do it.

GRACIE: I thought you hated men!

PEG: I hate men, but I love Russell.

PEG opens a beer.

GRACIE: Well, how are we going to kill off all the men in the world if you're not willing to kill Russell?

PEG toasts with beer.

PEG: Obviously, if I'm not willing to kill Russell, we can't do it.

PEG drinks beer.

GRACIE: Dammit!

Lights fade to black and then come up on the nightclub stage.

GRACIE joins THE BAND on the nightclub stage. She carries a large pair of hedge clippers.

GRACIE:

    Song: JILL THE RIPPER

I saw you walking home one night, so safe and sure and smug.
So unafraid of mugger, rapist, robber, punk or thug.
I followed right behind you,
Hoping someplace dark I'd find you,
Where I'd rope and tie and bind you,
And I'd squash you like a bug.

The next night as I followed you, you seemed as if in shock.
You walked a little faster and your knees began to knock.
And when I bared my clippers,
An enormous pair of snippers,
With a grin like Jack the Ripper's,
You went running down the block.

Last night as I was following, you muttered and you prayed.
You crossed the street at least four times, my presence to evade.
I thrilled to the sensation,
In my mad imagination,
Of your imminent castration,
With my razor-sharpened blade.

Tonight I will wait patiently, 'til you come into sight.
I'll hear your heaving heartbeat, smell your sweat and feel your fright.
There's no hope of escaping,
You are done with all your raping,
And your crotch I'll be reshaping,

Or—if not—tomorrow night.

Lights Fade To Black.

Scene 4
Meeting The Parents: Before

The next Friday. 5:30 p.m.

AT RISE: An empty stage. PEG rushes in. She is wearing a dinner jacket over her best bowling shirt.

PEG: Honey, are you ready?

She looks around.

God dammit!

She searches for a note. Finds a piece of paper. Reads it aloud.

"How do I love thee? Why do I love thee? Thou art strong, but not long. Thou art large, not unlike a barge."

She crumples paper, throws it away. GRACIE enters, wearing a large colorful coat and wonderful shoes.

GRACIE: I'm here.

PEG: Where have you been? We're late!

GRACIE: Almost late, but not quite.

PEG: We have to be at the restaurant in fifteen minutes.

GRACIE: It's only a five minute drive from here.

PEG: Let's go.

GRACIE: What's the hurry? I think I want a drinkie-winkie first.

PEG: You want a drink? You must be nervous.

GRACIE: I just want a little drinkie-winkie before we meet my parents.

PEG: Well, since you're having one…

PEG pours two drinks and hands one to GRACIE. PEG slugs hers down. GRACIE sips her drink slowly and noisily.

PEG (con't): Come on, come on. We're gonna be late. I know we're gonna be late. And if we're late, your parents will blame me.

GRACIE: (*Still sipping.*) We won't be late.

PEG: How do I look?

> *PEG turns around with her arms out, so GRACIE can inspect her.*

GRACIE: (*Pause.*) Good. Very good.

PEG: Not great?

GRACIE: Not great. But, very good.

PEG: What's wrong? Come on, tell me what's wrong. I can take it. Spit it out.

GRACIE: It's the shoes.

PEG: The shoes? (*She regards them.*) What's the matter with the shoes? I polished them.

GRACIE: The heels are very rundown.

PEG: That's a very small detail.

GRACIE: I didn't say it was important. It just keeps you from looking great.

PEG: (*A bit distressed.*) I am not a rich person. I only have one pair of shoes, so the heels get run down. Is that such a terrible thing?

GRACIE: You could have gotten them fixed.

PEG: (*A bit more distressed.*) How can I get them fixed when they're the only pair of shoes I have? What am I supposed to wear on my feet while the heels are being replaced? Banana leaves?

GRACIE: I think black plastic garbage bags would be more appropriate.

PEG: (*Greatly distressed.*) Your parents are going to hate me because my heels are rundown. I'll walk on my knees so they won't notice.

> *PEG gets on her knees and mimes shaking hands with someone.*

Hello, M and D. So nice to meet you.

GRACIE: That could make things even worse.

PEG: Worse? You mean they're bad now? I thought your parents were anxious to meet me.

GRACIE: Anxious…that's an appropriate word.

PEG: What did they say about me?

GRACIE: My father said, "I see, I see," while my mother cried softly in the background. But sometimes they switched places and my mother said, "I see," so my father had a chance to cry.

PEG: I see.

She cries softly.

GRACIE: It must be catching.

PEG: Why do they want to meet me if they're so upset?

GRACIE: I didn't say they wanted to meet you.

PEG: Why are they willing to meet me?

GRACIE: I didn't say they were willing.

PEG: What exactly did you say to me, then, when you told me about this dinner engagement?

GRACIE: (*Pause.*) I said they were going to meet you.

PEG: Let me ask you a question.

GRACIE: Shoot.

PEG: Do your mother and father know they are going to meet me tonight?

GRACIE: No.

PEG: Wonderful.

GRACIE: I thought it would be a nice surprise.

PEG: A nice surprise.

GRACIE: Maybe not a nice surprise, but…a surprising surprise. After tonight they will have met you. That part of the ordeal will be over.

PEG: Thanks a lot.

GRACIE: Then, maybe next time we see them, you and I can hold hands. And maybe after that, we can kiss.

PEG: You plan these little dramatic scenes without thinking of anyone else, don't you? What if your parents are rude to me? What if they walk out on me?

GRACIE: They won't. They're very well trained. They have excellent manners.

PEG: Believe me, manners can fly right out the window when your child's a queer. I've seen it happen before, in my own family.

GRACIE: Come on. Don't tell me that your mother was ever rude. I don't believe it.

PEG: You should have seen her with my first lover. She wouldn't even speak to her. Turned her back on her.

GRACIE: You're kidding!

PEG: It was shameful.

GRACIE: (*Pause.*) I hope I haven't made a big mistake.

PEG: Don't worry. You haven't.

> *GRACIE embraces PEG.*

GRACIE: Oh honey, I'm so glad you feel that way.

> *PEG pushes GRACIE away.*

PEG: You haven't made a big mistake because I refuse to meet your parents for dinner tonight.

GRACIE: Oh no!

PEG: It's out of the question under the circumstances.

> *PEG takes off her jacket with great ceremony.*

GRACIE: But it'll be so interesting.

PEG: Interesting! You don't care what happens, do you, as long as there's some action for you to observe! You'll probably write it all down in your journal tonight, won't you?

GRACIE: What's wrong with that?

PEG: I know you. I won't act in your little play. I'd love to meet your parents, but not like this. Besides, I couldn't possibly make a public appearance tonight. My heels need to be replaced.

GRACIE: Oh please…please…pleeeeeeeeeaaaaasssssseeeee…

> *GRACIE gets down on her knees, begs PEG… No response.*

GRACIE: I guess I better get going then.

PEG: Yes, I guess you'd better.

GRACIE: You're not mad at me, are you?

PEG: No, I am furious!

GRACIE: I just wanted to get it over with. (*Pause.*) What are you going to do for dinner tonight?

PEG: I'll stay here and fix something.

GRACIE: There's nothing to eat. I didn't have a chance to go shopping today.

PEG: You're doing everything right, aren't you? Well, I think I'll just fast.

GRACIE: Oh, please come to dinner. It's a fancy French restaurant. The food is supposed to be great. You can order whatever you want. Even escargot.

PEG: (*Ears prick up.*) Escargot?

GRACIE: I'll order them, too, and you can have my share.

PEG: Two orders of escargot?

GRACIE: I just cannot bear the thought of you starving here while I'm sitting in a beautiful, elegant restaurant, stuffing myself with delicious, rich…

PEG: After all, your parents couldn't be that bad.

GRACIE: Of course not.

PEG: You're not that bad. So how could your parents be that bad?

GRACIE: Exactly!

PEG: And I am hungry. Very hungry.

GRACIE: It would mean so much to me. (*Inspiration strikes.*) I'll wash all the dishes for a month if you come!

>   *Pause.*

PEG: All right, I'll do it!

GRACIE: Yay!

>   *She throws her arms around PEG, kissing her.*

GRACIE: Thank you, sweetie. I'll never forget this.

PEG puts her jacket back on and they exit.

Lights Fade To Black.

Scene 5
Meeting The Parents: After

Later that night. 9:00 p.m.

AT RISE: PEG and GRACIE walk in, slowly, separately. PEG throws her jacket on the floor and slumps in the big chair. GRACIE hangs up both their jackets.

PEG: Well, that certainly was a lovely evening.

GRACIE: How was I to know?

PEG: How were you to know? I told you it was going to be awful. That's how you were to know.

GRACIE: I didn't believe you.

PEG: Oh no, you never believe anybody. You've got to experience everything for yourself, firsthand. Well, next time you decide on a nice little confrontation to clear the air, count me out.

GRACIE: Why did they have to be so…so creepy?

PEG: I think it's written somewhere. Ah yes, I remember. The eleventh commandment. I believe Moses brought it down from the top of whatever mountain he was on. "Thou shall not be civil to thy child's homosexual lover."

GRACIE: "Thou shalt make thy child feel like shit for being queer."

PEG: Yes, something like that. I forget the words, exactly. But I'm sure it's in the Bible somewhere. (*Pause.*) And the escargot were tough! They were, without a doubt, the most disgusting escargot I have ever had in my life.

GRACIE goes to PEG, hugs her, sitting on the arm of the chair.

GRACIE: I'm sorry.

PEG: (*Not looking at GRACIE.*) So am I.

GRACIE: No honey, I'm really sorry they treated you so badly. I apologize.

PEG: I think it was when your father refused to pass me the salt after my third request that I started to get upset.

GRACIE: They never looked at you or said a word to you.

PEG: Well, thank goodness for that! I'd hate to hear what they would have said if they had.

GRACIE: It was really hard to reach all the way across the table and get the salt for you.

PEG: I imagine so. That must be why you spilled wine all over your mother when you did it.

GRACIE: No, I did that on purpose.

PEG: (*Greatly cheered.*) You did? Isn't that sweet. Thank you, baby. She deserved it.

GRACIE: They deserved a lot more.

She stands, starts pacing.

Why did we sit all through that horrible meal? Why didn't we storm right out after my mother refused to shake your hand?

PEG: I don't know. We should have. I was taking my cue from you.

GRACIE: Why do I always do this? Why do I always figure out what to do after the opportunity has passed? I'm such a wimp. I can't stand it. Especially around my parents. Why don't I just tell them off and leave it at that? Why do I keep trying to make them understand my life?

PEG: (*Softly.*) Because they're your parents and you love them.

GRACIE: I don't love them. I hate them. They're jerks, they're creeps, they're bigots, they're… Oh Peg, I'm so disappointed in them. Why do I let them do this to me? Why do I even care what they think? I hate them. I'm going to disown them.

PEG, still sitting in the big chair, opens her arms.

PEG: Come here, baby.

GRACIE goes to PEG. She caresses, comforts GRACIE.

PEG (con't): I know it's hard, isn't it? When you really see your parents for what they are.

GRACIE: Goddamn phony liberal Jews. Goddamn gutless, conventional, cowardly…

PEG: That's it. Get it all out.

GRACIE: Oh Peg, I feel awful.

PEG: They don't understand. But maybe they will someday.

GRACIE: And maybe they won't.

PEG: That's right. Maybe they won't. But we know what we've got, don't we? We don't need them to tell us it's good.

GRACIE: I do want them to tell me it's good. That's what I want. I know it's stupid. But I want it.

PEG: You've got to let go of that one, baby, or you'll never be happy.

GRACIE: I know. I know. (*Pause.*) Peg?

PEG: Yes?

GRACIE: Could you just hold me?

PEG: Oh, my love.

> *PEG holds GRACIE. She snuggles into PEG's lap. Lights fade as PEG kisses GRACIE's shoulder tenderly.*
>
> *Lights Fade To Black.*

Scene 6
Depression

The next Friday. 5:30 p.m.

AT RISE: PEG is pursuing the Want Ads. GRACIE is looking through the index of a book.

GRACIE: Let's see…abstinence…coitus…fellatio…impotence…masturbation…Oops! I've gone too far. Ah, here it is! Lesbian, page 191.

> *GRACIE finds the page and reads.*

"The top rung on the ladder of eroticism can be the first rung on the ladder of perversion." Ooooh. That sounds hot. "These pathetic women lead lives of hopeless desperation. They frequent seedy saloons looking for a partner in perversion to satisfy depraved cravings. Despised by humanity, scorned by their families, these forlorn females are neurotic and depressed." (*To PEG.*) Are you depressed?

PEG: (*Very matter-of-fact.*) No, I'm happy.

GRACIE: But it says right here in this book that all lesbians are unhappy.

PEG: I know. I'm totally out of sync. It makes me feel terrible.

GRACIE: Maybe I can think of something to depress you so you won't feel so bad.

PEG: That would be nice.

GRACIE: Let me see…You're an outcast and considered a pervert by society. Does that depress you?

PEG: Considering what society is like, I prefer to be an outcast.

GRACIE: Me too. Especially since I'm Jewish. I'm more comfortable as an outcast. It's in my blood. But I've never felt really oppressed as a Jew. Maybe someday I will.

PEG: Being black is still a very good oppression.

GRACIE: That's true, but there's no way you can choose it. No, when you get right down to it, homosexuality is the oppression of choice. Anyone can be queer, regardless of sex, race, religion, creed or age. Homosexuality—the equal opportunity oppression! (*Pause.*) Do you feel bad that you can't have a penis stuck inside you?

PEG looks up, does not deign to reply.

How about a big strong man to protect you? Do you ever miss that?

PEG: Not having ever had a big strong man to protect me, I find it a difficult thing to miss.

GRACIE: I see your point.

PEG: How about you?

GRACIE: Me? I'd much rather be protected by a big, strong woman.

She approaches PEG in a cartoon of a seduction.

PEG: Aw shucks, ma'am.

They embrace.

GRACIE: What about children? Does it depress you that you can't have children?

PEG: Children? Are you kidding? All that work, all those dirty diapers, all that money, and for what? So some little brat can grow up and do exactly what she wants to do with her life? Forget it. Look at my poor mother. She worked and slaved and ended up with a lesbian. I was a terrible child. My mother had to put a leash on me to control me. (*Pause.*) Still…

GRACIE: What?

PEG: Sometimes it makes me sad that you and I can't have a child together.

GRACIE: I know. I feel the same way sometimes. But imagine what our child would be like. It would be completely obnoxious.

PEG: It would be unbearable. And I'd end up doing all the work.

GRACIE: What are you talking about? I'd make a great mother!

PEG: Don't be ridiculous. You are the most undomestic person I've ever met. You don't like to cook, you don't like to sew, you don't like to clean, you don't like sweeping, you don't like doing the dishes, you don't like ironing....

GRACIE: I love doing the dishes!

PEG: And what else? There's a little more to having a baby than doing the dishes. Tell me one other thing you like to do around the house.

No response.

You'd make a rotten mother.

GRACIE: That's true. I'm not the nurturing type.

PEG: Some people would call it lazy.

GRACIE: I told you, I did all that stuff for men when I was with them.

PEG: You're always telling me all the wonderful things you did for men. Why don't you do some of those things for me?

GRACIE: I told you, I'm sick and tired of all that crap. I've had my life quota of cooking and cleaning.

PEG: Well, it seems to me that the men got a hell of a lot better deal than I'm getting.

GRACIE: All right, all right. You've convinced me. I'd make a rotten mother. Anyhow, what if it turned out to be a little girl who liked frilly dresses and makeup and boys?

PEG: Or a little boy who liked to kill butterflies and hit little girls. Or twins? A boy who liked frilly dresses…

GRACIE: And a girl who killed butterflies.

PEG: Disgusting.

GRACIE: Insupportable.

TOGETHER: It's better we can't have a child.

GRACIE: Well, have I succeeded in depressing you?

PEG: No! I don't understand. They must have lied to me when I was growing up.

> *Lights up on THE BAND, who now sport cowgirl hats and bandanas. PEG sings. GRACIE joins her on the last chorus.*

PEG:

        Song: MISERY LOVES COMPANY

They taught me when I was a tyke
There's no one sadder than a dyke.
We seek out others who're the same
In lonely bars to share our grief and shame.
Because,

Misery loves company
I was taught that that was true,
Misery loves company
And that's why I love you.

I grew up frightened and alone
My special sadness was my own.
I thought that I was just no good
Because I didn't yearn for motherhood.
You know that,

Misery loves company
'Specially when I've had a few,
Misery loves company
And that's why I love you.

But I discovered as I grew
That straight folks can feel lonely too,
And let me tell you how it looks
The saddest folks are those who write those books.
Saying,

Misery loves company
Don't let them tell you that it's true,
Misery loves company
And that's why I love you.

Now I am happy as a clam

>   Since I have found out what I am,
>   And since it seems I must be one
>   I wish every woman was a lesbian.
> **PEG & GRACIE:** Because,
>
>   Misery loves company
>   Just like the grass loves the dew,
>   Misery loves company
>   But not like I love you.
>
>   *PEG and GRACIE look at each other, then embrace, then kiss. PEG starts unbuttoning GRACIE's shirt. GRACIE starts to unbutton PEG's.*
>
>   *Lights fade to black, THE BAND continues to play in the blackout.*

Scene 7

Sex

Later that night. 9:00 p.m.

AT RISE: PEG and GRACIE have just gotten out of bed. They are both wearing bathrobes. PEG is sitting tensely in a chair on one side of the stage, GRACIE is sitting tensely in a chair on the other side of the stage. PEG has a beer. GRACIE has a bag of potato chips. They are both upset.

GRACIE: Sex is so difficult for me.

PEG: Don't get upset. You're good at other things—like typing.

GRACIE: It's a problem. I have to solve it.

PEG: Everything for you is a problem you have to solve. Why can't you just be happy with what you have?

GRACIE: You know, when I slept with men, sex was never that important. Of course, if I didn't have it, I was obsessed with it. But once I was in a relationship, I'd always think, why do I make such a big fuss about it? But ever since I've been with women, sex has always been a big deal.

   PEG relaxes a little, she goes to get another beer.

PEG: That's because all lesbians are sex maniacs.

GRACIE: That's another thing. I always thought that women had a weaker sex drive than men. So I assumed that one advantage of being a lesbian is that my partner wouldn't always be bugging me to have sex. But if there are women besides me with a weak sex drive, I haven't found them yet.

PEG returns to the big comfortable chair with beer.

PEG: That's because all perverts are sex maniacs.

GRACIE: I'm a pervert, and I'm not a sex maniac.

PEG: That's because you are a perverted pervert. And everybody knows that perverted perverts never have any fun because they think too much. When you're making love, everything is OK.

GRACIE: If everything is OK, then why isn't it OK for me to think? Why isn't it OK for me to be uptight and repressed if everything is OK?

PEG: You're always expecting the earth to move. But sex isn't like that all the time. Sometimes it just feels good. Sometimes it's pleasant. And sometimes it stinks.

GRACIE: I should never have read *Lady Chatterley's Lover* that first semester in college.

Pause.

PEG: I hesitate to ask, but what does *Lady Chatterley's Lover* have to do with us?

GRACIE: Those sex scenes are engraved on my brain. I was a virgin then and I thought that's what sex was really like. You know, (*Standing to act this out like a modern dance.*) the waves crashing on the rocks and the tide rolling in and rolling out, rolling in and rolling out.

PEG: It's high tide for us sometimes, isn't it?

GRACIE crosses to PEG, stands next to the big chair.

GRACIE: But not all the time. Why can't it be all the time?

PEG: God, I am so sick of this. Everything's been just fine this week. So you get bored and you poke around and you poke around for something to get upset about, and when you can't find anything else, you pounce on SEX! We'll probably have our money argument tomorrow.

GRACIE: What's wrong with trying to improve our sexual relationship?

PEG: It's not our relationship! It's you! It's your problem! Leave me out of it!

GRACIE: Let me just ask you a question.

She sits on an arm of the chair. PEG puts a pillow over her face.

If you had to choose between having sex every single day...no, twice a day for the rest of your life and never having sex again, at all, ever... what would you choose?

No response.

All right, let me ask you another question. Which would you rather do: have sex or...read the newspaper?

Still no response.

But honey, the newspaper is very dependable. Whereas sex... sometimes sex is a waste of time. Maybe the Catholics are right. Maybe we should just have sex to procreate. Otherwise it's a big waste of time.

PEG removes the pillow from her face.

PEG: That would totally eliminate homosexuality.

GRACIE: Good point, good point, Peg. You know, when I was with men, I used to fantasize about being with women all the time. And now that I'm with women, I fantasize about men. Isn't that terrible?

PEG: Yes, it is.

GRACIE: Ever since I heard that a woman reaches her sexual peak at thirty-five, I always thought, "Oh boy, I can't wait! Some day, I'll be a drooling maniac!" But now I'm thirty-four, and let me tell you, unless things start improving rapidly, my sexual peak is going to be a sexual foothill. Maybe a valley. Yes, a sexual valley would be a good way of describing it. And then, when I think that after thirty-five, it's all downhill...I'll go into a canyon. By the time I'm fifty, I'll probably be at the bottom of the Grand Canyon of sexuality! It's very depressing, very depressing.

PEG: If it upsets you so much, why don't you ever say anything when we're actually making love?

GRACIE: I do.

PEG: When?

GRACIE: Sometimes.

PEG: Not very often. Not very goddamn often. I can't read your mind, you know. I need to be told.

GRACIE: And told, and told, and told, and told.

PEG: Have you ever considered celibacy?

GRACIE: You know, it's interesting you brought that up.

PEG: Just as a joke! I was only joking!

GRACIE: But that's the new "in" thing, celibacy. It's becoming very chic.

PEG: For straight people and monks, it's chic. Not for lesbians.

GRACIE: You are so narrow-minded.

PEG: Listen, it takes two not to tango, and I ain't interested.

GRACIE: You're not interested in not tangoing?

PEG: That's right.

GRACIE: So, I guess I should have sex just because you want it, right?

PEG: Something like that.

GRACIE: You sound just like a man.

PEG stands.

PEG: Don't you say that to me. I'm a woman and I sound exactly like a woman. If you don't think women talk this way, you're wrong, because I'm a woman and I talk this way. So forget about me sounding, looking, walking, talking or acting like a man. I'm a woman, got it?

GRACIE: No, I don't "got" it. What's the point of being a woman if you're going to act like a man?

PEG: What's the point of being a lesbian if you don't like sex?

GRACIE: I didn't say I didn't like it. I'd say I'm ambivalent.

PEG: Well, what the hell point is there in being an ambivalent lesbian? If you're a lesbian, everyone defines you by who you sleep with. If you don't care that much, why go through all the hassles?

GRACIE: I like the hassles.

PEG: Why?

GRACIE: Because it gives me something to write about.

PEG: Is that all I am to you? Are we just "soon to be a major motion picture?"

GRACIE: A movie! I never thought about a movie before!

PEG: I was not put on this earth as a device to stimulate your creativity.

GRACIE: Well, why are *you* a lesbian?

PEG: Because I love women and I hate the way men are. Because sex with men was boring and sex with women isn't…usually. Because all the people I fall in love with happen to be girls.

GRACIE: I wish it was that simple for me.

PEG: Don't you like being a lesbian?

GRACIE: Oh yeah. I love it.

PEG: Why?

GRACIE: Because it's very chic, because it's politically correct, because I'm fed up with men, because it upsets my parents, because it's a little dangerous, because I like being oppressed, because I like breasts, because a lot of men don't like women like me, because I cannot stand the idea of being possessed by a man, because I love possessing women, because I never really felt free until I slept with you.

PEG: But do you love women?

GRACIE: I trust women. I understand women. But I don't think I love women the way you do.

PEG turns away from GRACIE.

PEG: I don't know why the hell we're together.

Pause.

GRACIE: I've written two poems for you.

She recites from memory.

Poem for You, Number One

They write poems, graphic poems
About making love, fucking, sexual intercourse
They write poems about men and women.

Then why am I afraid to speak
    Of the golden dolphin I rode once as your tongue
        played with my clitoris?
    Or the fir tree that shot up inside me when your finger
        entered my vagina?

> Or when you told me of the rose quartz crystal mountain that
> Shattered when I buried my face in your cunt.

Am I still afraid to speak of such things?
No, not any longer.

> *Pause.*

PEG: You said there were two poems.

GRACIE:

Poem for You, Number Two
Ducks

> Very few poems are written about ducks.
> And, with good reason,
> Clumsy, silly, cute, obnoxious…
> They waddle like ducks.
> They quack exactly like ducks.
>
> And have you ever seen one take to water
> > as easily as a duck takes to water?
> Amazing.
> Or have you noticed the water rolling off their backs
> > like water off a duck's . . .
> Etcetera, etcetera.
>
> The stuff of aphorisms, ducks are.
> Yes.
> But poems?
> No!
> Very difficult to write a poem about a duck.

> *Pause.*

Which one do you like better?

PEG: You're right. It is very difficult to write a poem about a duck.

> *They kiss.*

>> *Lights Fade To Black.*

Lights up on nightclub stage. PEG and GRACIE join THE BAND and sing.

PEG & GRACE:

Song: I DON'T CARE (reprise)

They say I'm crazy, got no sense, but I don't care.
They may or may not take offense, but I don't care.
You see, I'm kind of independent, of a clever race descendant,
My star is on the ascendant,
That's why I don't care.

I don't care, I don't care
What people think of me.
I'm happy-go-lucky
They say I am plucky
So jolly and carefree.

I don't care, I don't care
If I do get the mean and stony stare.
If I'm never successful, it won't be distressful
Cause I don't care.

Some people say I think I'm it, but I don't care.
They say they don't like me a bit, but I don't care.
'Cause my good nature effervescing
is one there is no distressing,
My spirit there is no oppressing
Just 'cause I don't care.

I don't care, I don't care
If people don't like me.
I'll try to outlive it.
I know I'll forgive it
And live contentedly.

I don't care, I don't care
If people do not try and treat me fair.
There is naught can amaze me, dislike cannot faze me
'Cause I don't care!

Lights Fade To Black.

End of Play

LILITH
WOMEN'S ★ THEATER
SAN FRANCISCO

FROM THE CREATOR OF DOS LESBOS

held over!

EGO TRIP
i'm getting my shit together and dumping it all on you

TERRY BAUM
in a one woman show

one woman's theater

TWO MONOLOGUES

1975

BISEXUAL CELIBATE

FROM
LILITHEATER

1982

COMING-OUT STORY

FROM
**EGO TRIP
OR
I'M GETTING MY SHIT TOGETHER
& DUMPING IT ALL ON YOU**

Bisexual Celibate—or Not!

First Production(s)

The original monolog, "Bisexual Celibate," was part of *Lilitheater*, the first production of Lilith Women's Theater Collective, which opened in the Fall of 1975 at Live Oak Theater in Berkeley, California. The monolog was performed by Terry Baum and directed by the other actresses, Charlotte Colavin and Shelley Fields.

The expanded monolog *Bisexual Celibate-or Not!* was performed in 2010 in New York City at the conference, "Lesbians in the 70s." Terry played both Young Terry and Old Terry. The monolog was produced by The Crackpot Crones and directed by Carolyn Myers.

PRODUCTION HISTORY

In the Fall of 1974, I still viewed myself as heterosexual. However, I realized I wanted to do theater with women only, and moved to the San Francisco Bay Area to start such a group.

I would name my theater Lilith, after Adam's first wife, who appears in early versions of the Talmud. God created them equally, from dust. But Adam, assuming he was top dog, commanded Lilith to lie beneath him. When she told Adam to go to hell, he complained to God. Lilith, fed up with the whole scene, stormed out of Eden in a fury. Then God created Eve from Adam's rib in a desperate attempt to guarantee her obedience. As a Jew, I honor Lilith, the first uppity woman of my own tradition.

I was very excited with the first group that came together—until the other three women showed up at a rehearsal to announce that they had all, individually and simultaneously, decided to quit. I picked myself up off the floor and found two other women, Charlotte Colavin and Shelley Fields. We formed a real team, and thus Lilith Women's Theater Collective began. This monolog was in our first show.

I wrote the "—Or Not!" part of this monolog in 2009. At that time Carolyn and I were performing as The Crackpot Crones, a sketch comedy and improvisation duo. The Crones were invited to perform at a conference, "Lesbians in the 70s," in New York City. We reviewed our theatrical writing from the 1970s, to find appropriate pieces to present. I was struck, not to say stunned, by the self-delusion in my old monolog. My writing had seemed so radically honest in 1975! In 2010, it was clear to me that I just couldn't face that I was moving away from loving men toward loving women. I decided to update "Bisexual Celibate" to include my current perspective, by dividing myself into two characters—Terry in 1975 and Terry in 2010.

CHARACTERS

One actress plays both parts.

YOUNG TERRY: A woman in her middle 20's. She has a lot of energy and she greatly enjoys revealing herself to the audience. The playwright was 27 when she wrote the original scene.

OLD TERRY: An older dyke, thoughtful, observant, with a wry sense of humor. The playwright was 62 when she wrote this scene.

TIME

For YOUNG TERRY: 1975.
For OLD TERRY: 2010.

PLACE

A bare stage.

AT RISE: As the lights come up, OLD TERRY is revealed, standing Upstage Center in a bright pool of light, looking at the audience. She's dressed in a rather dykey fashion—a man's jacket, open-necked shirt, sensible shoes.

OLD TERRY: (*To the audience.*) In 1975, when I was 27, I joined a theater where I was the only woman. In response to that very alienating experience, I decided to start a theater of only women. Lilith Women's Theater sprang into existence with an original play in which I and two other women joined together to act out stories from our personal lives. Each of us had one monolog exploring an intimate personal issue. Charlotte's was about her frustrations with different types of birth control. Shelley's was about her fear that she was too old to have children—she was 35. Mine was about…Well, you'll see.

As OLD TERRY crosses Downstage Right, the center light fades out and another light comes up Downstage Right. This light has a more amber quality, reflecting that the actress is becoming her past self. Throughout the scene, these lights brighten and dim as the actress enters and leaves them.

Although OLD TERRY is in no way decrepit, there is a clear physical and vocal difference between the two. YOUNG TERRY'S voice is a bit higher, her movements a bit more bouncy.

Throughout the piece, OLD TERRY hears everything YOUNG TERRY says and speaks to both YOUNG TERRY and to the audience. But YOUNG TERRY is completely unaware of OLD TERRY. She speaks only to the audience.

YOUNG TERRY: (*To the audience, very brash.*) My mother thinks I'm undersexed. Isn't that weird? She's even asked me on a couple of occasions, "Don't you ever just get the urge to go out and sleep with someone?" The truth is: Yes! I do get the urge to just go out and get laid. But I can always think of a really good reason why not to go to bed with someone.

She points to the invisible young men as she thoughtfully rejects each one.

He's too pushy…He's too passive…He'll get dependent on me. (*To the audience, quite proud.*) I'm celibate. I threw out my diaphragm jelly because it had calcified.

I always used to feel that if I had a really good relationship with a man, my stable and calm life would transform me. I would become more creative, more disciplined. I would start brushing my teeth twice a day. In short, I would find myself. And then a terrible thing happened. I had a really good relationship with a man. But I still couldn't find myself. So I decided to be celibate.

OLD TERRY: (*To the audience, she cannot remain silent any longer.*) I'm sorry, but my 62-year-old lesbian self just has to say something to my 27-year-old quote celibate unquote self.

(*To YOUNG TERRY.*) What does this "I couldn't find myself" business really mean? In fact, you stopped sleeping with men because you got bored. You had not one but two really great boyfriends, but you wanted more intimacy. You're an intensity junkie. You wanted something other than what you could find with a man, so you…

YOUNG TERRY: (*Not having heard OLD TERRY, she picks up where* *she left off.*) So I decided to be celibate. It's been a beautiful, exhilarating time. I taught drama, I traveled in Europe. I started two theaters. But recently, I thought, OK, I've done my homework. I've found myself. And what I found is pretty damn good! So how about a relationship?

I stepped out of my cocoon of self-improvement. (*She does so.*) Here I am, all you nice men in your twenties and early thirties. I'm smart, funny, assertive, a feminist—just what you've been looking for! (*She looks around with great surprise, shock even.*) Where are all the fantastic men who are dying to relate to me? There are very few! There isn't anybody that I want to have sex with. Damn it!

So, even though I had chosen to be celibate, once it got started, it seems to roll along of its own accord.

OLD TERRY: (*To YOUNG TERRY.*) You are really deluding yourself. The truth is that you weren't celibate—except in your head. You were having sex with men every once in a while. (*To the audience.*) But there was a huge change: She cared less and less about the men she was sleeping with. (*To YOUNG TERRY.*) Remember that poor poet? He wrote a beautiful love poem to you on the back of your food stamp application, and you went and just filled out the application and turned it in! That was really heartless. (*To the audience.*) And it was a good poem! That poor guy was devastated. If that's not pre-lesbian behavior…

YOUNG TERRY: (*Very thoughtful.*) I've been wondering if I'm not really attracted to women and just afraid of making that leap.

OLD TERRY: (*To the audience, throwing up her hands in frustration.*) DUH!

YOUNG TERRY: (*Very dry, intellectual.*) I've had erotic fantasies and dreams about women. Maybe I should just come out as a lesbian and THEN I'll have sexual relationships! But after lots of talk with my friends, I'm facing up to my true nature. I'm not a lesbian.

OLD TERRY: (*To YOUNG TERRY.*) That is a total lie. Now, the concept that you've been celibate for a long time is a delusion, but it's not a lie. You really do believe in your celibacy. But this latest idea, that you actually sat down with your friends and talked about the possibility of sleeping with a woman…No, I'm sorry. Never happened. Ever. It never even occurred to you to talk to your friends about this.

(*To the audience.*) You know why? Because one of them probably would have said, "It makes a lot of sense to me." One of them might have even been sexually attracted to her. No, that was too dangerous. But somehow, at this moment in her life, she needs the fictitious support of her friends to declare that she is not a lesbian.

YOUNG TERRY: (*Very clear, emphatic, calm.*) I'm not a lesbian. I'm bisexual—a bisexual celibate.

OLD TERRY: (*To YOUNG TERRY.*) Yes, that's how you always escape from uncomfortable conclusions—with a joke. (*To the audience.*) Of course, today, the idea of a "bisexual celibate" is not a joke at all. It's just another sexual choice. But in 1975, it was a joke. (*To YOUNG TERRY.*) You know, I do admire you for having the courage to bring all of this up, even if you don't have the courage to follow it where it's obviously leading.

YOUNG TERRY: Of course no sex doesn't really mean no sex. To me, masturbating is an intense confrontation between my independence, which I value very highly, and my aloneness, which I'm not all that sure about. I have this image of wires leading from me connecting back into my body instead of connecting with someone else. So the current just goes in circles.

I do feel isolated sometimes, but I'm also doing what I want by myself.

OLD TERRY: (*To the audience.*) This is brave. Am I this brave now at 62? I'm not sure.

YOUNG TERRY: I always had this idea that I wanted to marry an artist. The man I marry will have a great sense of humor, be creative, outgoing, politically aware…But now I know I want to be that artist, not marry one. All those things—the artistic activity, the politics… even the sexuality—I am doing it for myself. (*Surprised and delighted with her conclusion.*) I'm becoming the person I wanted to marry.

OLD TERRY: (*To YOUNG TERRY.*) This is your great feminist transformation. You already have become the person you want to marry. As you speak this monolog, you are being your full self, instead of waiting for a man to complete you. And this frees you to love women.

(*To the audience, very proud of YOUNG TERRY.*) She's speaking her truth to the world. Admittedly, her truth is riddled with lies and self-delusion. But she's being as honest as she can be. Hey, at 62 I'm probably still only speaking a partial twisted truth. And when I'm 82, I'll look back on some of the things I'm saying now, and I'll just laugh.

> *Lights fade to black as OLD TERRY softly chuckles, shaking her head, laughing at herself.*

End of Monolog

Coming-Out Story

From *Ego Trip or I'm Getting My Shit Together & Dumping It All On You*

Premiere Information

"Coming-Out Story" premiered as part of *Ego Trip or I'm Getting My Shit Together & Dumping It All On You*. *Ego Trip* opened at Bethany Church in San Francisco, CA on May 14, 1982. The monolog was performed by Terry Baum.

>Director ……………………….. Carolyn Myers
>Producer ……………………… Terry Baum
>Set and Lighting Design ……… Margo Tufo

PRODUCTION HISTORY

This is an autobiographical monolog written in 1982, when I was 36 years old. It was part of my first solo show, *Ego Trip or I'm Getting My Shit Together & Dumping It All On You*. At the time, solo shows were uncommon, so it was a rather daring thing to do. My motivation was more economics than ego. I desperately wanted to stop working as a temporary secretary and start making a living in theater. Being alone onstage seemed the easiest way to get there.

The production travelled to Bear Republic Theater in Santa Cruz, CA later in the year. It also toured the Northwest and Midwest in 1984 as part of *Baum and Tufo, the Official Lesbian Music and Comedy Act of the 1984 Olympics*.

Ego Trip is a compilation of monologs. I play eight different characters, some invented, some observed. There are, among other scenes: A mother speaking at the memorial service of her son who died from AIDS; a 5,000-year-old virgin with a unique view of the war between the sexes; a secretary whose best friend is Elvira, her computer; and a wacky cooking show hostess who demonstrates how to make "mock tofu" from hamburger and talcum powder when unexpected vegetarians show up for dinner. For me, the heart of *Ego Trip* was my "Coming-Out Story."

A note about language

Currently (2019), a wide variety of people, including heterosexuals, use the word "queer" in describing themselves, to indicate they consider themselves sexually subversive in some way. But in 1982, "queer" meant "homosexual" and it had a challenging in-your-face edge to it.

TIME
1982

PLACE
A bare stage.

AT RISE: TERRY is discovered standing center stage, eager to tell the audience her story.

When I was in college, my best friend, Lizzie, and I agreed that it was a terrible shame that I wasn't a boy. You see, my best qualities were exactly what girls looked for in a boyfriend—and exactly what caused boys to run very rapidly in the other direction. Lizzie and I fantasized that if I were a boy, she and I would fall in love. We knew we would make a great couple because we adored each other and spent every second together. Plus we both thought the other was totally hilarious. My transformation into a boy was the perfect solution to the major cause of our unhappiness, which was our rotten relationships with college boys— or our lack of rotten relationships with college boys. (*Pause.*) It never occurred to us that two girls could be lovers. It also never occurred to us that Lizzie could also be the boy.

I graduated college in 1969 and moved to New York City for graduate school. Feminism was happening, baby! I went to a meeting of the New York Radical Feminists. They handed out a mimeographed sheet of all the ways that women were oppressed. I read it and the proverbial light bulb went on. I realized that the reason I had never quite fit in was because I didn't fit the conventional definition of a woman. I was too outspoken, too opinionated. What an enormous relief! It wasn't *me* who needed to be fixed, but *Society*!

I was the first feminist on my block, so all my friends brought their boyfriends to me for an introduction to Feminism 101. I joined a consciousness-raising group. Twelve of us met once a week and shared our experiences. Sisterhood wasn't just a word. It was a feeling of love and solidarity that flowed through all women. It had always existed, unseen and unspoken until now.

There was one lesbian in my consciousness-raising group. This was my very first encounter with an "out" homosexual. Charlene wore turbans and bright red lipstick and talked in a very artificial way, exaggerating the pronunciation of her words. She was just plain weird. When she stopped showing up at the group, I was relieved. Two months later, Charlene was back and told us why she'd been gone.

She had been sexually assaulted by her neighbor in the hallway of her building. Fortunately, she had some knowledge of martial arts, so she threw her attacker down the stairs. Then *he* went to the police to demand that she be arrested, which she was. When Charlene went to trial, she told the judge what had happened. But her attacker testified that he couldn't possibly have sexually assaulted her because she was a lesbian and therefore repulsive to any man. Furthermore, everyone knew that all lesbians hated men and were just waiting for the opportunity to throw them down the stairs. Well, it made perfect sense to the judge and off Charlene went to jail for six weeks. It's an improbable story, isn't it? But I believed her at the time, and I still believe her.

I went to all the big women's conferences in New York City. On May 1, 1970, at the opening session of the Second Congress to Unite Women, I was sitting in an audience of 200 women, listening to the first speaker. I have no memory of what she said because suddenly a bunch of young women stormed the stage, shouted down the speaker and grabbed the microphone. They were the Lavender Menace, a very articulate and angry bunch of lesbians, led by a young Rita Mae Brown. At that time, feminist organizations were actually kicking lesbians out, in a desperate effort to appear unthreatening to the public! The Lavender Menace took over the whole damn conference to demand that dykes be given their rightful, open place in the women's movement! It was a historic moment, and I was there. The conference schedule, with its plenaries and workshops, was tossed out, and everyone met in small groups to talk about lesbianism. In my group I stood up and said I could imagine sleeping with a woman, but I could *not* face telling my mother about it. I felt very brave.

After the discussion, a woman approached me. The first honest-to-goodness butch woman I had ever talked to. A.J. had a crew cut, motorcycle boots, and a black leather jacket with studs on the back that spelled out "Jewish Defense League"—the most macho Jews in the world. I mean, this woman was tough.

A.J. challenged me. "I don't believe you're worried what your *mother* will think of you. You're worried what *you* will think of *yourself.*" Which seemed perfectly ridiculous to me.

Then she asked me out to dinner. I was terrified of her, but I was also broke and I assumed since she was so butch, she would treat me. So I got on the back of A.J.'s motorcycle, and off we roared. All through dinner, we argued over why I was afraid to be a lesbian and whether the Jewish Defense League, which espoused violence, made things better or worse for Jews. When the check came, she didn't offer to pay for me.

But she *did* offer to take me to the womens' dance that was the culmination of the conference. I was really worried this bulldyke was going to try drag me off to bed. What would I do? I would be strong! Even if she got violent! But, as it turned out, I needn't have worried. A.J. dropped me like a hot potato once we got to the dance. Just turned her back and walked away! I was so insulted.

So there I was in the gloomy, grimy basement of a church. A few women were kissing each other rather passionately in the corners. Most of us just stood…waiting.

> *Looking around expectantly.*

All wallflowers.

> *She straightens her collar, tries on a smile, tries looking serious, then bored, then a smile again, stretches, notices her shoe is dirty and rubs it on the back of her pants, clears her throat, taps her foot while she hums a little tune.*

It seemed like being a lesbian was just as awful as being straight! I gave myself fifteen minutes for something to happen. *I* wasn't going to ask anybody to dance because *I* wasn't a *dyke*. But I *was* open to being swept off my feet by…Princess Charming…or failing that…(*She looks around.*)… A.J. (*She checks her watch.*)

Right before my time limit was up, a very small, very scared-looking young woman came up and asked me to dance. (*She takes a step toward the woman.*) Just our luck, they put on a *slow* record. (*She groans.*) So we had to *touch*.

> *Full of dread, she puts her arms around the imaginary woman, trying to touch her as little as possible, and dances very awkwardly with her.*

We were both shaking. We didn't look at each other. We didn't say a word. It was *horrible*. It was the longest slow song in history. When the music finally ended, I fled.

> *She runs across the stage, stops and turns to the audience.*

(*With pride.*) I took some big steps that day. I danced with a woman for the first time and rode on a motorcycle behind a big butch dyke. But it was to be seven more looooong years before I finally fell in love with a woman. I blame the lesbians for this. No one tried to seduce me! I had to move to San Francisco and start Lilith, a women's theater and then wait three more years until finally in 1976, three lesbians joined the collective. One of them was Sherry.

The company was creating a new play, *Moonlighting*, on women and work. We created material by doing improvisations inspired by actual stories from the work lives of the actresses. One scene took place in a day care center. Sherry and I were assigned to be little kids in the background. You know, creating atmosphere. We started wrestling. (*Dreamily.*) And the rest of the world disappeared. At some point, the improvisation ended and one of the actresses was kind enough to tell us we could stop wrestling.

Sherry Sherry Sherry Sherry. Sherry was wild and fun and worked hard and had lots of crazy ideas. As an actress, there was something unpredictable about her, something intriguing. She was kinda butch and kinda androgynous…and very attractive.

A week later, we had a photo session to get some pictures of Lilith rehearsing, and one of the women said, "Terry and Sherry, do your baby act for the photographer!" "Yeah! Yeah!" Everyone wanted to see the quote baby act unquote again. Sherry and I complied, (*Dreamily.*) and once again the rest of the world disappeared.

Sherry Sherry Sherry Sherry.

Next up: Sherry and I went to a big feminist conference in San Francisco at one of the big hotels downtown. When the session was over Sherry invited me for a drink at The Top of the Mark—a bar with a view of the whole city. The Top of the Mark! I'd never been there before.

I have no memory of what we talked about before she said, "How does it make you feel that I'm a lesbian?" I replied, "It makes me want to sleep with you." And we got up to leave. Much later, Sherry told me that, although she'd known her whole life she was gay and had had relationships with women, that moment at The Top of the Mark was the first time she had ever said the words "I'm a lesbian."

Sherry paid the check—unlike A.J.—and took me back to her place, an attic room in a flat in the Mission that she shared with the two women who ran the feminist bookstore. That first night, Sherry just held me. I was freaking out because I could feel my life was totally changing in that moment. For the first time I felt…FREE. Not that I had ever been aware that I was UNfree. But now that I was finally in the arms of another woman, I realized I'd been dragging heavy shackles my whole life without knowing it. While Sherry gently held me, I felt the shackles of trying to be part of the patriarchy falling away. This was not an intellectual experience. I felt the shackles falling off! There was no path back to who I had been. I was a lesbian and that was that—even BEFORE I had sex!

I would describe my sex life with men as ranging between perfectly fine and lousy. Men and women fit together in a very obvious way. But that's part of the problem. Men are just so happy to have a hard penis, they don't think they have to do anything else! Many of my male partners thought because *they* were having a good time, *I* was having a good time. That's my definition of a pig.

When I'm with a woman, I make love to her and then she makes love to me. It's sequential, not simultaneous. It's a matter of possession and surrender. When I seek to possess a woman, it's about her pleasure, not mine. Although there's no pleasure like *giving* pleasure.

I don't think I ever possessed a man. Let's face it: It's no big deal to make a man come. They're always worried about coming too soon. But to make a *woman* come…that's an accomplishment. To sexually possess another woman can be very time-consuming in the most delicious way.

So Sherry and I were madly in love in that "can't-keep-our-hands-off-each-other" way. But along with that ecstasy…I was also depressed. I was 30 years old. I'd had three long-term relationships with men. I was acutely aware of what I was losing. I was leaving the comfort of belonging to Society with a big "S." I was giving up the right to walk in public with my arm around my beloved. I was losing the chance to make my mother happy by finding my true love and getting married. I was risking getting thrown into jail for defending myself, like Charlene. And, just like I'd told A.J., I *did* feel terrible when my mother told me she was ashamed of me. And, just like A.J. had told *me*, I felt confused and even degraded, knowing I had become something I'd always regarded as pathetic and sick. All of the accoutrements of homophobia are a great big drag, let me tell you!

But still, I had no second thoughts. Being free and having great sex made up for everything else. And my depression slowly lifted as I realized that while I was losing my place in the Big "S" Society, there was a place waiting for me in the Society of Queers—admittedly a much smaller group, but a hell of a lot more fun.

When I told my old college friend Lizzie that I was a lesbian, she said that she was jealous, that she wished we had shared that kind of intimacy. By that time, Lizzie was a librarian in Providence, Rhode Island. I said, "Lizzie, would you consider sleeping with a woman now?" She told me, "I know I could be sexually happy with a woman. But I am just too conventional. I'm not brave enough to be a lesbian."

Not brave enough to be a lesbian. I felt really sad then that we hadn't done anything about the incredible closeness and attraction we had felt for each other when we were eighteen.

It's hard to talk about all of this. On the one hand, there are the dykes, who get pissed off if I don't say that lesbianism is paradise on earth. And on the other hand, there are straight people: "Listen, Terry, of course you can do whatever you want. But why do you insist on _talking_ about it? Look, Terry, you've already written a play about lesbians. And now there are some movies out about gays. Isn't that enough? Why can't you people shut up?"

Well, why can't you straight people shut up? You straight people have been going on about men and women for four thousand years, and you're still at it! Nobody ever says, "Oh no, not another play about heterosexuals. I've already seen one this year." You straight people have an insatiable appetite to see yourselves reflected in plays and movies and billboards and television. Well, I want to see myself reflected too! So do all the other queers. Now, I figure if ten percent of all the people in the world are homosexual, then ten percent of all the plays in the world should be about homosexuals. We have a long way to go to reach our quota. And I'm going to keep writing plays about queers until we do.

Lights fade to black as TERRY looks at the audience, a challenge in her eyes.

End of Monolog

1983

IMMEDIATE FAMILY

Premiere Information

Immediate Family had its premiere at the National Festival of Women's Theater at the Art Center Theater in Santa Cruz on May 20, 1983. At that time, the play was titled *Death's Angel, Requiem for a Marriage*.

Director .... Carolyn Myers
Producer .... Terry Baum
Technical Design & Direction .... Margo Tufo

CAST

VIRGINIA .... Terry Baum

PRODUCTION HISTORY

I was initially inspired to write this play by news stories describing a nurse in a nursing home accused of killing patients by secretly removing them from life support. She was vilified by the press as "Death's Angel." She was inhuman! A monster! I thought, "Maybe she is a monster—and maybe not." In the early 1980s, there was very little discussion of the unnecessary suffering of people who were dying. I could imagine "Death's Angel" pulling the plug for reasons of compassion. So I wrote a monolog from the viewpoint of the nurse.

Then I realized if my own lover was unconscious and near death, I would never have the legal right to remove her from life support. As a lesbian, my relationship with my lover had no legal existence! And I realized that the "Death's Angel" of my play needed to be the lover of a woman who was dying. So I tossed out the nurse's monolog and started over.

Many versions of me appear as characters throughout this anthology, but Virginia is decidedly NOT me. For the first time, I experienced channeling someone else's voice. It's a wonderful feeling—the story is out there in the ether, waiting to be told. You, the writer, are only a vehicle to get it to people. It gave me a strong sense of purpose, which helped me overcome my discomfort at writing, for the first time, something that was basically serious in tone.

With Virginia, I began to explore what it means to be butch. I have always been fascinated by butch lesbians who were in the closet in their heads, while their physicality communicated to everyone that they were gay. Virginia is such a person. I find this struggle, between the need to hide and the need to be one's self, very moving.

Since being published in *Places, Please!*, the first anthology of lesbian plays, *Immediate Family* has been performed throughout the U.S. and in Canada, England, Holland, Belgium, Australia, New Zealand, Sweden, Germany, Austria, Israel, and Cuba. It's been translated into Dutch, French, and Spanish.

I've toured the play in the U.S., Canada, Israel and much of Western Europe, including the Boston Women's Theater Festival (1984), the Fifth International Women's Festival in Amsterdam (1985), and Stockholm's Gay Cultural Festival (1992).

Vivian Kleiman, an award-winning filmmaker and fan of *Immediate Family*, produced a short film of me as Virginia that was seen at gay film festivals in San Francisco, Berlin and Milan. And in 1989, *Naaste Familie*, with Dutch film star Nellie Frijda, was shown on prime time network television in Holland.

In terms of my personal life, *Immediate Family* got me invited to the Boston Festival, which caused me to be invited to the Amsterdam festival, where I met and fell in love with a Dutch woman, which caused me to move to Amsterdam, which supplied the material for *One Fool*, the performance of which caused me to meet the woman who inspired *Two Fools*.

Immediate Family has also been my most politically useful play, and I'm very proud of that. A well-known Canadian actress chose to come out to her public by playing Virginia. In the 1990s, activists in Boise, Idaho and Pittsburg, Pennsylvania fought anti-gay ballot initiatives by producing the play to raise money and educate people. I performed *Immediate Family* countless times in 2008, to raise funds to defeat Proposition 8, the anti-gay marriage initiative in California. And in 2015, I brought *Immediate Family* to Mejunje, in Santa Clara, Cuba. This "diversity" center, was the only venue in the country for gay culture.

I remember thinking when I was writing *Immediate Family*, "Nobody's going to want to see this play. It sounds so grim. I don't even think *I* would want to see it!" I never expected it to find an audience. Ironically, it's been my most produced play and has taken me all over the world.

CHARACTER

VIRGINIA is in her fifties. She wears an official U.S. Post Office uniform. She ws born butch. That is, she always knew she ws destined to love women, and she scorned all feminine attire and mannerisms as soon as she was old enough to scorn. In her lifetime, the world has been a dangerous place to be gay. But Virginia has never aspired to change that world. All she ever wanted was a decent job, a little house, and a loving wife to share it all with. She has achieved her goals. She was very happy before Rose became ill.

TIME

The year is 1983. Gay people have no marriage rights. Thus, Virginia has no say about the hospital's treatment of Rose. She is not legally part of Rose's immediate family.

PLACE

A hospital room in a big city.

Scene One

The play begins in darkness. The relentless pulsing sound of a ventilator is heard, very loud and harsh. When VIRGINIA starts to speak, the volume is drastically lowered, but the noise of this mechanical inhale-exhale, with its inexorable precise rhythm, is an undercurrent to the whole play.

AT RISE: *The lights slowly fade up on a hospital room.*

SETTING: *There is a rectangle of intense light on the floor where the bed would be. There lies the invisible ROSE in her invisible hospital bed. Next to the bed are a chair and a nightstand. On the nightstand is a water pitcher, a glass, and a vase filled with wilted flowers. A waste basket sits on the floor. Upstage is a half-open door which leads to the hospital corridor. Downstage left is the ventilator, which is invisible.*

VIRGINIA enters through the upstage door. She is in her middle fifties and is wearing a post office uniform, as she has just come from work. She is a bulldyke. That is, her manner, walk and haircut are "masculine" in a stereotypical way. She walks with a swagger, her feet wide apart. Her hair is very short. She carries a bag of groceries and a bunch of flowers. Several letters stick out of her back pocket.

Out in the corridor, VIRGINIA has just learned from ROSE's

> doctor that ROSE will die soon, without coming out of her coma. She pauses inside the door, surveys the hospital room, shakes her head, sighs. She seems frozen in that spot, incapable of movement. But she has come into that room to make one last attempt to awaken ROSE from her deathly sleep. She believes she can do this, through the force of her will, through her love. She slowly walks around the invisible bed, studying its occupant. She puts down her grocery bag, looks at ROSE, plasters a smile on her face and speaks in a loud, falsely cheerful voice to the place where ROSE's head would be.

Hello there, Rosie. How's my girl? Look what I got for you today! Flowers! (*Waves the flowers in ROSE's face.*) Pretty, aren't they? They're called…Hell, I've been making a garden with you for 27 years, and I never can remember the names of the flowers. Can you smell them? I'll just throw out the old ones and put these pretty yellow ones in the pitcher. (*She stops, surprised.*) Look at these poor flowers I brought yesterday. All wilted up already. I'm tellin' ya, my girl, this hospital air'll kill anything that breathes.

> VIRGINIA glares at the old flowers, then tosses them in the wastebasket and carefully arranges the new ones in the pitcher. She regards them with satisfaction.

There! That's better.

So, Rose, how's your coma going?

> *Crosses downstage to confront the invisible ventilator. With bitterness:*

I see the old ventilator's doing its thing, bob-bob-bobbing along.

> *She turns away from the machine. With tenderness:*

How're you feeling today, Rosie? (*Pause.*) *Are* you feeling today?

> VIRGINIA sits slumped in the chair, suddenly feeling her exhaustion. Her cheery façade gone, VIRGINIA speaks to ROSE as she has every day for decades, recounting the mundane, intimate details of her day.

Had a hard day at work, my girl. Got a whole shitload of mail dumped on us. Had to work like hell. And then I spent my lunch hour shopping for groceries.

> *She pulls a very large tomato out of her shopping bag.*

You know, they had heirloom tomatoes on sale today. Look-a here. Only six-fifty a pound! How about that!

(*Conciliatory.*) Now Rose, I know you think that's extravagant. But you spoiled me by growing tomatoes every year. And now you've let a little thing like this cancer get in the way of growing them this year. What am I supposed to do? (*Feisty, argumentative.*) I don't care what you say. I think six-fifty a pound is a bargain. I'm gonna have this baby for dinner tonight when I get home, and I don't wanna hear another word about it!

> *With great finality, she puts the tomato on the nightstand. She pulls a cheap bamboo back scratcher out of the shopping bag.*

Oh, and I got one of these things. I'm telling you my girl: no home-grown tomatoes, and an itchy back with no one to scratch it. Hard times! (*Pause, feeling a bit foolish.*) I don't know why I brought all this stuff in. I guess I thought you might like to look at a tomato.

> *She regards the tomato with disgust and returns it to the shopping bag. She searches for a topic of conversation.*

Rose, you will never guess what I had for dinner last night, not in a million years. (*With urgency.*) Come on, try! (*Pause.*) Aw, you give up too easy. (*Dramatically.*) Brussel sprouts! Can you believe that? Smelly green golf balls, I used to call 'em. Stunk up the whole house. I just ate 'em because you love 'em. And you say I'm not the romantic type and here I am gobbling up your favorite foods just so's I can…(*Hesitantly, softly.*) I don't know…have you inside me somehow.

> *Performing with mockery her great transformation:*

Oh Rose, how I've changed. I'm doing all the things you always wanted me to do. I'm tellin' you, if you came home today, we'd never fight for the rest of our lives. (*Leaning forward.*) For example: I admit it: you were right. It's not so tough to keep the house neat as a pin. You've just got to keep on top of it. Once you've let it slide…oh, for five or six weeks or so, then you've got a mess on your hands. But if you attend to it every fifteen or twenty minutes, it's not too bad! (*Strutting around the room.*) I'm tellin' you, my girl, you are looking at a new woman. House so clean I'm eating Brussel sprouts off the floor!

> *She looks for a response from ROSE. Nothing. VIRGINIA pauses, searching her mind for the next topic. She remembers she has an important story to tell. She tells it with great animation, acting out the parts.*

Did I tell you I talked to the head nurse yesterday? (*Irritated.*) "Now listen here Nursie," I says to her, "I don't get off work until 5:30. By the time I get down here, it's six o'clock, six-fifteen. And then the damn visiting hours are over at six forty-five! Do you mind if I stay a little longer," says I to the nurse.

When she speaks as the nurse, she imitates her cold, officious manner.

"Well Miss Sedgeway," says the nurse to me, "What is your relationship to Miss Belbasio?" (*Pause.*) I am Miss Belbasio's…best friend. "Oh! Just a friend. Then I'm sorry, Miss Sedgeway. You will have to adhere to the official visiting hours. Only the immediate family is allowed to come and go as they please. Those are the hospital rules."

(*With bravado.*) Rosie, I gave that woman such HELL! "Now listen here Nursie," says I. "I am Miss Rosa Felicia Belbasio's immediate family. You are never gonna find anybody more immediate than I happen to be. And I don't care how hard you look. So the next time you want me out of that room, you'd better call the police to drag me away. Because I'm staying until I'm damned ready to go."

Boasting of her triumph.

Rose, I damned near punched her lights out!

Silence. Her pose crumbles.

Well, that's not exactly the way it happened. Actually, that's not the way it happened at all. You know me, Rose. I did think all those things. I just never got around to saying a single one of them. (*Mocking herself.*) Big bad Virginia. Oh, I think big, don't I? But when it comes right down to it…I don't know…I clam up. I get confused.

Recalling the humiliation.

The truth is, I begged her. I said "please" a lot more times than I'd like to remember. Maybe I shoulda got down on my hands and knees. (*Bitterly.*) Begging some stranger to let me see my girl just a little bit longer.

(*A new thought.*) Maybe I *shoulda* punched her lights out…

Realizing something about herself for the first time.

All the times I've talked about punching people's lights out, and I've never done it. Not once. Frankly, I don't think I'd even enjoy punching somebody's lights out. (*Awash in self-pity.*) Big bad Virginia. I'm all bark and no bite. Actually, I don't bark much either, do I?

(*A flicker of redemption.*) Of course, I did get them to switch you to a new room now, didn't I? (*She stands.*) Oh, they wouldn't believe that your old room was colder than the rest of the hospital, would they? Oh no!

> *VIRGINIA strides around the room.*

I said to them, look at this room! It's a mess! You got two ceiling tiles missing over here…(*Points up.*)…and a crack between the wall and the window over there. (*Points to the invisible window.*) Why, this isn't a room. It's a goddam walk-in freezer, says I! (*In her nurse's voice.*) "Oh no, Miss Sedgeway. Every room is the same temperature. Those are the hospital rules."

I had to bring in the goddam thermometer from home to prove to them that your room was colder. And it was, wasn't it, Rose? Four whole degrees colder! (*Reveling in her victory.*) Oh I tell you, when I shoved that thermometer in the head nurse's face and she promised to switch you to a new room right then…That was a gooood day!

> *Pause. The simple truth, at last.*

Actually, I didn't shove it in her face, Rose. I just kinda showed it to her. But I got your room changed, didn't I? I'm good for something after all, aren't I, Rosie? (*Flirtatious.*) Oh I bet you'd say I was good for a lot of things. (*Pause.*)

(*Doubtful.*) Maybe you wouldn't. I never could predict you. Sometimes I'd feel so close to you and then—bingo!—you'd be a million miles away. It used to bother me a hell of a lot. (*Softly, with longing.*) Where are you now, my girl? Where are you? I'd sure like to know.

Rose, I'd like to hold your hand. But it's got a tube in it, and it's tied down. Goddamit!

> *Intently studying ROSE's hand.*

Your hand's so thin. Spindly. Used to be a big hand, didn't it, Rose? Now, how many times have we put our hands together to see how big yours were compared to mine? Why did we do that? I can understand doing something like that once, just out of idle curiosity. But we musta done it a hundred times. (*Laughs.*) The things people do when they're spending their whole lives together. (*Pause.*) Comparing hands.

Rosie, remember the first time we held hands?

> *They've told each other this story many times, but not for a long while.*

Oh, I sure do. We'd known each other a few months, and I was so confused. I knew you liked me a hell of a lot. But did you know what I was? And if you did know what I was, were you one, too? Were we just good friends? Were we falling in love? What the hell was going on?

Finally, I couldn't take it anymore. I decided I had to take action— even if it meant losing you as a friend. (*Very dramatic.*) So I took your hand in mine. (*Laughs.*) I was scared to death that you were gonna jump up and run out of that movie theater screaming at the top of your lungs. But you didn't. You stayed right where you were. (*With great wonder.*) And later that night, you kissed me.

I will never forget that moment. Just been kissed by the girl of my dreams…and I step in a pile of dog poop. I thought, that's it for you, Virginia. You have done it this time. How can this…beautiful…elegant…lady possibly love somebody so stupid and clumsy? But you just laughed. As a matter of fact, you laughed a lot.

Come to think of it, you couldn't stop laughing, could you? You're always laughing at me, aren't you, Rose? You don't take me seriously at all! And here I thought I had found me somebody who would make me a nice little wife. Somebody I could talk to without fear of contradiction. (*Laughing at herself.*) Without fear of contradiction… Some nice little wife you made me…

> *Regarding ROSE with great fondness, she shakes her head at her own foolishness.*
>
> *New topic! Maybe this one will wake her up!*

Hey Rosie, did I tell you that everybody at work asks about you? Now that's nice. Makes me feel real good. Almost like a normal human being instead of some crazy old…whatever. Except Arthur. Now Arthur, he makes a big point of not asking about you. But you know Arthur. He's always hated…people like us, hasn't he? He's the only one left. All the others have come around. (*Thoughtfully, to herself.*) The post office isn't such a bad place to work nowadays. Maybe all that gay liberation stuff has done some good.

(*Lest ROSE get the wrong idea.*) Now, I didn't say for sure. I said maybe. And don't you start in about that Gay Pride Parade. You could have marched in that damn thing all by yourself if you had wanted to.

(*Sarcastically.*) Gay Pride. Gay vanity is more like it. Okay, I'm gay! Damn it, isn't that enough? Why the hell do I have to be proud of it too? What's the sense of being proud of something that you just are? That's like me being proud that I have…blue eyes. Okay, I confess: I have blue eyes and I happen to be gay. But I fail to see why I should paint a great big sign advertising those simple facts and march up and down the street with it!

(*Defending herself against ROSE's imagined reply.*) Besides, you never can tell who's gonna see you at one of those things. They've got TV crews there and everything. Why, just suppose I had marched in that Gay Pride Parade of yours and I'd been on television! And… somebody… (*Searches in her memory for the perfect somebody.*)…Aunt Ida in Fort Wayne, Indiana! Yes! Aunt Ida sees my face on the 7 o'clock news, realizes her favorite niece is a hoh-moh-sexual…and has a heart attack…and dies! (*Pause. Looks at herself.*) Ahhh, who'm I kidding? Everybody already knows I'm a hoh-moh-sexual…even Aunt Ida in Fort Wayne. (*Pause. Softly, to herself.*) I'm afraid to march in that parade, and that's the truth. Big bad Virginia. (*Sudden inspiration.*) Rosie, if you come out of that silly coma, I'll march in that parade with you! That's a promise! How about it, my girl? (*Looks for a response. Nothing.*)

> *Putting her hands on her hips, she finds the letters in her back pocket.*

Oh, I almost forgot. I brought your mail.

> *Brings the letters out, goes through them as she talks.*

A whole shitload of letters from the Gay Task Force and all those other do-good organizations that you send money to. Friends of the "this" and people trying to stop the "that." I'm tellin' you, Rosie, you musta sent ten dollars to every good cause on this earth. Now, that is a lot of ten dollarses. (*Pause.*) Come to think of it, considering how many groups are out there doing good, I wonder why the world hasn't gotten itself saved yet. Probably because I haven't sent in *my* money. Oh yes, they're all waiting for ten dollars from Virginia Sedgeway to put 'em over the top!

> *Catches ROSE's face out of the corner of her eye, rushes over to the bed.*

Did you smile? Did I see a smile? I swear to God, Rose, I think you smiled. (*Loud.*) Honey, are you there? Can you hear me? (*Pleading.*) Please, Rose. (*Ordering ROSE.*) Wake up and come home. I need you! Rose! Rose. Rose?

> *Stares at ROSE, then slowly sits down.*

I'm losin' it, my girl. I'm imagining things.

(*Pulling out her last strategy.*) Alright, I guess it's time to stop fooling around and haul out the big guns.

She rummages in her grocery bag and pulls out a plastic container, which she waves around as she talks.

Now Rose, I've been going easy on you, letting you just lie there and pretend you don't hear or see anything. But this foolishness has got to stop! You know what we called your kind in the army? A malingerer. You are malingering! You just don't want to get out of bed and come home and do your share of that damn housework, do you?

Takes the lid off the plastic container, which holds some red sausages.

Well, my girl, I've got something here that'll put an end to your lazy tricks.

She sticks the container under ROSE's nose.

Italian sausages! Your favorite! Goddamit, Rose, do something! Way deep down, don't you want to grab these smelly old things and sink your teeth into 'em? (*Long pause.*) I guess not.

She collapses into the chair. She's out of ammunition.

They say the sense of smell is the last to go, and somehow I got it into my head... (*Ruefully.*) You're laughing at me now, aren't you, my girl? I deserve it. You're married to a fool, there's no doubt about it.

(*To herself.*) Maybe the doctor's right after all. (*To ROSE.*) I just talked to him out in the hall and he told me that there was...no hope. I said, "Doc, what about a miracle?" (*In the doctor's voice.*) "Oh no. It's too late for a miracle." (*Scoffing.*) Too late! Too late! says I. A miracle can happen whenever it damn well pleases. That's what makes it a miracle. (*Doctor's voice.*) "I'm sorry to have to tell you this, Miss Sedgeway, but the cancer has spread to her lungs." He says, "There's no hope." And then he skulks off down the hall.

Focusing on ROSE, demanding a response.

Rose, is the doctor right about no hope? (*Pause.*) I don't know what I expect you to do. Pop out of your coma and say... (*Very brightly.*) "Yes Ginny, the doctor's right. I'm as good as gone." And then pop back down again. (*To herself.*) That would be nice, wouldn't it?

(*Leaning forward, with intensity.*) Rose, are you here anymore at all? Do you want to be here? You see, I gotta know because the doctor says that...maybe it's time to...the best thing now is to turn off that ventilator that's keeping you breathing. (*Pause.*) Is that what you want, baby? My sweet baby. (*Pleading.*) Help me, Rose. Can you hear me? Can you blink your eyelids, wiggle your fingers…(*Desperate.*) …anything?

(*With great frustration.*) Dammit, Rose, why didn't you tell me what you wanted when you could tell me? Why did we just pretend you were gonna get better?

She walks over to the bed, stands.

Alright, Rose. I'm gonna stand right next to you and be real quiet and you tell me…you don't have to make a sound or move a muscle. But somehow just tell me…Do you want to stay or do you want to go?

Long pause as VIRGINIA concentrates with all her energy on ROSE. Finally she let's out a strangled howl and crosses to ventilator, furious.

Jesus Christ! All I can hear is this goddam ventilator howlin' away. (*Turns back to ROSE.*) What'm I supposed to do, Rose? You know how I hate to make decisions. It's your life, anyhow. It's not fair! Oh, I know just what you'd say right now. (*Brightly, mimicking ROSE'S voice.*) "Ginny, my little pet, life's not fair, but it's fun." How many times have I heard that when everything was a big mess? "Life's not fair…"

(*Pause, with great thought.*) I guess I gotta do for you what I'd want you to do for me. And I know I'd want the plug pulled. That's it, isn't it, Rose? That's it.

The full realization of what she's saying hits her.

Oh god, Rosie. Oh god oh god oh god. (*Pulls herself together.*) Well, my girl, if you want it…you shall have it.

I'd want the same thing if I was in your shoes, that's for damn sure. Let me tell you, as soon as this whole mess is over, I'm going to hire me a lawyer and have him put down on a piece of paper that I do not want to be hooked up to any goddam machine when it's time for me to go. I don't want to be in a hospital at all. Nosiree, I want to be on a beach in Hawaii…. No! In the backyard under the plum tree! Yes! That's where I want to be. Under that plum tree. I don't care if it's raining and freezing and…and hail is coming down the size of golf balls. I'm gonna put that in writing so there'll be no mistake about it. Because I know I don't want to be here.

Looks around her with great distaste.

I don't want to be here ever again. You know, Rosie, I've never hated anywhere so much in my life as I hate this hospital. (*Vehemently.*) I hate it.

Standing up, she claps her hands together, gearing for action.

Now I've got to go see about getting that damn machine turned off. Doctor says he needs permission from somebody in your immediate family. So I've got to talk to your relatives. What a crew. Who's the nicest one, Rose? Your sister, Roxanne? Roxanne…As I remember, she was almost civil to me the last time we talked, years ago. It won't be any trouble for her. She just has to sign a piece of paper. I'll drive down and bring it to her. Hell, I'll bring her a ball point pen to sign it with. (*Almost cheerful.*) No fuss, no muss, no bother.

(*With great tenderness.*) I'll take care of you, baby. I know you're suffering. I can feel it. It'll be a big relief, won't it? (*With deep sadness.*) It seems like you've been dying for such a long time. I'm beat, honey. I don't sleep good. I wake up— I don't know how many times during the night—and I wonder, has it already happened? Is it happening now?

Leans intently toward ROSE.

It seems to me that even if I'm not with you, I should know when you… Hell, the whole world'll be different when Rosa Felicia Belbasio isn't in it anymore. Maybe the air'll turn purple, the wind'll start to howl… earthquakes, volcanoes…something.

She moves the chair closer to the bed.

Rose, it bothers me that it could happen and I wouldn't know until the hospital called me. If they did call me. That's why I want to be here. (*With great urgency.*) I want to go with you as far as I can go. You always were dragging me to places I never heard of and had no interest in. Maybe if I was here…I don't know…I would see a puff of smoke rise up from your body…feel an invisible butterfly touch my cheek … something.

It dawns on her what she's really after.

I guess I want to catch your soul. (*Pause.*)

Smiling as she recalls her dream.

Rose, I had a dream last night that we both came back to life as eagles. Bald eagles. You know, when an eagle falls in love, that's forever. Even if one of them dies, the other one just stays on alone. Guess it's too much damn trouble to get used to another eagle. (*Joyful.*) Oh honey, what a dream. We were flying and soaring and playing. A nice life. No post office, no head nurse. Just trees and sky and you and me. I woke up feeling so good. (*Pause, then with great excitement.*) Rose, maybe that's where this whole thing is leading! We're gonna be eagles together someday! Sounds like fun, doesn't it? Do you think it's possible? I do. I know it is possible.

> *She looks at ROSE and, instead of seeing her dreams of what was or her fantasies of what might be, VIRGINIA sees what ROSE is right now: a wasted, comatose body in a hospital bed. Her eyes travel to the ventilator and then to her watch.*

(*Surprised.*) Looka-here, it says 6:45. Goddamit, I don't feel like leaving. (*Folds her arms resolutely.*) Let 'em call the police. We'll show 'em, won't we?

> *There is a long silence as VIRGINIA waits for nurse to arrive. She walks to the door, checks the hallway. She feels more and more uncertain of her plan to defy the nurse as time progresses.*

Wait a minute, I've got a better idea! You know that nurse usually sticks her head in and goes on down the hall. I'm gonna hide behind your bed! She'll never know I'm here. Now, don't you make a sound. It would be just like you to come out of your coma right now so's you could give me away and embarrass me.

> *She starts to hide behind the bed, stops.*

Oh Rosie, you know what this reminds me of? Remember when we went to visit your old college buddy Adele and she put us in separate bedrooms? And I snuck down the hall in the middle of the night into your room and we were having such a good time…you know…fooling around. And then Adele knocks on the door. She wants to have a little midnight chat with her old college buddy! So I hide in the closet. But I couldn't stop giggling.

(*Starts to laugh at the memory.*) So Adele's chattin' away, and you are coughin' to beat the band trying to cover the sound of me giggling in the closet. But Adele hears me anyhow and she throws open the closet door. And there I am standing, stark naked. Oh, I stopped giggling then, didn't I?

So Adele tears out of the room, we pack our bags and skedaddle in the middle of the night and you never see Adele again. Oh, I always remember that night whenever they talk about homosexuals being in the closet.

Uh-oh. Here comes the nurse.

She ducks behind the bed. Pause. VIRGINIA slowly stands and sheepishly looks at the invisible nurse who has discovered her. She tries to be casual.

Oh, hello, Nurse. I…I…just dropped something! That's right. I think maybe it rolled under the bed somewhere.

Pretends to look under the bed, then glances at nightstand.

Oh there they are! The Italian sausages! On the nightstand the whole time. How about that? I must be blind!

Listens to the nurse, with astonishment.

Visiting hours are over?

Scrutinizes her watch in disbelief.

My my. How time flies when you're having fun, doesn't it, nurse?

To ROSE, in a hearty public voice.

Well, my dear, it's time for me to go.

She gathers her things together and puts the chair back in its original position. Then VIRGINIA bends low over ROSE's head. She speaks softly, insisting on a private moment despite the nurse's presence.

I love you. You remember that. You're my girl. I'll take care of everything. I'll make everything alright.

She picks up the grocery bag, gives the ventilator one last look, and turns to the nurse.

Goodnight, Nurse.

VIRGINIA exits. Lights fade to black, except for the rectangle of light that is ROSE's bed. The sound of the ventilator strengthens as the lights dim.

Scene Two

Lights fade up. The sound of the ventilator recedes into the background. VIRGINIA enters in a rush, filled with anxiety.

Hello there, Rosie. You're right. I'm here early today, my girl. I just got fed up at work and told them I was done for the day. They understood.

She sits but immediately springs up and starts pacing.

You know what I did when I left here last night? I got in my car and I drove. I drove and I drove and I drove. All over the city. Just couldn't stand the thought of going home to that damn empty house. That's not the first time I've done that either, my girl.

Do you know what I did when I finally got home? Even before I ate my heirloom tomato? First I fixed myself a good stiff drink. And don't you reprimand me. I needed it before I phoned your relatives.

Your sister Roxanne…You remember her, the nice one? She wouldn't speak to me. In fact, she hung up on me not once but three times. Now, your brother Roland …I've got to hand it to him. He did talk to me. Explained how it was God's will that you were on this ventilator as a punishment for your sins. You see, Rose, according to Roland… and God…you loving a woman just made you destined to end up like this. And, seeing as Roland is such a good Christian, he doesn't want to interfere.

That left your daddy, so I went to the rest home. He was downright friendly to me, for the first time. Unfortunately he didn't remember who you were. Poor fella. (*Pause.*) And that was it for your immediate family. (*Pause.*)

I just spoke to the doctor out in the hall and he says that there's nothing he can do if the family doesn't want to get involved. He says we'll have to "let nature take its course." I'm sorry, baby. (*VIRGINIA is broken.*) I'll tell you, Rosie, between God's will, the hospital's will and the doctor's will, there's not too much left over for you and me, is there?

> *She walks over to the ventilator. With bitterness.*

I do believe this ventilator's got more say in the situation than I have.

"Let nature take its course." (*Furious.*) What the hell has this machine got to do with nature? Hell, if you were out in nature, some wild animal would come along and kill you. Nature would never allow you to suffer like this. (*Bitterly.*) Machines.

And doctors! That's another real disappointing subject, isn't it Rose? Can you imagine, I thought they knew it all. Isn't that funny? Not like gods exactly. But something between a human and a god. But guess what, Rosie: They're just stumbling around in the dark like all the rest of us. Isn't that sad? I wish they were gods.

> *Pause.*

Your doctor...oh, he's not so bad. He didn't give you the cancer, after all. I have to keep reminding myself of that. I just wish he cared a little bit more. But he's too busy. Doesn't have the time. Besides, I guess he'd be real sad if he did care. If he understood that you, Rosie Belbasio, were dying in that bed. Not just anybody. But you.

You know Rose, when we fell in love it was so beautiful...beautiful. And now it's come to this. Would I have had the guts to fall in love if I had known? This love business is pretty tricky, isn't it? Sets you up for a big fall. Reels you in nice and slow and then slaps you down.

(*Turns on ROSE.*) Goddamit, Rose, why did you have to go and get sick? And why didn't you go to the doctor when you first saw the blood? (*Sarcastic.*) Oh no, Rosie doesn't believe in doctors. So Rosie waits six months before she even says a word to me. And then I had to drag you to the doctor. (*Spits the words out with anger.*) Maybe they could have saved you if you'd gone in earlier! That's stupid, woman. Just plain stupid.

(*She's shocked at herself. The words tumble out.*) Rose...I don't know why I said...I didn't mean it. I'm sorry, Rose. I'm sorry. I'm sorry. (*Pause. VIRGINIA is drained.*) I'm sorry for so many things. For not going to the Gay Parade with you. For not keeping the house clean. I'm sorry for all the times I drank a little too much and embarrassed you. (*An agony of remorse.*) Maybe I should have borrowed more money and taken you to another doctor, a better doctor. Maybe I should have moved you to a better hospital. (*Pleading.*) What do you think, Rosie? What do you think?

You know what I regret the most? That I never told you that I forgave you for having that...that affair with Sandy, way back when. Every day I'd come here and I'd say to myself, "Tell her you forgive her, goddamit. Just spit it out." But...I don't know...you'd be in a bad mood or I'd be tired. Somehow it was never the right time.

(*Pause.*) I guess I might as well say it now. (*With great generosity and love.*) I forgive you, Rose. Out of 27 good years, a few bad months. What difference does it make? Can you hear me, Rosie? It doesn't matter anymore. And it hasn't for a long time.

  VIRGINIA is spent, calm.

You know, last night, when I couldn't go to sleep, this song kept going through my head. I learned it when I was a little girl at church camp. (*Sings.*)

> *Death is a long, long sleep.*
> *Sleep is a short short death*
> *That softens but never ends life's grief.*
> *Death is a long long sleep.*

That's a hell of a song to teach little kids, isn't it? I loved it, though. It's a round. You know, one person starts singing and then another person comes in and another and another. So the song never ends. I used to love to sing rounds when I was a little girl.

(*She looks at her watch.*) Well, Rosie my girl, visiting hours won't be over for a while. But I'm done in. I think I'll go.

> *She stands up, stretches, turns to ROSE with a flirtatious smile.*

How about a little goodby kiss?

> *She goes to the door, looks out.*

The coast is clear. Nobody's coming down the hall.

> *She bends down to kiss ROSE, then jumps up, turns around, and walks toward the door again.*

I think I hear someone.

> *She stops.*

(*Distraught.*) Jesus Christ, look what they have done to me, Rose. For all I know, I might never see you again. And I'm still afraid that somebody might catch me kissing you on the lips. (*A realization dawns.*) I've been hiding and pretending for so many years that it doesn't matter anymore if there's anyone actually watching. Because there's always somebody watching…inside of me. I been walking around my whole life with a great big rock on my chest.

(*Angry, crying.*) And now they tell me that after living with you for 27 years and coming to visit you in this stinkin' hospital every single day, that I'm nobody to you, that I got no rights.

(*Her fury builds.*) Oh, if I was some man who met you and married you two months ago, that would be different. A man would have the right to say, "This person cannot speak for herself anymore, but I love her and I know she wants to die." Oh, they would listen to a man, wouldn't they? But me, I'm just queer old Virginia. They can tell me when I have to get out of this room. Those are the rules. Those are the rules! THOSE ARE THE RULES!

(*Taking a deep breath, then with great force, to the world.*) Well, who the hell made the rules? (*Turns to ROSE.*) They've got no right to make rules that come between you and me, my girl.

(*With deep sorrow.*) Rose, I've always wanted to walk with my arm around you, in the sunshine. Just you and me, out on a beautiful day, not afraid if somebody notices…that we love each other. We've never done it, not once. And now it's too late.

(*Close to ROSE, fiercely.*) Oh baby, I want to hold you so close right now. (*Wrapping her arms around herself.*) I want to press you, squeeze you to me so hard. I want to wrap myself around you. (*In an agony of frustration.*) But you got all those goddam tubes running in and out of you. Damn them. Damn them all with their tubes and rules and papers and machines!

She turns to face her enemy, the ventilator.

Oh Rosie, do you want me to turn that machine off right now? With my own hands? I could. I know which dial it is. I've seen the nurses fiddling with it a hundred times. I could turn that big blue dial… (*Suddenly panicked.*) What if I get caught? That's murder! (*Pause. She thinks it out.*) But I could turn the machine off, give you time to go, then turn it back on before anyone knew what happened. The nurse never comes in here until 6:45. (*Looks at watch.*) I've got time.

(*With rising panic.*) Rose, what am I gonna do without you? At least now I can come here and sit and talk. It's better than nothing. When you're gone, people will think I'm crazy to talk to you. Now they just think I'm a damn fool. I don't know how to live without you. I'm scared, baby.

(*She feels a message coming from ROSE.*) You want me to do it, don't you? (*She fights against it.*) I love you too much to do it! (*The final realization.*) And I love you too much not to do it. Damn damn damn.

(*This is the last time she will speak to the living ROSE.*) Rose, you have blessed my life. Nobody's luckier than me. Nobody. We had 27 fine years together. I wouldn't have minded a few more, but…My sweet baby, my best friend, my honey, my lover…my wife. (*Fervently.*) You are my wife. You and I both know that. I've got a right to do this, don't I? I've got a right.

> VIRGINIA *walks to the door, and looks out into the hospital corridor. She softly closes the door. She pulls the chair as close as she can to the bed and speaks softly to ROSE.*

You're my girl, Rosie. You remember that. Always were and always will be.

> VIRGINIA *walks over to the ventilator, which has gotten much louder, the sound dominating the space. She slowly reaches toward the dial and then pauses, struggling with herself. She stares at her hand, wills it to move to the invisible dial. She touches the dial and very slowly turns it, as the sound of the ventilator slowly fades away. Finally, for the first time in the play, there is silence.* VIRGINIA, *stunned by what she has done, stands perfectly still, listening to the silence. Then she rushes to the chair and sits close to the bed, her whole body leaning toward* ROSE.

(*Softly, urgently.*) Don't forget about being eagles, now. You wait for me.

> *Lights slowly fade as* VIRGINIA *stays intensely focused on* ROSE. *Eventually everything is dark except for a pinpoint of light on* VIRGINIA's *face and the rectangle of light that represents the hospital bed. These lights get brighter. Then the light on the bed fades. The last thing we see before the blackout is* VIRGINIA's *face, watching* ROSE *as she dies, trying to catch her soul.*

End Of Play

1985

ONE FOOL

ONE FOOL
OR
HOW I LEARNED TO STOP
WORRYING & LOVE THE DUTCH
OR
THE ASTONISHING & TERRIFYING
ADVENTURES OF A YANKEE DYKE
IN THE LAND OF DIKES & TULIPS
OR
HOW SHE FOUND LOVE & LOST
LOVE & FOUND LOVE & LOST
LOVE, ETC.

Premiere information

One Fool had its first performance at Sonderbar, the one lesbian bar in Vienna, Austria, on March 25, 1987. Terry Baum played The Fool.

The United States premier was August 1988 at Theatre Rhinoceros in San Francisco. Andrea Snow directed.

"Ballad of Clitoral Self-Stimulation" by Ronda Slater

PRODUCTION HISTORY

In Fall 1985, I went to Amsterdam to perform my play *Immediate Family* at the International Women's Cultural Festival. I met a Dutch woman there, fell in love, and moved to Holland. It didn't work out with the woman, but it did work out with Amsterdam. What was to become *One Fool* began at the Suikerhof (trans: Sugar Shack), an old-time Dutch cabaret with dark wood and flocked red wallpaper.

The first shows were solo improvisation, built on suggestions from the audience. However, the third night, I could not get anyone in the audience to volunteer a single word in *Dutch*. I was devastated, and I still had six performances to go. My best friend, Mary Wings, encouraged me to buid a new show around stories I had told onstage about my life in Amsterdam. *One Fool* is a good example of creation through chutzpah and serendipity. On one night, I was inspired to incorporate a coatrack, that happened to be backstage, into my act. On another night, I realized the outrageous dress I was wearing was big enough to throw over my head. Each night, I came to the Suikerhof with an outline and added and subtracted bits. I made tapes of my performances, transcribed them, and put together a script. *One Fool*, as it stands now, is a mixture of true fact and wild flights of imagination, with the former being by far the more bizarre.

I toured *One Fool*, along with *Immediate Family,* to Germany and Austria in March, 1987. Subsequently, I performed the play all over Holland and at festivals in London, Stockholm, and Boston.

One Fool had a very successful run in San Francisco at Theatre Rhinoceros, and was named one of the ten best plays of 1988 by the S.F. Bay Guardian. In 1992, *One Fool* was published in *Tough Acts to Follow, One-Act Plays on the Gay/Lesbian Experience.*

Although I haven't performed *One Fool* in many years, the first scene, with The Fool in the audience, has become a staple for the Crackpot

Crones, Carolyn's and my current sketch comedy duo. The Crones have taken The Fool's search for love in the audience to many venues in the U.S.—and a few in Mexico.

CHARACTER

THE FOOL: Not a realistic character, but rather a clown. A romantic idiot who chases love all over the world. In terms of age, The Fool must be old enough to have had all those relationships before she runs away to Europe. The Fool is never pathetic. She is heroic in her reckless adventuring to discover the woman who is The One for her. She is a lover of life, of women, and—ultimately—the city of Amsterdam, the most seductive and maddening mistress of them all.

NOTE: In the bar scene, The Fool describes her body, which happens to be my body. I encourage the actress playing The Fool to rewrite that particular part of the play so that it fits her. I would be happy to assist in the rewriting.

TIME
The 1980s

PLACE

When The Fool is in the audience, the location is San Francisco. But the producer is welcome to change it to whatever town where the performance is taking place. Once she leaps onstage, The Fool is in Amsterdam, Holland, the specific location morphing according to the needs of the script.

AT RISE: At the moment when lights usually go down on the Audience and up on the stage, the opposite happens. The house lights become brighter, and the stage, which was dimly lit, becomes dark. THE FOOL enters from the back of the theater. She is wearing a rather amazing dress. It is red and shiny and billowy with lots of ruffles. She is wearing silly shoes. She looks a bit like a clown, and definitely like a fool. She wanders through the audience, stopping and pondering as she stares at different women. Several times, she shakes her head "no" and moves on.

Finally she finds a woman who possesses what she is seeking. She addresses the woman she has chosen: The One.

THE FOOL begins tentatively, shyly, but her certainty grows rapidly.

Excuse me, are you The One? You're The One, aren't you? You're The One I've been searching for, waiting for! I've found you at last! Everything is different with you. (*She's overwhelmed by a totally new sensation.*) I've never felt this way before! I love you. We're destined to spend the rest of our lives together. Let's make a home right here in San Francisco. Oh darling. Oh darling.

She dances ecstatically, reveling in her love.

Love darling love darling darling love love love…

What began in ecstasy becomes mechanical in repetition and finally slows to a stop.

…love… darling… (*To herself, puzzled.*) Something is wrong. (*Horrors!*) I'm bored! I'm in a rut. (*To The One.*) You too? (*Very matter-of-fact, cheerful even.*) Look, let's admit it. We made a mistake. I mean, we hardly have sex anymore. I'm not saying it's your fault. I'm just stating an objective reality. We've grown apart. Hey, no hard feelings. It's time for both of us to move on.

THE FOOL shakes The One's hand absentmindedly and turns to search again. She chooses another woman.

Are you The One? (*Pause. Not the answer she expected, but she is stunned by the deep insight of the response of The One #2.*) You're right! That is a stupid question. (*To the audience, absolutely thrilled.*) I have finally found The One who sees me for what I really am—an idiot! (*To The One #2, she is admiring, obsequious.*) You are so perceptive. I am lazy and greedy and dishonest. (*Abjectly but joyfully begging.*) You'll help me, won't you? You'll shape me, mold me, change me from this revolting worm into someone beautiful and fine, like you! (*Groveling.*) I need you desperately. (*Overwhelmed by a totally new sensation— again!*) I've never felt like this before. I love you…as much as a wretch like me is capable of love. (*Triumphantly.*) I want to spend the rest of my life with you! (*The One #2 responds unpleasantly.*) Maybe it is a stupid idea, but that's how I feel right now. (*The light finally begins to dawn.*) Nag, nag, nag. That's all I ever hear from you. You don't like anything I say. You don't like anything I do. (*Dawn has fully arrived, and with it, outrage.*) You don't love me, do you? You are not The One. You never were The One. You lied to me from the beginning. Goodbye forever.

Full of righteous outrage, she flees from The One #2 into the arms of The One #3. THE FOOL arrives a broken woman.

(*Hesitant.*) Are you The One? (*Confiding, very intimate.*) I want to tell you right away, I've been deeply hurt. I need to be treated gently. I need understanding and kindness.

Luxuriating in the security of The One #3, she wraps her arms around herself, swaying peacefully.

Please enfold me in your arms and fill in all the tiny little cracks in my psyche. I love you! (*Overwhelmed by a totally new...well, you know.*) I've never felt like this before. (*So peaceful she's melting...*) So relaxed, so safe, so warm, so...so...so...

Gradually, her arms rise toward her neck until she is strangling herself. She croaks in horror.

...so suffocated!

Consumed with irritation, she pulls away.

Don't you ever think of anything but me? You need a life of your own. You should get a job. Or at least a hobby! (*With compassion.*) How about stamp collecting? Listen, I'll give you a stamp to get you started!

She backs away, arms flailing.

Please! Get away from me! I need space, stimulation, freedom. (*She notices #3's distress, nonchalantly.*) Oh, please don't cry so hard. Things were destined to be like this. I'm sure someday we'll be great friends.

THE FOOL condescendingly pats #3's shoulder and saunters away, on the hunt again. A man in the audience catches her eye. She dismisses him.

You couldn't possibly be The One. You're a man.

THE FOOL continues to wander through the audience. A woman catches her eye. She regards her for a moment, then shakes her head.

Oh no. You couldn't possibly be The One. (*Points to the woman sitting next to her.*) You're already with her. (*Pause.*) She's going away for two weeks? Oh, alright. Just a teeny tiny affair. (*To the audience, very very rational.*) After all, what could be the harm? We're both adults. We know how to control our emotions. (*But guess what! This is The One #4!!*) Oh, baby, I now see the truth. You are The One. I love you. (*And once again a totally new...*) I've never felt this way before! Leave her and run away with me forever! (*Pause.*) She's coming back tomorrow? (*Overflowing with empathy.*) It's going to be tough breaking the news to her. I feel for both of you. Still, it's got to be done. (*Pause, then incredulous.*) What do you mean that you have no news to break to her? (*Pause. With mounting outrage.*) So what if you've known her for seven years and me for two weeks! What has that got to do with anything? We're talking quality here, not quantity! (*Haughty.*) I cannot believe that after two ecstatic weeks of bliss with me, you still think that she's The One.

> THE FOOL *loses control.*

What's she got that I haven't got, huh? What's wrong with me? Tell me. TELL ME! (*Pause, totally shocked.*) You're telling me! SHUT UP! Did you think I really wanted to know? You have broken my heart. Goodbye forever.

> THE FOOL *sweeps off with tragic fury. She's magnificent. To the audience.*

Can you believe her? (*Points to The One #4.*) She wants to stay with her (*Points to the woman sitting next to her.*) instead of running away forever with me because… (*Very sarcastically.*) …they love each other, they're happy together, and they have great sex. (*Disgusted, to #4.*) You are really self-destructive. You'll regret this. I won't, but you will!

> *To the audience, crushed.*

Oh, my heart is broken.

> *But somehow she finds the courage to go on with her search.*

Hello… You're her ex-lover?

> THE FOOL *moves on to someone else.*

You're her sister?

> *Panic growing, to someone else…*

You're her sister's ex-lover?

> *…and someone else…*

You're her lover's ex-sister?!? (*She's devastated. To the audience.*) It's a very small world, isn't it? Tiny, really. I'm already connected to every single lesbian in the San Francisco Bay Area. (*Desperate.*) I've got to get out of this place! Everything reminds me I'm not with her.

(*Hope—or idiocy—springs eternal!*) I know! I'll go to Europe! Nobody will know either of us there! (*Dreamily.*) I'll drown my sorrows standing in line at tourist attractions. I'll be insulted in languages I've never even heard before. (*Considerably revived.*) Europe, here I come!

THE FOOL runs down the aisle and leaps onstage. As she hits the stage, the lights come up there, and go down on the audience.

SETTING: Onstage are two chairs and a table, all painted in many bright colors. One particularly fabulously painted chair sits Center Stage. The other chair is in the Upstage Left corner. The table, placed Downstage Right, has on it a large bunch of tulips in a vase, a newspaper, a pen and a small notebook. A coatrack stands Downstage Center. It is wooden, with a round flat bottom. It "wears" a knitted cap on top with a long woolen scarf hung around the hooks and tied in front. Street noises can be heard: traffic, people speaking Dutch, the sound of a calliope. The sounds slowly fade as THE FOOL speaks. She looks around her, dazzled, and spots the tulips in the vase.

Ah, Amsterdam! It's so beautiful! It's so old! Look at all the people in cafes, laughing and talking. I want to be one of them. It's so…

She steps in something unpleasant.

…It's filthy. (*Oh, the pain of it all…*) And I'm still so heartbroken.

The Coatrack onstage, heretofore unnoticed, says something to her.

Excuse me? Would I like to dance? Well, yeah…I guess so. (*To the audience, a bit defensive.*) Look, my heart is still broken, but a little distraction couldn't hurt.

She dances without inhibition or grace around The Coatrack. Approvingly, to the audience.

She's a good dancer!

She listens to The Coatrack, laughs hysterically. To the audience.

She's got a great sense of humor. And she speaks perfect English, with such a cute Dutch accent. (*She gazes at The Coatrack.*) And she's tall. I just love tall women. (*She has been dancing all this time. She listens to The Coatrack.*) Would I like to go for a walk? You bet!

THE FOOL takes a walk around Amsterdam with The Coatrack by lifting it up and carrying it to various parts of the stage, where The Coatrack points things out. THE FOOL finds everything very interesting.

So this is the famous red light district! Everything is so open and tolerant here! (*Looking somewhere else.*) Amsterdam has more canals than Venice? I had no idea. (*To the audience.*) I'm learning so much!

She walks towards something interesting.

That crazy building with all the wavy brick, what's that? Amsterdam School Style? You're right, it does look like the architect was stoned when he designed it! I love it. (*To the audience, more and more delighted.*) She knows everything about architecture in Holland! What an intelligent, witty, articulate, well-read, attractive woman! (*Pause.*) However, my heart is still… (*The Coatrack says something.*) I beg your pardon? (*What she hears pleases her immensely. Her voice turns husky with desire.*) I thought you'd never ask.

She slowly and seductively approaches The Coatrack, making little sexy growly sounds. She impetuously flings its hat on the floor and then sinuously unwinds the scarf, flinging that aside too, laughing a throaty laugh. She lightly kisses the tips of The Coatrack's hooks and massages them as if they were nipples, getting more and more excited. Now she is moving around the stage, rubbing The Coatrack up and down, moaning, rubbing herself on The Coatrack. She sits on the chair, The Coatrack upended, its pedestal in her lap and facing the Audience, which can see a pair of underpants velcroed on the bottom. THE FOOL slowly slides her hand beneath the underpants. She is salivating, delirious.

Oh, baby, you're so wet.

She tears the underpants off and performs oral sex on The Coatrack. This leads to further mad, passionate and athletic lovemaking. THE FOOL ends up exhausted, sprawled in the chair, with The Coatrack lying over her. To the audience.

She's magnificent in bed!

THE FOOL gently caresses and kisses The Coatrack. This is a very intimate, post-orgasm conversation.

You need a lot of love? What a coincidence! I happen to have a lot of love to give. And don't worry about giving me a lot back. I'm very strong. I don't need much. (*The Coatrack confides in THE FOOL.*) You're an alcoholic? (*THE FOOL becomes increasingly sympathetic as The Coatrack catalogs her faults.*) Ohhhh…You're a workaholic and don't have time for a relationship? You had a miserable childhood? You're terrified of being loved? (*Overjoyed.*) You hate yourself? Fantastic! (*To the audience.*) She's so honest. I love it.

(*To The Coatrack, full of love and understanding.*) Oh, baby, I can see that you're a total mess, but I don't care. I want to take care of you, heal you, make up for all the bad things that all those other people have done to you. I…How do you say "I love you" in Dutch? (*Pause.*) "*Ik hou van jou*"? It rhymes! That's adorable. (*The Coatrack doesn't like that.*) Oh, I'm sorry. I didn't mean to insult your language by calling it adorable. (*She receives a revelation.*) Sweetheart, I have an idea. What do you think about me moving to Amsterdam and saving you with my love? Would you like that? (*The Coatrack would like it.*) Great!

She stands herself and The Coatrack up. To the audience.

After all, love is more important to me than my friends, my family, my career, my country, and my entire life up to this point. And besides, I really like Amsterdam.

She embraces The Coatrack.

Oh, darling, we'll be so happy. We'll spend the rest of our lives together. I've never felt like this before… (*A tiny bit of doubt.*)…at least as far as I can remember.

She gives The Coatrack a great big smacking kiss.

You wait here. I just have to go home to America and pack a few things.

She starts to rush offstage, then turns to the audience.

Moving six thousand miles for Love! My friends will be so jealous. (*To The One #4 in the audience.*) You know, I'm glad you didn't run away forever with me. This is working out much better.

THE FOOL runs offstage and returns lugging a very large battered suitcase, which she drops Downstage Left.

Honey, I'm home from America! Oh, darling.

She throws herself on The Coatrack for a lengthy embrace. Too lengthy for The Coatrack's taste. THE FOOL backs away.

You need time to yourself? Of course, I understand.

She walks away, calming herself.

After all, she's used to being alone. This is a big change for her. (*The Coatrack calls her back. Joy oh joy!*) You need me again? Oh, sweetheart, I need you too!

She throws her arms around The Coatrack.

You don't like it when I'm dependent on you? Well sure, I understand.

She backs away. To the audience, boiling.

Ooh, she's pushing me away. That really turns me on. I want her, I want her so bad. Oh darling.

She rushes in—and stops abruptly.

Your mother's coming and you need time to prepare?

She walks away from The Coatrack, a bit slowly.

Anyone could understand that. It's a no-brainer.

The Coatrack summons her again—or so she thinks.

Oh, darling.

She stops abruptly.

(*Incredulous.*) Your mother just left and you need time to recover?!? I… guess I understand.

THE FOOL backs away once again, rushes forward with "Oh, darling," then away with "I understand." This repeats and builds into a frenzy, with THE FOOL eventually standing in one place, swinging wildly back and forth saying "Oh, darling, I understand." She collapses in total frustration.

This is driving me crazy. I am really suffering. I am filled with pain. (*But on the bright side…*) Oh, well. At least I know I'm alive—because I'm in agony!

She stands up groggily.

One more time!

She rushes in and throws her arms around The Coatrack.

Oh, darling. I'm so happy to be with you. I've never felt like… (*Pause.*) Why should I sit down?

THE FOOL obediently sits.

(*Still desperately cheerful.*) Well, I'm in love too, sweetheart. *Ik hou van jou.* That's the whole point of my moving to Amsterdam. I'm in love with you and you're in love with…WHO? (*She takes a big breath.*) Now, let me get this straight. You're in love with somebody else? (*Pause, then pleading.*) Are you sure you're in love with her? Maybe you just think you are, but you really aren't. (*Pause.*) Uh-huh. Well, does that mean you don't love me anymore? (*Pause, enraged.*) And why can't you love two people at once? Everybody else is doing it! (*Arrogant.*) She can't possibly be a better lover than I am! (*Stunned.*) Are you telling me that you have better sex with her? (*THE FOOL loses it once again.*) What's so fabulous about her? What's her magic trick? What's she got that I haven't got? (*To herself.*) This is starting to sound familiar, but I can't help myself. (*Back to the tantrum.*) What's she got? Tell me, tell me! (*Long pause.*) Long thick fingers?

> *She stares at her own hands in horror, then rises to the pinnacle of contempt.*

So that's what you go for. My sensitivity, imagination, stamina mean nothing compared to her long thick fingers. (*With great contempt.*) You're just a size queen. I suppose my tongue isn't big enough for you either.

> *She sticks her tongue out.*

These things happen? No they don't. This is the first time in the history of the human race that one person has moved six thousand miles to be with another person, only to be dumped immediately for a third person with long thick fingers! I hate you. You have ruined my life. I never want to see your stupid face again. I hope you suffer!

> *She wrestles with The Coatrack, pushing her offstage. She comes back to find The Coatrack's hat and scarf. As she throws these offstage, she yells.*

And you know what? Sleeping with you was like sleeping with a…with a COATRACK!

(*Mumbling, arguing with herself.*) What a terrible thing to say. I'm an awful person. No wonder she doesn't love me. What am I saying? I'm lucky to be rid of her. She's a sadist. That woman enjoyed my suffering. I have to face the fact that she is essentially an evil human being. (*Pause.*) But then why did I fall in love with her? I must have very very bad judgment. That does not bode well for the future. (*Panic.*) The future! Yeouggh! How can I go on without her? Oh, I miss her so much already. I still love her. She's so wonderful… (*She appeals to the audience.*) How could somebody so wonderful be such a monster? Doesn't anyone know the answer to that? (*Nobody does.*)

(*A bright idea!*) I know. I'll go to sleep. What a lovely idea. In fact, I may stay in bed for the rest of my life. Just pull the covers over my head and forget about the world.

> *She curls up on her chair and pulls imaginary covers over her. Then she uncovers herself and looks up. Strange thudding noises are heard above her.*

What the hell are they doing upstairs? Moving the furniture for the fourth time this week? Are they bowling? Yes, that's it. Wait a minute. It's not bowling. They're training horses! I'm positive. They are training horses to bowl in the upstairs flat. Amazing what Dutch people can do in such a tiny space. I'll never get to sleep with all that racket.

(*Terrified.*) I'm alone. Me. I can't even go to sleep. I am alone and awake in a strange country! (*Mumbling to herself, very upset.*) I'm alone. I can't believe it. I'm alone, alone…

> *She runs to her suitcase and takes a small, stuffed, hand-crocheted dog out of it. She cuddles the little dog, visibly relaxes.*

Ahhhhhh. That's better.

> *During the following scene, THE FOOL manipulates Snarky like a puppet. The stuffed animal seems to be alive and responding to her, although it never makes a sound.*

Oh, Snarky, what would I do without you? Thank you for being here for me when I need you. You're so understanding, such a good listener. You're different from all the rest, aren't you? You love me, don't you? Why didn't I realize it was you…you…you all along? Come to me, my Snarky-Warkums.

> *She embraces Snarky passionately. This is followed by a horrible moment of self-knowledge.*

This is pathetic. Here I am, an intelligent mature woman, reduced to nibbling the armpit of a stuffed animal. (*To Snarky, outraged.*) I deserve better than someone with a crocheted head and a heart full of cotton. This is all your fault, Snarky. How could you? I hate you, Snarky.

> *In a frenzy of anger, she beats Snarky's head on the back of the chair while repeatedly yelling "I hate you!" She suddenly stops.*

Oh my… (*To the audience, overwhelmed with guilt.*) I don't know what came over me. Don't tell anyone about this, okay? (*Examining Snarky.*) Your head is an entirely different shape now. (*Clasping Snarky to her bosom.*) Thank goodness you're washable. (*To Snarky, imploring.*) Oh Snarky, I'm so sorry. Can you ever forgive me? No, no. Don't blame yourself. You did nothing to deserve this. It's just that…ours is such an unequal relationship. We need to work on that. I'd feel better if you beat me too. Would you do that? Please, hit me hard. I'm begging you. Wipe away my guilt.

> *Snarky hits her a few times, but the little pup's heart isn't in it.*

It's no good, Snarky. It's no good. The magic is gone.

THE FOOL throws Snarky back in the suitcase. Then she throws herself on the floor in despair, howling. She suddenly pops up, like one of those dolls that cannot be pushed over.

Oh well, at least I'm not in prison or starving. At least I don't live in a dictatorship—yet. Yep, it would definitely be worse to live in a dictatorship, where you would get shot if you said what you think, than to lose the love of your life after two months. Let's face it: On the cosmic seismograph of human suffering, all of this would hardly make a blip. I'm making a huge fuss over nothing, aren't I? Look at me.

She leaps around the stage with joy.

I'm free. I'm healthy. I live in a beautiful city. I can look out my window and see ducks on a canal. I can hear them quacking. I can hear and see. I've got my legs, my arms. I've got my hands…

She stops joyfully leaping to closely examine her hands.

My hands…Hands, you're too small. That's been established. But I'm still very attached to you. You're so useful. You do so many things well. (*The light dawns.*) And there's one thing you do really superbly.

THE FOOL goes to her suitcase and finds a pair of castanets, which she puts on. She sings while dancing, Flamenco-style, clattering her castanets.

Song: THE BALLAD OF CLITORAL SELF-STIMULATION

I give myself good vibrations
With clitoral self-stimulation.
No broken hearts, no frustration
With digital manipulation.
I do not have any lover
So you may be shocked to discover
Me ahh-ing and ooh-ing at what I am doing
Myself underneath the bedcover! Ole!

Dance break. THE FOOL dances Flamenco-style.

I slather my body with lotion.
My hands become poetry in motion.
Ain't it sublime to take so much time.
Who else would show such devotion?

THE FOOL turns her back on the audience and masturbates, using the castanets. The audience hears their vigorous clack and THE FOOL's rising moans as she writhes toward a climax. She builds to an enormous orgasm. She slowly turns to face the audience, smiling blissfully.

That was a truly fabulous orgasm.

She collapses into the chair.

Sometimes I wonder why I even bother to have sex with anybody else. Oh hands, I love you.

She kisses her hands.

And now I'm going shopping! My mother sent me a check that comes to three hundred euros at the current exchange rate. I've got to go out and spend it before the dollar goes down any further. What a perfect day. First, a big orgasm. And now, shopping. Boutiques, here I come!

THE FOOL skips around the stage, humming The Ballad of Clitoral Self-Stimulation *to herself, trying on imaginary clothes and rejecting them. Finally, something special catches her eye.*

Oh. What an exquisite pair of orange-and-turquoise high-topped leather sneakers. (*To the audience.*) They'll look smashing with this dress, don't you agree? I must have them.

She goes to the invisible saleslady. THE FOOL speaks Dutch to her with a very thick American accent.

Mevrouw, ik denk dat ik dese mooi schoenen nemen. (*She listens to the saleslady and then turns to the audience.*) Now, why do they always speak English to me when I speak perfectly beautiful Dutch to them? (*To the saleslady.*) Mijn geld is in mijn tasje. Mijn tasje…

She looks around her.

My purse…it must be here somewhere. Oh no. Now I remember. I left it over…it must be…

She rushes around the stage, searching for her purse.

It's gone! (*To the audience.*) Somebody must have taken it! But I don't understand. Here I am in peaceful, honest Amsterdam for two months and my purse is stolen. How is that possible, *Mevrouw*? (*She listens to the saleslady.*) Oh, you think an American stole it? Well, it's only fair then, I guess.

Dazed by tragedy, she drags herself home.

They must have seen me coming. They took one look at my face and they knew, there's a sap with more euros in her *tasje* than she's ever had before. Three hundred! What a catastrophe. (*Pause.*) Oh well. At least I don't live in a dictatorship—yet. At least I've got fifty tulips that only cost me five euros. Flowers are so cheap in Amsterdam. I've still got my tulips. I've still got my...

She waves her hands, looks knowingly at the audience, starts humming The Ballad *and puts on the castanets. Then she turns her back to the audience. But things don't go so well this time. The audience sees her sporadic gyrating and jumping up and down. The castanets get faster and then...*

(*Very loud.*) Ouch!

She turns to face the audience, glowering.

It's. Not. Working.

She takes the castanets off and slams them down on the table. She paces the stage, thinking hard.

I have a very serious problem. I've got to figure this out. This morning, I masturbated and I had a gigantic orgasm. Immediately after that, I went out shopping and my purse was stolen with three hundred euros in it. I just tried to masturbate again... (*She finally figures it out!*)...but I couldn't do it because I felt like I couldn't afford it!

Yes! My unconscious thinks my purse was stolen to punish me for having too much pleasure! Not only having too much, but having it all by myself! (*To the audience.*) Listen, it was a great orgasm, but definitely not worth three hundred euros. Seventy-five, tops. What am I going to do for the rest of the day?

She sits, takes her phone out, and stares at it.

I cannot believe that sleazy shithead hasn't phoned yet. Just because I told her I hated her guts and never wanted to see her again—is that any reason not to call a person? My phone must be broken.

She presses a button, listens.

No no. There's a dial tone. But maybe I can call out but nobody can call in. That does happen. I bet that sleazy shithead is dying to talk to me right now. She's probably been dialing for days, sitting by the phone crying her eyes out. That poor baby. Maybe I should call her.

She starts to call, then stops.

What am I saying? She dumped me. She has to make the first move. She can damn well wait until the phone is fixed.

She puts the phone down.

After all, I've got my pride. (*Pause.*) Wait a minute. Maybe I haven't got my pride. (*She feels herself all over, trying to find the pride.*) There doesn't seem to be any pride in here.

She grabs the phone. Stops.

(*With fine dramatic agony.*) Stop it! Do I want to pile humiliation on top of humiliation?

She puts the phone down.

(*Cheerfully.*) Oh, why not? I've never piled humiliation on top of humiliation before.

She grabs the phone, starts to dial. Stops.

Oh, wait a minute. I have piled humiliation on top of humiliation before. It's coming back to me.

THE FOOL slowly puts the phone down. She sits, can't think of anything to do. She can't help staring at the phone. Finally, a bright idea strikes!

I know! The newspaper!

She picks the paper up from the table, reads the headline out loud.

"Pope Clarifies Church's Position on Homosexuality." Oh goody. I love to hear what the Catholic Church has to say about sex. It's always so kinky. (*Reading from the article.*) "A spokesman for the Pontiff affirmed that practicing Catholics who feel a homosexual tendency must remain celibate." Those wacky Catholics! (*Hysterical laughter, which is gradually replaced by a look of distress.*) A terrible thought just occurred to me. I'm not using birth control. I won't need an abortion. I'm not having sex with anybody. I can't even masturbate anymore. I might as well be a practicing Catholic! (*Growing horror.*) I have become a Practicing Catholic without even realizing it!

She flings herself around the room in an agony of despair.

This has got to be the absolute bottom of human experience. I can't go on. I'm so bored. I'm so lonely. I swear, if a Jehovah's Witness comes to the door, I'm going with her, just for the company. (*Deeply yearning.*) There must be somebody out there for me. But how do I find her? (*Suddenly, it hits her.*) How silly of me! I've completely overlooked the modern route to romantic bliss. An online Personals ad!

She gets paper and pencil.

Let's see. "Attractive." (*Writes.*) "Intelligent." (*Writes. Then stops.*) No no no. Everybody is attractive and intelligent. You never see "ugly and stupid" in a Personals ad. I've got to go all out if I want to get attention. "Gorgeous…brilliant…" That's it. (*She continues to write.*) Ah-hah. Oh yeah. Mmmm. That'll do it. Hee-hee. Okay. Great. Finished!

THE FOOL reads aloud what she has written.

"Gorgeous, brilliant, charming, warm, sensitive lesbian is abandoned, lonely and desperate. I need a woman who will appreciate me, sweep me off my feet…" Do I really want to be swept off my feet again? No. (*Erases that.*) Yes. (*Writes it again.*) No! (*Erases it.*) Yes! (*Writes it again.*) NO NO NO NO! (*Erases it furiously and continues reading.*) "I need a woman who will appreciate me, take care of me and show me a good time. Sense of humor essential, as I have lost mine. I am looking for the love that lasts a lifetime, but will settle for a good fuck." (*With great satisfaction.*) That ought to do it. (*Pause.*) But the people who answer this ad will be the kind of people who answer Personals ads! Oh well. They must be a higher caliber than the kind of people who put them in.

(*The phone starts ringing. Ecstatic.*) The phone works! She's calling at last! I'll make her beg for forgiveness. But I won't give it to her. Oh no. It's too late. She had her chance and she blew it. I've moved on. (*Pause.*) On the other hand, maybe I'll take her back.

She picks up the phone, with great relish.

Hello, you sleazy shithead. (*Pause.*) Oh. Hello, Mother. No, no, I was expecting somebody else. No! There's nothing wrong! I'm having a fantastic time, Mom. Friends? Dutch people are so friendly. I have dozens of fantastic friends! As a matter of fact, I'm surprised you could get through. Usually my phone is ringing off the hook with dozens of invitations to parties and dinners and all kinds of things! (*Pause.*) Be careful? Mother, Holland is the safest country in the world! They've got gun control and everything! Don't worry about me. I'm doing fantastically. (*Pause. With real tenderness*). I love you too. Bye.

She hangs up the phone, smiles wistfully.

I wish my mother would call more often. I always feel so much better about my life after I've lied to her about it.

She's staring at the phone again.

I wonder if that sleazy shithead thinks about me as much as I think about her. I wonder if she's sitting home thinking about me right now, waiting for me to call. (*Pause.*) Maybe she's not. Maybe she's out having a good time with Big Finger and she thinks that I'm sitting at home waiting for her to call! Hah! That'll be the day! (*With great determination.*) If she's out having a good time, then I have to go out and have a good time too. I cannot stay home alone. I'm going to the lesbian bar. I'm going to pick somebody up and bring her home with me. Yes I will. (*She hesitates.*) Maybe I should dress up.

She rummages in her suitcase, finds a pair of polka-dot gloves and puts them on.

These make my hands look bigger, don't you think? Well, off we go.

She doesn't make a move. She surveys her room.

Look at this place. It's a pigpen.

She runs around picking up things, making all neat and orderly.

I can't bring a woman home to this mess. Of course, eventually she'll discover that I'm a slob. But maybe by that point, she'll be madly in love and it won't bother her so much.

She sees the castanets.

Oh no!

She grabs them and throws them in the suitcase.

I can't leave my sex toys lying around. She'll think I'm a pervert.

Looking around the room with satisfaction.

That's better. Well, off we go. (*She doesn't move.*) Either you do or you don't. (*She still doesn't move.*) Either you do or you don't.

She begins to move.

Either you will or you won't. Either you can or you can't. Either you have or you haven't. Either you do or you don't.

She repeats this rhythmically and does a little dance to it as she walks towards the disco. Suddenly, above her head, a fluorescent sign begins blinking. It shows an image of two stereotypical Dutch girls with wooden shoes and traditional hats, kissing. THE FOOL looks up.

This must be the place. (*Hesitantly.*) Well, here I am. (*Gathering all her confidence.*) Either you do or you don't.

> *Resolutely, she pushes open the invisible door and is confronted with a blast of disco music, flashing colored lights, and the cacophony of many women talking Dutch at the top of their lungs. This sound fades to a low level and continues throughout the bar scene. THE FOOL strolls around, surveying the scene.*

I'd better position myself so that people can get a good look at me.

> *She moves to a strategic spot center stage.*

Yep, the revolving globe is bouncing off me very nicely in this spot.

> *She looks around expectantly.*

Eye contact, eye contact. Anybody in the market for a little eye contact? (*Panic.*) Nobody's looking at me. They don't want me. I'll go home alone tonight…and tomorrow night…and the night after that… and every single night for the rest of my life! (*Calms herself down.*) Get a grip on yourself. Don't allow yourself to be desperate. Desperation is extremely unattractive. Dutch lesbians are very cool, and that's what they like. Just be cool, be calm.

> *THE FOOL attempts to be cool, with no great success. She drops it and talks to the audience.*

I really don't understand what people have against somebody who's desperate. In my experience, it puts a very nice edge on things if one or both participants are totally, flat-out desperate. Desperate sex can be fabulous.

> *She notices someone noticing her.*

Is that woman over there in the chair looking at me? Maybe she's not. She's probably just looking around me.

> *She turns away and quickly turns back.*

Yep. She *is* looking at me. And she's smiling.

> *THE FOOL smiles back, suavely, she hopes.*

She's very attractive. I should go over and say something to her. (*Testing it out, with her most suave and phony voice.*) Gosh, you're attractive. Hello, I think you're very attractive. When they handed out attractive, you got a whole shitload of it! (*She has reach suavity lift-off.*) Okay. I've got it down.

> *She walks with a debonair swagger to the invisible woman and speaks debonairly.*

Hi, little lady. Are you attracted to me? (*Pause.*) No? (*She's crashed and burned.*) Oh. Sorry I bothered you. I'll never speak to you again, for the rest of your life. I promise.

She stumbles back to her place, dazed.

What did I say? It wasn't what I planned. (*Pause.*) She said she wasn't attracted to me! And I always considered myself so attractive. I wonder if you can still be attractive if nobody's actually attracted to you. Come to think of it, the only person interested in me lately was a man. He was nice, too. Good-looking, intelligent, funny. The only reason I didn't go to bed with him was because he was a man. Silly to be so prejudiced when you're desperate. I can see it now. It's just like that old stereotype of the woman who becomes a lesbian because no man will have her. I'll become a heterosexual because no lesbian will have me. (*She shudders.*) What a tragic fate for a dykaholic.

Maybe I should leave this bar and go out and seduce a straight woman. But the one time I tried that, I spent the whole night apologizing. I told her, if sex with a woman was that bad all the time, I wouldn't be a lesbian either. No, I'd better stay right here.

Ooooh, I have to go to the bathroom right now.

She looks around desperately for the toilet, which she can't find. She asks someone.

Pardon, *waarom is de toilet*?

She looks to where she's being pointed.

Beedankt. (*To the audience.*) Why are they all laughing at me?

She walks to the Upstage Left corner, opens the invisible door and sits on the upstage chair, which has now become a toilet. As she does this, lights dim in the bar and a light focused on this small area comes up.

(*With great satisfaction.*) I just love Dutch toilets. American toilets are so boring in comparison. In America, everything plops into a big bowl of water and falls apart. But here in Holland, it all sits on a nice little dry platform so you can carefully examine your work before you flush it away.

She does so.

(*Very proud.*) I made a question mark! How about that! (*The sound of a knock.*) Someone's knocking. How the hell do I...

Looking around.

In America, there's always a little silver handle on the side of the tank. But Holland must be the world leader in developing new and innovative ways to flush a toilet. Here, it could be a cord hanging from the ceiling…

She pulls something above her head. The light goes off.

No, that's the light.

She pulls the cord again, light comes back on. She finds something on the wall.

A switch on the wall…

The sound of a loud fan is heard.

That's the fan…

She turns the fan off.

Or a secret tile in the floor that you have to stomp on…

Starts stomping heavily

Or a section of pipe that needs jiggling…

The knocking is getting louder. She yells through the door.

I'm sorry… s'il vous plait… (*To herself.*) No, that's French…How do you say "please wait" in Dutch? I can't remember… (*Yelling.*) Hold your horses! (*To the audience, beginning to panic.*) I can't let her in here to see my question mark! There must be some way…

She starts flailing around, stomping on the floor, pushing on the walls, anything. Finally, the very loud sound of a flush. THE FOOL is triumphant.

At last! I haven't the foggiest idea how I did it, but I did it.

She opens the door to leave, peeks out, quickly shuts the door.

There's a whole line out there. Oh well.

She exits the toilet, giving a weak smile to those waiting.

Buenos dias.

(*She returns to the spot where she was standing. Suddenly it hits her.*) I know why nobody's paying attention to me! It's this dress! They think I'm fat because this dress is so loose. Dutch lesbians are allergic to fatness. They're afraid if they're in the same room with a fat person, they'll catch it. Dutch lesbians think "Fat American" is one word. (*Righteously angry.*) They call themselves feminists, but they've swallowed the patriarchal beauty trip lock, stock and barrel.

I'm wearing this dress because it's beautiful, not because it hides my body. I think I'm gorgeous. I just said so in a Personals ad. I'm not ashamed of my body!

> *She pulls her dress in with her hands, to show her waist. This is not effective.*

Oh, what the hell.

> *She throws her dress over her head. She is wearing a shiny white body suit with patriotic red-white-and-blue underpants and a gold stretch belt with an enormous rhinestone buckle. THE FOOL continues speaking with her face hidden by the dress, her body exposed. She can't see a thing. She addresses the women in the bar.*

Well, girls, what do you think? Not too shabby, is it? I mean, what's not to like? The legs— see, girls?—are definitely above average. I admit the breasts are extremely large. But you'll get used to them. Everybody does— unless you have a very small apartment. Then it might be a serious problem. (*Pause. To herself.*) Oh my gosh, I forgot to pull my stomach in.

> *She pulls her stomach in as hard as she can. She turns so that everyone in the bar can see her.*

Girls, this is the real me! See? Hardly any bulges at all! I was just sticking my stomach out before to tease you! Ha-ha! (*To herself.*) I wonder if anybody's looking at me.

> *Even with her dress over her head, THE FOOL can see through an opening where the dress buttons at the top. She peeks through the little slit, turning around slowly, examining the bar scene.*

(*With wonder.*) Nobody's looking at me. Damn, these women are cool.

> *She shakes her dress to get a little air.*

It's hot under here. It's like a sauna. What time is it anyhow? You have to stay up until four in the morning to get laid in Amsterdam. I can't do it. I'm an American. I need to be in bed by midnight. I think it says so on my passport.

> *She checks her watch through the slit.*

Just as I thought. It's past my bedtime. (*Plaintively.*) I want to go home! (*Pause.*) I'll just leave. .

> *She marches this way and that, but she cannot see.*

I'll never find the door with my dress over my head. (*Pause.*) But if I pull my dress down, I'm going to have to look all these people in the eye. All these people who have just seen me with my dress over my head. (*Long silence. Uh-oh.*) I think…maybe…I've made a little mistake. Sometimes you take a big risk and it doesn't work out, right? Happens to everybody. Happens all the time. (*In an agony of embarrassment.*) What was I thinking when I threw my dress over my head in a crowded lesbian bar? (*To the audience, accusingly.*) Why didn't one of you stop me? Oh well. It's too late now. I might as well get this over with. Here goes.

> *THE FOOL takes her dress down from over her head and speaks with great bravado to the whole bar.*

I'm leaving, girls. I don't know if I'll be back here again. And if I do come back I don't know if I'll throw my dress over my head again. You've had your chance, girls, and you blew it. Buenos dias!

> *She sails out of the bar onto the street. The disco music fades. Lights change from "disco" to "night outside." THE FOOL is greatly relieved.*

There's a lesson to be learned from all this, but I have absolutely no idea what it is.

> *She walks along, laughing softly, then slows to a stop. She allows herself, for one moment, to feel the full weight of her loneliness.*

For some reason, I feel like crying. Isn't that silly? What have I got to cry about? I'm not starving…not in prison…And yet, I'm so sad. Sad and tired. (*She stares into the distance, exhausted. Then she gathers herself together once again.*) Oh well. At least…at least… (*She looks around her.*) it's a beautiful night. Look at that dark blue-green sky. I've never seen that color anywhere but Amsterdam. And the golden street lights reflected in the canals. (*Thoughtfully.*) You know, even an ugly building is beautiful when it's reflected in water. I wonder why that is. (*The moment is over. Briskly.*) It's too beautiful a night to go home. I wonder what's going on at the Leidseplein, the big outdoor square with all the free entertainment. Maybe I'll see what's happening there. As they say, when all else fails on a summer night, head for the Leidseplein. And all else has failed.

> *As she says these words, she marches jauntily in a circle around the stage, arriving at the Leidseplein, where the sounds of a crowd and several kinds of music can be heard. The lighting changes from a romantic night to the much harsher brightness of a well-lit square. The music of Peruvian flutes and drums gets*

louder.

Oh look. There's a Peruvian Indian band over there…Somebody's eating fire over there…and a very stoned and raggedy hippie pretending to be a robot, there…There's always one of those.

A blues band with women singing starts out tentatively.

And there's an all women's blues band, surrounded by their motorcycles.

The music gathers confidence, volume. It continues through the end of the play.

They're good. They're really good. Look, somebody's started dancing. Now, she's rather unusual looking, even by Amsterdam standards. About eighty years old, wearing a purple see-through blouse, skin-tight leopard print pants and black patent leather high-heeled boots. Now, that woman has style with a capital "S." (*Joyously.*) I'm telling you, people come from all over the world just to make fools of themselves right here on the Leidseplein.

She starts to move to the rhythm, then stops herself.

I'd dance too, but I didn't come here to make a fool of myself.

She moves again, then stops.

I came here just to watch…just to listen…

Her body moves, despite herself.

I can't help it. I can't keep still. I gotta join the dance.

THE FOOL really lets go, dancing wildly.

It feels so good to be crazy, with so many different people, dancing out in the fresh air.

She stops dancing and looks around her with great affection.

Oh Amsterdam—with your mysterious toilets and quacking ducks and arrogant lesbians and cheap flowers and purse snatchers and golden-lit canals—Amsterdam, I love you. (*Confidentially, to the audience.*) You know, I've never felt this way before.

THE FOOL returns to dancing—wildly, ecstatically—as the music swells and the lights fade to black.

End Of Play

1996

TWO FOOLS

**OR
LOVE CONQUERS ALL – NOT!**

Premiere Information

Two Fools opened February 1, 1996 at Noh Space in San Francisco. At that time, the play was subtitled *A Cross-Cultural Romance*. The subtitle was changed to *Love Conquers All—Not!*, for the 2004 production.

Director .... Terry Baum
Producer .... Lilith Theater
Dramaturg .... Paoli Lacy
Set Design .... Iva Walton
Lighting Design .... Caroline Boyden
Sound Design .... Dixie Treichel
Stage Manager .... Retts Scauzillo

CAST

GRACIE .... Blancett Reynolds
LUNA .... Catherine Castellanos

PRODUCTION HISTORY

In 1993 I was living in Amsterdam, performing *One Fool*, my play about a very impulsive lesbian seeking—and never finding —love. After every performance, I read the audience comment book in the lobby. One night, someone wrote, "Dear Fool: Come to the Clit Club tonight—or was this "just" a play???" The Clit Club…A new lesbian disco with naked go-go dancers… Hmmmmm…

I betook myself to the Clit Club. An attractive woman approached me and asked, "Are you The One?" —which is the opening line of *One Fool*. Clearly the woman I had come to meet! She almost immediately told me that the ending to *One Fool* didn't work. This would not be a turn-on for most writers, but for me, it was. I crave feedback from perceptive, brutally honest people. When this perceptive, brutally honest woman spoke, I knew immediately:
  1. What was wrong with *One Fool*'s ending
  2. How I could fix it
  3. I was destined to spend the rest o my life with her.

It is strange that a woman, with enough self-knowledge to write an autobiographical play titled *One Fool*, could still be a fool. But there it is.

I didn't end up spending the rest of my life with this wonderful and perceptive woman. But I did get a play out of the relationship—it shouldn't be a total loss. (By the way, she insisted that she had never written anything in the comment book.)

The original 1996 version of *Two Fools* was way too long and complicated. It took place in Amsterdam, the Greek island of Lesbos, and San Francisco. It was also a play within a play, wherein the characters acted out, and argued about, a play they were writing based on their relationship as they were living it. Whew! There was the scene of Luna fleeing the bar pursued by the INS (the precursor to ICE). But she escaped. Somehow Luna being deported seemed terribly melodramatic to me. Luna left because she could not tolerate Gracie writing about her.

I moved to New York City and directed two productions of *Two Fools*: at W.O.W. Theater (1997) and Wings Theater (1999). I cut out the play-within-the-play, making *Two Fools* simpler and shorter. In the 2004 version for Theatre Rhinoceros, the play was finally reduced to one location, San Francisco. As gay marriages were actually taking place for the first time in the U.S. at that moment in City Hall, the marriage scene ws rewritten to include that reality. And now, for this anthology I've made a major change in the ending, rewriting it so that the women are torn apart, not by emotional disagreements, but because Luna is caught by the INS and deported. Sadly, what had once seemed melodramatic to me now seems realistic.

Two Fools was a finalist for the 1996 Jane Chambers Playwriting Award, and was published in *Intimate Acts*, an anthology of lesbian plays, in 1997.

CHARACTERS

GRACIE: A Caucasian American. She dresses in brightly colored clothes. Her outfit is a bit theatrical.

LUNA: A Costa Rican woman. She wears a t-shirt and jeans. She is definitely to the butch side of the butch-femme spectrum.

NOTE ON AGE: The women could be any age between 30 and 50. It is important that they be approximately the same age. They have many differences, but age is not one of them.

NOTE ON RACE: Since race is an artificial construct, it is common for "white" people to be darker than "non-white" people. However, race is also a perceptible visual reality. For this play to work, Luna needs to be darker than Gracie—if not in skin, then in eye and hair color. It is not essential that Luna be very dark, although she refers to herself as "black." As she makes clear, outside the U.S., "black" is a category that includes all people not defined as "white."

TIME

The year is 2004, when the first (illegal) gay marriages take place in San Francisco. The federal agency that pursues undocumented people is the INS (Immigration and Naturalization Service) not ICE as it is today.

PLACE

The play takes place in San Francisco—except for the scene where Luna phones from Amsterdam, at which point the stage becomes both cities at once.

SETTING: *The main portion of the stage represents GRACIE's apartment. There is a bed Stage Right with a nightstand and a wireless landline phone. A small table and two chairs are Stage Left. All of the furniture is painted playfully in tones of pink, orange, yellow and turquoise. This is not a realistic set because these areas also serve as other locations. For example, the foot of the bed becomes two seats at the opera. The table and chairs become a café and later a bar. At these times, the lighting defines the smaller area. Upstage Left is a doorframe with no door. This serves as a portal to and from the world offstage. The*

Downstage area serves as many locations: a bookstore, a city street, a park, the airport, and where LUNA lives when she's not in San Francisco.

Scene One

AT RISE: Lights up onstage. GRACIE stands Downstage Center, holding a book, in a pool of light. She speaks to the audience.

GRACIE: I first saw her in Modern Times bookstore. I was part of an evening called New Lez Lit. A bunch of us were reading our writing. I noticed her in the audience.

LUNA enters Downstage Right and stands, studying GRACIE.

She stared at me intently while I read my story. It was a little disconcerting.

GRACIE reads aloud from her story:

"The plaza was filled with people on this perfect balmy night. People dancing to a rather large and very good salsa band, playing for free, for the joy of playing, of making people move! And what a crowd: Young people, old people, normal people, weird people. All swirling and laughing on this beautiful night. My feet seemed to move of their own volition, sweeping me into the dance, the only one without a partner. Even though I was alone, at that joyous moment, I belonged. And I knew I would be alright."

(*Pause. To the invisible audience.*) Thank you.

Applause. GRACIE walks downstage. LUNA approaches her.

LUNA: That was quite a story.

GRACIE: Thank you…I think. I'm Gracie. And you're…

LUNA: Luna.

GRACIE: Luna? What a beautiful name.

LUNA: It means "moon" in Spanish.

GRACIE: I know. Where are you from, Luna?

LUNA: I'm from Costa Rica. But I live in Amsterdam. And now I'm on vacation in San Francisco.

GRACIE: Costa Rica! Wow! There's something special about it, I can't remember…

LUNA: We don't have an army. We're the only country in the world that has a constitutional prohibition against an army.

GRACIE: That's incredible. So how did you end up in Amsterdam?

LUNA: I'm an editor and translator for the International Press Service, which supplies news to what you call "the developing world." It has its main office in Amsterdam. They had an opening for an editor who was fluent in Spanish. I leaped on it, because of course Amsterdam is famous for its wonderful gay life. I wanted to experience what it was like to live totally outside of the closet.

GRACIE: And what do you think of San Francisco, now that you're visiting?

LUNA: A magical place. The Victorians look like colored candy. And the sun shines so brightly! Living in Holland, I miss the sun so much… It's a high price to pay for living openly as a lesbian.

GRACIE: (*To the audience.*) Of course I should have mentioned the notorious San Francisco fog right then. But she was so thrilled with the sun, I couldn't bring myself to shatter her illusion.

LUNA: The sky in Northern Europe is like an enormous gray helmet that sits on the earth for months. It's not easy for someone from the tropics. But San Francisco—I've never seen a city that sparkles before. And you also have a wonderful gay life!

GRACIE: I'm so glad you like my city. Now tell me what you thought about what I read.

LUNA: Gracie, you must not give up hope! You will find the right woman someday. Or was that "just" a story that you read tonight?

GRACIE: It's the story of my life! I'm a lesbian on the loose!

LUNA: I'm so happy to hear that. So am I!

GRACIE: Oh! That's very nice. But you still haven't told me if you liked my story.

LUNA: Do you think I would have wanted to talk to you if I didn't?

GRACIE: Sometimes people get pleasure out of telling writers everything that's wrong with their writing.

LUNA: Well, as a matter of fact, the ending didn't work.

Pause.

GRACIE: Why not?

LUNA: You show a person whose life is a series of disasters—and then suddenly the end comes and she's happy and dancing with a bunch of crazy people. I don't believe it.

Silence.

GRACIE: You're right!

LUNA: Of course I'm right!

GRACIE: Nobody ever mentioned it before. But I know exactly how I'm going to fix it! I've got to plant little seeds all along the way, little clues that she's falling in love with the city…

LUNA: You've read this story to other people?

GRACIE: Oh, sure.

LUNA: You're telling me that nobody's ever noticed before that the ending doesn't work?

GRACIE: If they did, they didn't have the guts to tell me. I was just happy to have any ending at all. Endings are always the hardest part. But now that you mention it, it's so obvious. The ending doesn't work! Do you have any other criticisms?

LUNA: No, no. I'd like to return to the subject of both of us being single. Perhaps you are free to celebrate with me my first night in San Francisco. I heard there's a bar near here with beautiful Latin music. Will you do me the honor?

GRACIE: Ummm…Uhh…Well, actually, all the writers are going out for drinks together. But…I think I'd rather go listen to music with you!

LUNA: Excellent!

GRACIE: It is very awkward to desert them. But it's not every day that you meet someone who tells you the ending doesn't work!

LUNA: This is true. Sad but true.

GRACIE: Let alone a very attractive woman from the only country in the world with a constitutional prohibition against an army, who tells you the ending doesn't work!

LUNA: In fact, it's an exceedingly rare occurrence, and you're very wise to take advantage of it.

GRACIE: I'll be right back.

> *GRACIE exits Stage Right. LUNA takes the moment to make sure the collar of her jacket is flat, smooth her hair, and holds the*

palm of her hand in front of her mouth to check her breath. Not satisfied, she takes out a mint. GRACIE returns.

GRACIE: What a whiny bunch! I'm sure they'll get over it after a couple of drinks.

LUNA: Ready?

GRACIE: That wasn't very nice of me.

LUNA: Oh, that's good. Nice girls bore me.

They exit the bookstore through the upstage portal and walk downstage. They are on the sidewalk.

GRACIE: It's true, I'm too damn nice. I said goodbye. That should be enough for them.

LUNA: I hate goodbyes. People should get on with their lives.

GRACIE: In a story, if a goodbye is done well, it can be the best part.

LUNA: I myself have a strong preference for beginnings. And I think you and I are beginning something. Come on. Let's go back to my hotel and listen to some beautiful Latin music.

GRACIE: Wait a minute! Wait a minute! I thought we were going to a bar!

LUNA: We were, but now that I know that you are not a nice girl, I've changed my mind. I want to get into bed with you as soon as possible.

Pause.

GRACIE: Listen, I'm extremely attracted to you, but you should know something about me. I made a very wise vow never to sleep with anyone who lives more than forty-five minutes from my home by public transportation.

LUNA laughs hysterically.

Because if we fall in love, we'll be so far away from each other, we'll be in agony all the time.

LUNA: By public transportation?

GRACIE: Let's face it: This car culture is strangling the planet in pollution and traffic jams! We have got to develop great mass transit, and get rid of all the private passenger cars, and soon!

LUNA: So you don't own a car?

GRACIE: Of course not.

LUNA: But you own a home in San Francisco?

GRACIE: Oh no. I just rent an apartment.

LUNA: You're only renting! Then you could decide to move somewhere else tomorrow!

GRACIE: That's true. When you really think about it, where *is* my home?

LUNA: Where is anybody's home? Look at me. My home is in Amsterdam as a lesbian, but my home is in Costa Rica as a Latina. So there is nowhere that is really my home. And here I am, standing outside a women's bookstore in San Francisco! And maybe I'll decide to move next week! In which case, I might be…how much?

GRACIE: Forty-five minutes…

LUNA: From your home…

GRACIE: By public transportation.

LUNA: Yes! By public transportation! So you see, your very wise vow makes no sense at all.

GRACIE: And besides, I think this is just a one-night stand.

LUNA: Absolutely. Tomorrow morning, I'm kicking you out of my hotel room and out of my life.

GRACIE: You promise?

LUNA: Listen, in Costa Rica, my nickname was Perrita, little bitch, because I slept with so many women. I couldn't care less about you.

GRACIE: Good. Then let's go back to my place.

They exit as lights fade.

Scene Two

Lights come up on GRACIE's apartment. GRACIE and LUNA are in bed.

GRACIE: This is the longest one-night stand I've ever had.

LUNA: Have we been in bed a long time?

GRACIE: Ummmm…Three days, I think. Oh my god, I have to get back to my writing. I have to start paying attention to my life!

She starts to get out of bed.

LUNA: No, pajarito de mi alma, you have to continue to pay attention to me!

GRACIE: "Pajarito de mi alma." I'm…little bird of your soul, after only three days?

LUNA: Yes! And what am I to you after three days?

GRACIE: You're…a big, sleek, beautiful cat.

LUNA: I am Gatito!

GRACIE: Gatito, tell me about Costa Rica.

LUNA: Costa Rica is a very special place. We have so many beautiful animals that you don't find in San Francisco.

GRACIE: Like what?

LUNA: Like big cats in the jungle, jaguars, with golden eyes and black spots on golden fur.

GRACIE: Tell me a story about a jaguar.

LUNA: But you are the storyteller, not me!

GRACIE: There are thousands of stories out there in the cosmos just waiting to be told. Start talking and the story will come.

LUNA: We just made love and now you want a story!

GRACIE: Yes.

LUNA: You're very demanding. Do you know that?

GRACIE: Just try it.

LUNA: (*She begins hesitantly, frequently pausing to search for words.*) Once there was a jaguar who lived all by herself in the jungle. Whenever she saw another animal, she would try to kill it and eat it, and of course it would run away from her. Because of this, she was very lonely and very hungry. The end. (*She is very pleased with herself.*)

GRACIE: Go on.

LUNA: (*Exasperated.*) I can't think of anything!

GRACIE: (*Gently urging.*) Don't think. Just tell.

LUNA: All right. (*She starts slowly and becomes more excited, inspired* *by her creation as it flows from her.*) One day, Jaguar saw on the ground between the trees, a quetzal.

GRACIE: What's a quetzal?

LUNA: This is a very beautiful bird with a long tail that has many bright colors. Red, green, yellow—a rainbow bird. Jaguar asked, "What's wrong with you, Bird? Why aren't you up in a tree?" And Quetzal replied, "I cannot fly because my heart is broken."

GRACIE: I didn't know birds couldn't fly with broken hearts!

LUNA: You didn't? Oh, it's impossible. The heart is too heavy. They can't get off the ground.

LUNA gets out of bed so she can act out her story for GRACIE.

So Jaguar said, "I'm very hungry and I'm going to eat you!" But Quetzal, thinking very fast, said, "No, don't eat me! Come home with me and I'll give you some delicious fruit stew." And Jaguar, who was so hungry, thought, "First I'll have the fruit stew and then I'll eat the quetzal." She said, "Get on my back and I'll take you home." So Quetzal jumped on Jaguar's back and hung onto her fur.

GRACIE: Wasn't she frightened?

LUNA: Of course! But what choice did she have? In fact, Quetzal was hanging on so tight that she was scratching Jaguar's back and even tickling her. Jaguar had never been tickled before. What a delicious feeling when you've been so lonely! Jaguar started to laugh, for the first time in her life.

GRACIE: What did it sound like?

LUNA: Like this. (*She makes the sound of a jaguar laughing.*)

GRACIE: (*Joining in the story.*) And then Quetzal started to laugh too! (*She laughs as a quetzal.*)

LUNA: They were laughing and tickling, laughing and tickling.

They tickle each other.

GRACIE: And Quetzal could feel that her heart had healed. She sailed up in the air.

GRACIE gets out of bed, dances around the room.

LUNA: But Jaguar said, "On no, don't leave me now, now that you've made me happy for the first time in my life."

GRACIE: (*Coming back to bed.*) So Quetzal came back down and stood on Jaguar's back.

LUNA: And they walked around the jungle, laughing and tickling, laughing and tickling—and eating fruit stew whenever they were hungry. And that's how Quetzal and Jaguar met. (*She is very proud of herself.*)

GRACIE: That's the greatest story I've ever heard in my life.

LUNA: You know, you're good for me. You push me to do things I've never done before.

LUNA laughs. Lights fade to black.

Scene Three

Lights come up on GRACIE's apartment. LUNA is in bed. GRACIE is at the table writing.

LUNA: (*Stretching as she wakes up.*) What are you doing, little bird?

GRACIE: Trying to fix the ending of that story I read in the bookstore. It's turning out to be harder than I thought.

LUNA: What's the weather like today?

GRACIE goes to look out the window.

GRACIE: It's another beautiful day in San Francisco.

LUNA: (*Sitting up abruptly.*) I need to get all the sun I can before I return to Amsterdam! I must spend this beautiful day lying in the sun with my lover.

GRACIE: Wait a minute! Wait a minute! Am I your lover already? We've got to talk.

LUNA: Yes? Is something wrong?

GRACIE: I just want to be clear. Are we having an affair or a relationship?

LUNA: Oh! An affair, of course.

GRACIE: That's how I feel, too. In fact, maybe it's not even an affair. Maybe it's just a fling.

LUNA: And what exactly is a "fling?"

GRACIE: It's an intense sexual encounter short enough that you never learn the other person's last name, but long enough that if you run into each other years later, you remember their first name.

LUNA: Yes! That's it precisely. I'm only here for four more days. That's not even time for a real affair.

GRACIE: No. That's fling length.

LUNA: Yes. A fling. I like that word. (*She savors it.*) Fling…

GRACIE: So we are not lovers. We're…co-flingers. We'll just have a nice fling here in San Francisco and say goodbye and never see each other again.

LUNA: That sounds perfect. Now, where can we find a nice place in the sun…

GRACIE: I can't possibly lie in the sun today. I have to start writing again. I have to fix that story!

LUNA: But aren't you entitled to a vacation every once in a while?

GRACIE: Absolutely not. Only people with real jobs are entitled to vacations.

LUNA: Well, I have a real job. Therefore I am entitled to a vacation, and I'm entitled to bring my…

GRACIE: Co-flinger.

LUNA: Yes. I'm entitled to bring my co-flinger to lie in the sun with me, and you are depriving me of that.

GRACIE: That's true. Maybe I could think of it as me helping you have your vacation. It wouldn't be like I'm having a vacation at all. Not only that, when you take the trouble to come all the way over here, I have a responsibility to lesbian international solidarity to show you San Francisco.

She grabs a beach towel.

GRACIE (con't): Let's go to Dolores Park. There's even a part of it called Dolores Beach, where people go to lie in the sun.

LUNA: Just imagine, the sun, oh the warm sun, heating our bones, as we lie with our arms around each other. Just you and me, me and you…

GRACIE: I could bring my journal and work on that damn ending that's driving me crazy! Oh, this makes so much sense. I'll really accomplish something.

LUNA: And I will lie in the sun and accomplish nothing! Listening to the little soft breezes and the sounds of the San Francisco birds.

> *Lights cross-fade. They exit through the portal and walk downstage to the park. GRACIE spreads out the towel and they sit. LUNA immediately relaxes, lolling in the sun. GRACIE tries to write, but is having a hard time. She stands, starts pacing.*

GRACIE: (*Bursting out.*) Oh, why are we spending all this time together? We'll just fall in love and make a big mess of our lives.

> *LUNA sits up.*

LUNA: We're not in love already?

GRACIE: How can you say that? We're just having a fling.

LUNA: Oh, of course. I forgot.

> *She lies back down. GRACIE continues pacing, getting more and more upset.*

GRACIE: But by the time you leave, we'll fall in love for sure.

LUNA: Don't be ridiculous. I'm not falling in love with you and that's that.

GRACIE: What's the point of us being more in love than we are?

LUNA: But you just said we're not in love.

GRACIE: (*Overcome with frustration and confusion.*) I hope we have a huge fight and end up hating each other! Then we'll be ecstatic that we're never going to see each other again!

> *LUNA goes to GRACIE, caresses her as she would a frightened animal.*

LUNA: Calm down, amor, calm down. You're like a bird flying in a storm of your own creation.

> *GRACIE stops moving, startled. She looks at LUNA.*

GRACIE: (*Slowly, savoring the words.*) "A bird flying in a storm of your own creation." Luna, that's so beautiful. And so…so…accurate. Yes, that's what I was just now. A bird flying in a storm of my own creation. Oh, Gatito, I've never met anyone like you.

LUNA: Graciela, when I'm with you, the words rise up inside me.

GRACIE: (*Writing in her journal.*) A bird flying in a storm…

LUNA: Come closer. I have something to tell you.

GRACIE puts her journal aside, sits on the towel. LUNA whispers in GRACIE's ear.

I'm very hungry.

GRACIE: Of course you are! We haven't eaten yet today. I'm not taking good care of you, am I?

LUNA: In some ways yes, in other ways no.

GRACIE: I know a wonderful café near here.

LUNA: How far is it?

GRACIE: About five blocks away.

LUNA: That's too far. I don't like to walk.

GRACIE: Okay. See that building at the end of the park? That's a café. I'll race you to it.

LUNA: I suppose you think you're faster than me.

GRACIE: I've got to be faster than someone who doesn't even like to walk!

LUNA: We'll see about that.

GRACIE: Ready, set, go!

They take off. They run offstage left. LUNA re-enters running through the portal and seats herself at the table, which is now the café. GRACIE runs in right after her.

GRACIE: You're so fast! I can't believe you don't like to walk.

LUNA: (*Waving her hand for service.*) Waiter! (*To GRACIE.*) I'm physically lazy. I'm just here to enjoy myself.

GRACIE: Do you mean on this vacation or on this planet?

GRACIE takes out her journal, starts to write.

LUNA: (*Laughing.*) That's good! You're getting to know me. (*Pause.*) What are you doing?

GRACIE: I'm writing down our conversation.

For the rest of the scene, she is furiously trying to record everything they say.

LUNA: Ah! Now you are accomplishing something!

GRACIE: Good! You're getting to know *me*! I believe we've been brought together to accomplish something.

LUNA: Oh, that's nice. I believe we've been brought together to accomplish nothing.

GRACIE: That's because I'm a do-er and you're a be-er.

LUNA: A do-er? What's that?

GRACIE: Someone who defines herself by what she does.

LUNA: Oh, a do-er! I see. And I'm a be-er. (*She tries to get the waiter's attention.*) Excuse me! (*Back to GRACIE.*) A do-er! This is a different point of view. We are from different planets.

GRACIE: Well, we are from different worlds. You're from the Third World…

LUNA: (*Angry.*) And you're from the shit world! Listen, in Costa Rica, we don't consider our world second to anything, let alone third!

GRACIE: Oh my god! I'm so sorry, Luna. I never thought…when you're an American, you never think…

LUNA: I'm just as American as you are. Everyone in the western hemisphere is an American. So please don't call yourself an American when you mean you're a citizen of the United States.

GRACIE: (*Bowled over by the realization.*) We call ourselves by a name that erases everyone else in North and South America!

LUNA: And all the rest of us resent it.

LUNA tries again to get the waiter's attention.

LUNA (con't): Excuse me! (*To GRACIE.*) The waiter isn't coming.

GRACIE: Talk about the imperialism of language!

LUNA: That's what we're talking about.

GRACIE: What can I call myself?

LUNA: Well, we call you "gringos" and the U.S. "gringolandia."

GRACIE: "Gringo." I can't call myself by a Spanish name. How about a "United Statesan"?

LUNA: Hmmmm…A little clumsy, but maybe…

GRACIE: Waiter!

She waves her hand. The waiter comes over.

I'd like an Irish Coffee. Amor, you should try one. They were invented in San Francisco, I think.

LUNA: (*Snarling.*) I don't want anything from San Francisco!

LUNA bolts out of the café through the portal and crosses downstage. GRACIE runs after her.

GRACIE: What's wrong with you?

LUNA: Didn't you see how he ignored me?

GRACIE: He was busy!

LUNA: He was too busy to see my little dark hand. But you lifted one great big white gringo finger, and he flew over to our table.

GRACIE: Are you telling me…

LUNA: He ignored me because I'm black.

GRACIE: Luna, you're not black.

LUNA: Believe me, in this world, there are only two skin colors: Black and white. I know, because I've been both. In Costa Rica, I was white. Then I moved to Holland and discovered I had become black, just like that. Obviously, in San Francisco, I'm black too. If I want to be white, I'll have to go back to Costa Rica.

GRACIE: But I get ignored too.

LUNA: It must be wonderful to know that when you are ignored, it is only because the waiter is busy!

Silence.

GRACIE: It must be terrible to wonder why you're ignored.

LUNA: (*Calming down a bit.*) Maybe he was just busy. It was very crowded.

GRACIE: Maybe he was ignoring you. We'll never know, will we?

LUNA: No.

GRACIE: So this is what it's like to be black in a white world.

LUNA: This is a very little taste of what it is like.

GRACIE: It's not right! And there's nothing I can do to make it better for you.

LUNA: You make it better for me when you get angry like this. (*Pause.*) I'm going to miss you too much when I go back to Amsterdam.

GRACIE: Let's make a plan to see each other. I can come visit.

LUNA: No! I don't want to hear this talk.

GRACIE: Luna, we can't just walk away from each other…

LUNA: Yes, we can. We must. I must, Pajarito. Now, I have four more days in your beautiful city. Let's go home and make love. We won't get out of bed until it's time for me to leave for the airport.

> *They start to exit, arm in arm. GRACIE stops, and looks at LUNA.*

GRACIE: But what happens after that?

LUNA: Nothing. The fling will have flinged itself out!

GRACIE: I don't think so!

> *Lights fade to black.*

Scene Four

> *Lights come up. We hear the sounds of the San Francisco Airport, with announcements of planes. We hear GRACIE offstage. "Hurry, hurry! You're going to miss your plane!" They enter. LUNA is carrying a suitcase.*

GRACIE: I'll just move to Amsterdam!

LUNA: Don't you dare! I don't want to be responsible for your happiness.

GRACIE: Alright, then. I want to be responsible for *your* happiness! So you should move to San Francisco!

LUNA: (*Embracing GRACIE.*) I hope you meet a wonderful woman and that you're very happy.

GRACIE: And I hope you never meet anyone and you spend the rest of your life grieving for me.

> *They hold each other tight. LUNA extricates herself, starts to exit.*

LUNA: Adiós, amor. Goodbye, Pajarito de mi alma.

LUNA exits through portal. Lights fade as GRACIE gazes after her.

Scene Five

LUNA enters and stands Downstage Left, holding a wireless phone. She is in Amsterdam. After much hesitation, she dials the phone. The phone next to the bed in GRACIE'S apartment rings. GRACIE enters and picks it up. She walks with it Downstage Right. During their conversation, they both walk around the Downstage Area, sometimes even crossing paths. But they never see each other. They are 6000 miles apart.

GRACIE: Hello.

LUNA: Hello, Pajarito!

GRACIE: Gatito! The little cat I dream about every night.

LUNA: It's been a whole week since I heard your melodiocious voice. And I miss your wonderful eyes so much it hurts.

GRACIE: And what is so wonderful about my eyes? Tell me.

LUNA: Well, for one thing, you have two of them.

GRACIE: Are you saying you wouldn't love me if I had three eyes?

LUNA: I would try, but…no, I don't think so.

GRACIE: How about just one eye?

LUNA: I have to think about it.

GRACIE: I'm sorry to say, Gatito, you're a very superficial person.

LUNA: I know. But it is my only flaw.

GRACIE: Oh Luna, my two eyes are drowning in tears every night. I'm so miserable.

LUNA: Me too. Nobody's as good a lover as you.

GRACIE: (*Playfully.*) Are you taking a statistical sample?

LUNA: Only one or two.

GRACIE: (*Shocked.*) One or two??

LUNA: Alright, two. But that has nothing to do with us.

GRACIE: (*Terribly hurt.*) I have been lying on the couch sobbing my heart out. And I assumed that you were six thousand miles away, lying on the couch sobbing too.

LUNA: Well, I grieve in other ways.

GRACIE: Yes. By fucking all the lesbians in Amsterdam!

LUNA: I only fucked two.

GRACIE: (*Furious.*) It's only been a week. I'm sure you'll get around to all the others before the month is up!

> *GRACIE slams the phone down, throws herself on the bed. LUNA looks at her phone in disgust. GRACIE jumps up and dials her phone. LUNA answers the ring immediately.*

Are you in love with somebody else?

LUNA: Amorcito, lying on a couch sobbing, it's just not my style. I was drinking and drinking but it didn't help. So I had to do something. It's all your fault for making me love you.

GRACIE: Ah! So it's my fault!

LUNA: And another thing, you were the one with the very sensible vow. Not to sleep with…what was it again?

GRACIE: Anyone who lives more than…

GRACIE & LUNA IN UNISON: …Forty-five minutes from my house by public transportation.

LUNA: That's right. I've never made a vow like that. If you had stuck to your vow, then nothing would have happened and you wouldn't be angry with me right now. Now we're in the big mess you were always afraid of.

GRACIE: Amorcito, you haven't answered my question.

LUNA: What question?

GRACIE: Are you in love with either of these women?

LUNA: Of course not. I don't even remember their names.

GRACIE: And do you remember my names?

LUNA: (*Tenderly.*) Gracie, Graciela, amor, amorcito, Pajarito de mi alma…

GRACIE: I'm still the little bird of your soul.

LUNA: There is no other. Everywhere I look, I only see you.

GRACIE: Luna, it hurts so much.

LUNA: Tell me, tell me.

GRACIE: It hurts so much that you slept with someone else. It hurts so much that I'll never see you again.

LUNA: Well, then, I'll just have to move to San Francisco.

GRACIE: Oh, amor!

LUNA: I was just joking.

GRACIE: Don't joke like that.

LUNA: I have to be practical. I have a very responsible, well-paid job… (*Pause.*) …but I hate my boss.

GRACIE: It's no small accomplishment to have a well-paid job with a boss you hate.

LUNA: People work their whole lives for that! And I have a beautiful apartment.

GRACIE: But does the sun shine into your beautiful apartment?

LUNA: No. Is the sun still shining in San Francisco?

GRACIE: Yes…I mean, well, sort of. And don't forget the Latino community. You didn't see much of it because we spent so much time in bed. But it's really big. You'd be at home here as a Latina, and as a lesbian!

LUNA: (*Scoffing.*) People our age don't move a million miles for love.

GRACIE: It's only six thousand.

LUNA: People our age don't even move six thousand miles for love.

GRACIE: That's not true. People our age move up to seven thousand miles for love. Then, when we turn fifty, it gets reduced to five thousand miles.

LUNA: I didn't know that. (*Pause.*) But I would be illegal!

GRACIE: (*Increasingly excited.*) We could find someone for you to marry so you can become legal. I'll support you until you get a green card. And then, with all your skills, you'll get a great job. And then I'll finish writing the novel about us. And it will be a best-seller, of course, and we'll live off the royalties for the rest of our lives!

LUNA: How can I possibly move for someone with all these foolish plans and ideas? I'd have to be a fool myself. (*Pause.*) Okay. You talked me into it. I'm coming.

GRACIE: You're joking again, aren't you?

LUNA: No. I've made a decision. A practical decision. I miss the sun, and the sun is in San Francisco. I miss Latino people, and they also can be found in San Francisco. The only serious problems are that I'll be illegal and that you are an unpractical dreamer and generally very impossible. But I've decided to come anyhow.

Pause.

GRACIE: Are you sure you want to do this?

LUNA: Are you sure you want me to do this?

GRACIE: I'm sure I want to go with you as far as I can go.

LUNA: Then I must come to San Francisco, so you can do that.

GRACIE: Oh baby, you have made me very happy.

LUNA: I'll see you as soon as possible.

GRACIE: I can't wait that long!

LUNA: Okay, okay. Sooner than possible.

They both slowly hang up the phone. GRACIE looks ecstatic and LUNA looks very alarmed at what she has just done. Lights fade to black.

Scene Six

Lights come up on the Downstage Area, which is now the San Francisco Airport. An announcer can be heard reciting all the familiar security announcements. GRACIE is standing, staring intently off left. She looks at her watch.

GRACIE: (*To herself.*) Where the hell is she? It's been over two hours! I should go to the ticket desk and find out if she was even on the plane. (*Pause.*) She changed her mind. She decided not to come. Well, of course I understand. Even moving a hundred miles for love is a big deal—let alone six thousand. Why did I push her to do it? Well, if she can't make the move, she can't. I respect that. (*Pause.*) But she could at least phone me, for god's sake! Okay, she's entitled to change her mind. But does she expect me to stand here for days until it slowly dawns on me that I've been dumped? I knew it, I knew it. It's just too big a step. Maybe one of those women she slept with called her up. Just because she couldn't remember their names doesn't mean they couldn't remember *her* name. Why should she take all the trouble to move here when she can just go to the bar…

LUNA enters.

Luna!

GRACIE throws her arms around her.

LUNA: Hold me hold me hold me.

GRACIE: What happened? What took you so long?

LUNA: They thought I had drugs.

GRACIE: For god's sake, why?

LUNA: Isn't it obvious? I'm a black from Latin America. Why would I be flying from a big drug capital like Amsterdam if I didn't have drugs? You see, a Costa Rican doesn't have the right to live in Amsterdam and also travel to Gringolandia. I didn't know that. So they gave me a lesson.

GRACIE: Oh, my poor baby. You're safe with me now.

She wraps her arms tightly around LUNA.

LUNA: Graciela, they searched me everywhere!

GRACIE: No!

LUNA: They do what they want. Everywhere, everywhere.

GRACIE: God damn them! Oh amor, I apologize for my country.

LUNA: Thank you. My stomach hurts.

GRACIE: Let's go home, Gatito.

LUNA: Yes. Home.

They exit as lights fade to black.

Scene Seven

Lights come up on GRACIE standing downstage.

GRACIE: (*To the audience.*) After the fiasco in Customs, San Francisco behaved beautifully in honor of her arrival. The sun shone every day, thank goodness. The frivolous Victorian houses glittered in the crystal air. And Luna went out to explore her new world—all by herself.

> *GRACIE sits at the table writing in her journal. LUNA rushes in through the portal with a big bag. She is very excited.*

LUNA: Amor, I was walking around in la Mision, one of the greatest barrios in the universe. I was looking at all the beautiful brown faces, hearing Spanish all around me, and I was home, even though I was not home. I could feel the ice cracking inside me.

GRACIE: (*Writing.*) "...the ice cracking inside me..."

LUNA: After all those years of living in a brown and gray land, now I'm in a land of colors.

GRACIE: (*Writing.*) "...a brown and gray land..."

LUNA: I found a great music store in la Mission! Discolandia! It was worth moving here just for this store. *Pura vida!*

GRACIE: "*Pura vida*"?

LUNA: That's what we say in Costa Rica. "*Pura vida!*" It's the greatest, it's wonderful, it's pure life—life at its purest!

GRACIE: Love it. (*Writing.*) "Pura vida..."

LUNA: Stop!

GRACIE: Stop what?

LUNA: Writing.

> *She gently takes the pen from GRACIE's hand and puts it on the table.*

Just listen to me, Pajarito de mi alma.

GRACIE: Okay.

LUNA: And I met a very nice Mexicano man working in Discolandia, Eduardo, and he invited me out for a beer. My first friend in Los Estados Unidos!

> *She burrows in her bag.*

GRACIE: Congratulations! I'm so happy for you.

LUNA: And, when Eduardo saw how much I love music, he told me San Francisco has a great opera company. I love opera almost as much as

I love you! I went right out and bought tickets.

She takes the tickets out of her pocket to show GRACIE.

GRACIE: The opera? I've only seen a couple of operas in my life.

LUNA: It's *Die Walküre* by Wagner. Oh, the music is glorious, luscious. You'll love it. And I found the most amazing CD…

LUNA dumps a pile of CD's on the bed.

GRACIE: But Luna, how much did all this cost? And opera tickets…

LUNA: Music makes me happy, Pajarito. Wait 'til you hear this…

GRACIE: If we're very careful about spending, then we can live on my savings for a while…

LUNA: No no no. I have always worked for a living and bought beautiful music with the money I earned. I'll get a job. You're gonna love this song…

GRACIE: But it's not legal for you to work here.

LUNA: Don't you worry, little bird. I'll find something. Your Gatito is not the kind of cat who likes to live off her lover's savings.

She pulls another CD out of her bag.

LUNA (con't): You won't believe what I found at Discolandia.

GRACIE throws her hands up in mock despair. LUNA puts on the CD.

This is a salsa, about the foggy hills of San Francisco, and the Mission… "*San Francisco tiene su propio son.*" "San Francisco has its own salsa."

GRACIE: It really says that?

LUNA: Yes! And it's true! San Francisco has its own salsa, its own rhythm, its own soul. And now, I'm going to dance my first dance in Gringolandia, with you!

LUNA sweeps GRACIE into her arms and they begin to dance. LUNA sings along.

"With the morning sun, *me vino esta inspiración y como una flor silvestre que nace ye crece en mi imaginación, una fragancia hecho ritmo…San Francisco tiene su propio son.*" *Así*!

Lights fade to black as they dance and LUNA sings.

Scene Eight

As the lights come up, the salsa music fades and the music at the end of Act One of Die Walküre is heard. Lights come up on foot of bed, which has now become two seats at the opera. GRACIE and LUNA enter and settle in their seats. They hold hands, gaze at each other adoringly and then focus on the music. LUNA begins to caress GRACIE. GRACIE responds, although they are both trying to maintain some sense of decorum. The girls go a bit too far and pull apart, turn their attention to the opera again. They hold hands. After a few moments, they hold more than hands. They do not actually have any of their clothes unbuttoned, but they are in fact making love while also trying to watch the opera—or pretending to watch the opera. They alternate between surrendering to their impulses and resisting them, all the while trying to pay attention to the great artistic achievement unfolding before them. The music rises to the crescendo, and so do they. End of the Act One of Die Walküre. The two women applaud, along with the large audience, looking around them to see if anyone noticed their shenanigans.

Lights fade to black.

Scene Nine

Lights come up on GRACIE, talking on the phone.

GRACIE: Hey, Sandy, has Luna dropped by your place, by any chance? (*Pause.*) She was supposed to be home a while ago, and I'm starting to get worried. (*Pause.*) Of course, you're right. I know it's nothing…but still… (*Pause.*) Yeah, she's great, isn't she? And she really liked you too. That was so sweet of you to have us for dinner. (*Pause.*) Come on, that is not the only way you can get to see me! You did the same thing when you got together with Chloe! (*Pause.*) Yes, you did! I told you I gave you six weeks, and then you had to start being my friend again. And it took you three months or something! (*Pause.*) Okay, I'm a little obsessed, but it hasn't been that long…

LUNA enters through the portal, exhausted, and lies down on the bed.

Oh, here she is! I'll call you back.

She hangs up the phone.

Where have you been?

LUNA: Eduardo took me to a lot of restaurants, looking for a job. Then we went out for coffee. We could hardly find the cafe, with that fucking gray mist everywhere.

GRACIE: Fog.

LUNA: Fog!

GRACIE: You do realize your visa expired today.

LUNA: I was reminded of it every time I asked for a job.

GRACIE: (*Angry.*) And then you drink coffee with Eduardo while I'm sitting at home, flipping out, thinking you've been picked up by the INS. Thanks a lot.

LUNA: (*Losing her temper.*) Do you think I had a nice day, walking around in that freezing fog, begging people for jobs I would never have considered doing before? They all wanted to see my passport. I told them that I left it at home. They knew I was lying.

GRACIE: At least *you* knew you weren't deported.

LUNA: And *you* know you never will be!

GRACIE: Pardon me for being a citizen!

Silence.

LUNA: Amor, I'm sorry. That wasn't nice.

GRACIE: Thank goodness you're safe.

They embrace. LUNA lies down again on the bed.

LUNA: My stomach hurts.

GRACIE: Let me rub it.

She sits down next to LUNA lying on the bed and starts to gently massage her stomach.

LUNA: Pajarito, why didn't you ever mention to me about the fucking fog?

GRACIE: I thought I did.

LUNA: No.

GRACIE: I guess...I was afraid you might not move here if you knew about it.

LUNA: I would have come even if you had told me San Francisco had blizzards of snowballs.

GRACIE is still rubbing LUNA's stomach.

Mmmm…my stomach feels better…Don't stop.

GRACIE: Amorcito, I went down to City Hall to see the lesbians and gay men getting married.

LUNA: It's really happening?

GRACIE: Right now in San Francisco for the first time.

LUNA: I can't believe it.

GRACIE: There was a long line of people outside, people like us, waiting to get married. It was one of the most beautiful things I have ever seen in my life. I wish we could go stand in that line.

LUNA: I do too. Oh, to be in a city where people like us walk into the most beautiful building in the city, and they say to the world, "I want to stop looking, right now! I'm finished! Here she is!"

GRACIE: Let's do it!

LUNA: You want me to go to the seat of government and sign my name, in front of everyone? I'm not legal!

GRACIE: I heard some people did it, even though they weren't legal.

LUNA: That is very unwise of them. No, no. Just talking about it gives me a sharp pain right here.

She puts GRACIE's hand back on her stomach.

Don't stop. Oh, that feels good what you're doing.

GRACIE: Listen, I've been thinking about our different options for making you legal. One is to find a gay couple for us to marry—an American with a foreign boyfriend. You marry the American, so you can stay here. And I marry the foreign boyfriend, so he can stay here. We trade marriages, so to speak.

LUNA: Ah yes. Eduardo told me that can be very dangerous for the American. I would be thrown out of the country, but you could end up in prison. No, I cannot let you take that risk for me. What are the other options?

GRACIE: You could apply for a student visa.

LUNA: I don't want to be a student. I want to work.

GRACIE: I know. But a student visa is really the easiest way to become legal. We have to try it.

LUNA: Really?

GRACIE: Yes.

LUNA: Alright.

GRACIE: The first step is talking to a good immigration lawyer. I've got some stocks that I could sell...

LUNA: Using your money. All the time we're using your money. Is there anything you wouldn't do to keep me here?

GRACIE: No.

LUNA: You are a very foolish little bird.

GRACIE: I want to marry you so bad. All those other lesbians and gay men are getting married, in my very own City Hall. And we can't. It's not fair!

LUNA: Let's marry each other, in our own way. Here we are, two souls who wish to hold hands forever. Please marry me immediately.

GRACIE: Right now? Right here?

LUNA: Yes! At this moment, in this room.

GRACIE: It's not enough for me!

LUNA: For me, either. But it's all we can have.

GRACIE: God dammit, shit, fucking hell...

LUNA: That's not nice talk for a bride. Now come on, we have to have a ceremony. Think of something. You're the writer.

GRACIE: Alright. Let's ask each other what Gertrude Stein asked Alice B. Toklas.

LUNA: What was that?

GRACIE: "Will you be fairly necessary to me?"

LUNA: That's perfect and beautiful. Are you ready to be married now?

GRACIE: Yes. Goddamit.

LUNA: No more cursing!

GRACIE: Alright, alright.

As "San Francisco Son" plays, they dress up the apartment and themselves, creating for the moment a "wedding" environment. When they're finished, they move towards each other very slowly as the salsa is overlaid by the Wedding March. LUNA drops to one knee and takes GRACIE'S hand. The music fades out.

LUNA: Pajarito de mi alma, will you be fairly necessary to me?

GRACIE: It would give me great pleasure.

She raises LUNA up and then drops to one knee.

Lunacita, my Gatito, my love, will you be fairly necessary to me?

LUNA: Yes.

LUNA raises GRACIE up.

I now pronounce us wife and wife.

They kiss as lights fade.

Scene Ten

Lights come up on LUNA in the apartment, talking on the phone.

LUNA: Yes, I have a lot of experience cleaning houses. (*Pause.*) Absolutely. All kinds of floors. I can mop, I can scrub… (*Pause.*) No, no. I would never scrub so hard that I ruin the finish. Don't worry about that. (*Pause.*) Next Tuesday? Yes. Absolutely. (*Pause.*) How about fifteen dollars an hour? (*Pause.*) Okay. How about twelve fifty for the first time? And then if you like my work and I'm fast enough, we can talk about fifteen. (*Pause.*) Thank you. I've been speaking English for a long time. (*Pause.*) Alright. Next Tuesday.

She slams the phone down.

And by the way, not only can I speak English! I can write and translate, and my work has been published in newspapers all over the world! And I charged them more than fifteen dollars an hour and they were happy to pay it!

GRACIE enters through the portal, holding several letters.

GRACIE: Mail! There's a letter from Costa Rica!

LUNA: Give me!

GRACIE hands her the letter.

From mi madrecita.

GRACIE: What does she say?

LUNA: She misses me, of course. She doesn't understand why I moved to San Francisco when I had a good job in Amsterdam.

GRACIE: Have you mentioned me?

LUNA: No, amor. She wouldn't understand. But someday I will take you to see my beautiful country, and you will meet her. She is a very dear woman

GRACIE: I will meet her as your "friend?"

LUNA: Yes. Mi madre is accustomed to my very important "friends."

GRACIE: So we would be in the closet.

LUNA: Except when we were with other gay people. Is that alright?

GRACIE: For a visit? Of course!

She looks down at the letter in her hand.

GRACIE (con't): Oh my gosh! This is a letter from a literary agent! I sent her a packet of my writing weeks ago.

LUNA: I remember! You spent a whole day sending out packets.

GRACIE: (*Opening the letter.*) It's probably one of those form letters—"Thanks but no thanks." (*She reads the letter.*) It's not a form letter. (*Pause.*) She wants to represent me!

LUNA: Fantástico!

GRACIE: (*Reading.*) She wants to submit one of my stories to *The New Yorker*! That's only the most important literary magazine in the country! Am I hot or what?

LUNA: You are hot!

GRACIE: Am I going to be famous or what?

LUNA: You are going to be incredibly famous!

GRACIE: And the best part is that it's the story about us!

Silence.

LUNA: About us?

GRACIE: It starts the night we met at the bookstore…

LUNA: So I am a character in this story?

GRACIE: We're both characters.

LUNA: Do you use my name?

GRACIE: No, of course not. It's fiction. But I've captured you precisely!

Silence.

What's the matter?

LUNA: No, I don't like it.

GRACIE: What don't you like?

LUNA: I don't like you using me.

GRACIE: I use everything. You know that. I'm a writer. I put everything down in my journals.

LUNA: Yes, I've noticed that. Every single thing.

GRACIE: And then I turn it into a story. That's what I do.

LUNA: But not to me. I didn't give you permission to grind my life up into hamburger meat and shape it into little story patties. I am a whole cow! I refuse to be ground up.

GRACIE: Are you telling me you don't want me to publish that story?

LUNA: I'm telling you I don't want you to write about me anymore. I don't want anymore to be examined, recorded, analyzed.

Pause.

GRACIE: Don't you see I want to capture you on paper because I love you?

LUNA: And the man who captures the butterfly and kills it and puts it in a glass case says he loves the butterfly. But nobody's asking the butterfly if it wants to be loved that way.

GRACIE: You don't believe I love you?

LUNA: How do I know? Maybe you just invited me here so you would have something to write about. And when you're done with the story, you'll be done with me.

GRACIE: Why are you saying these terrible things?

LUNA: Every move I make, you're writing it down.

GRACIE: Because I'm so in love with you.

LUNA: Why do you have to do something with your love, accomplish something, make use of it?

GRACIE: But we're both characters in the story. In fact, you're a much better character than I am. The reader is going to love you.

LUNA: I don't want to be loved by a reader. I just want to be loved by you. And how can I be sure that you love me when you are always exploiting me?

GRACIE: Exploiting you! You're my muse! You should feel honored that you inspire me.

LUNA: No. I don't feel honored. Here I am. That's all you have. Just Luna. I am enough. Even if we never do another damn thing in our lives but be happy, we are both enough, all by ourselves.

GRACIE: Listen! I'm always understanding you. Why don't you try for two seconds to understand me? I am not enough all by myself. This is what I do. This is who I am. You knew that from the beginning. I felt from that first night, when you told me the ending didn't work, that we were brought together to accomplish something.

LUNA: Then I'm sorry I ever told you the ending didn't work.

GRACIE: Don't you understand, when I write, I can step back, I have a little power. Otherwise, you have all the power.

LUNA: I have power! You are grinding me into a hamburger, and you tell me I have power!

GRACIE: You can do whatever you want with me. We both know that. But I have power to turn our life together into something that touches other people. Then everything we've gone through will have some use.

LUNA: (*With contempt.*) Use?

GRACIE: It's beautiful to be useful.

LUNA: You are choosing to be useful. I am only being used.

GRACIE: Why the hell can't you choose to be useful, like me?

LUNA: So that you, a transparent one, can use me, a black, for your transparent story for a transparent reader?

GRACIE: Are you saying I can't speak of our life together because I'm white?

LUNA: Oh, you can speak. You use up all the air so no one else has a chance to speak. But you can never really know me, see me. Maybe it's the blue eyes. All transparents are half-blind. Only we blacks with our dark brown eyes can see everything. You are mining me for a character just like the gringos mined Costa Rica for gold.

GRACIE: Luna, this is me! Gracie! How can you say that I'm just a greedy…big white gringo to you?

LUNA: You want to prove that you're something more? Then stop writing about me, right now, today, and promise me that you will never write about me again.

Silence.

GRACIE: So if I don't publish the story, and I stop writing about you, you'll know that I love you for yourself.

LUNA: Yes.

Pause.

GRACIE: I'm sorry, Luna. I have a chance to make a big leap, if *The New Yorker* publishes that story. I am a writer. I wouldn't mind being a more famous writer. I'm not going to withdraw it.

LUNA: I don't like that.

GRACIE: You've made that clear.

LUNA: And what about the future?

GRACIE: I do understand what you're saying about feeling objectified by me…

LUNA: Objectified! Yes!

GRACIE: So I won't write about you anymore. That's hard for me because I always have written about my own life…No I can't commit to forever. How about six months? I won't write about you for six months, and then we'll talk again. Does that satisfy you?

LUNA: I'm going to say the same thing in six months…but…alright.

GRACIE: (*Trying to lighten things up.*) It's all your fault anyhow. You keep saying such wonderful things. I can't help myself!

LUNA: Okay! I'll stop saying wonderful things.

GRACIE: Promise?

LUNA: I promise until the stars fall out of the sky and all the pastel Victorians crumble to the earth!

GRACIE: You see? You see? How can I not write that down?

LUNA: But you're not, are you?

GRACIE: No, I'm not.

LUNA: Good! (*Pause.*) I'm a terrible person, aren't I, amorcito?

GRACIE: The worst.

LUNA: I told you I only have one flaw, but it turns out I have two. I'm superficial and I hate to be written about.

GRACIE: Don't worry about that, Gatito. It turns out I also have a flaw. I'm obsessed with you.

LUNA: But that still leaves me with one more flaw than you.

GRACIE: You could even say twice as many flaws!

LUNA: I'd better stay with you, Pajarito. I don't think anyone else will have me.

GRACIE: I don't think so either.

They embrace as lights fade to black.

Scene Eleven

Lights come up on LUNA and GRACIE getting dressed in their party clothes. The "San Francisco Son" song plays in the background.

LUNA: (*Singing along with the music.*) San Francisco *tiene su propio son!* (*Speaking now. She is very excited.*) My first party in los Estados Unidos. All Latin Americans, and two Ticos, besides me.

GRACIE: Ticos?

LUNA: From Costa Rica, like me! Now you'll see what a good party is really like.

She watches appreciatively as GRACIE dons a black sequined sweater.

Ahh! Qué bonita!

GRACIE: Do you think Eduardo and I will like each other?

LUNA: Of course! Now, what am I going to wear?

GRACIE: (*Admiring herself in the invisible mirror.*) You don't want to look like a schlump next to me.

LUNA: Schlump! What's a schlump?

GRACIE: It's Yiddish for a sloppy dresser.

LUNA: "Schlump." I like that word. Schlump, schlump. No, I don't want to be a schlump at the party.

GRACIE: And that's why you're going to wear…this!

She brings out a brocade evening jacket she had hidden away.

Surprise!

She holds out the jacket to LUNA.

GRACIE (con't): Come on.

LUNA: It's too flashy for me.

GRACIE: It suits you.

LUNA puts on the jacket, studies herself in the mirror.

LUNA: I don't look like a fool?

GRACIE: You look spectacular! Like Gatito on the town!

LUNA: The schlump becomes Gatito.

GRACIE: Y yo puedo practicar mi español.

LUNA: Yes, you can practice your Spanish! Vámonos!

GRACIE: Sí! Vámonos!

LUNA: Oh, it's been a long time since I've been with my compañeros.

They leave the apartment through the portal. Lights cross-fade as the sound of the party, with laughing and Latin music is heard. As GRACIE and LUNA re-enter from offstage left, they are on the street, going home after the party. LUNA is very high, from both alcohol and camaraderie. GRACIE is rather low.

Now that was a great party! Qué bonita, esta noche. Look at the view from this hill.

She sings at the top of her lungs.

San Francisco tiene su propio son!

Speaking now, she turns around, admiring the view.

Una ciudad maravillosa, San Francisco. *Pura vida*! Oh, I can hardly walk. I ate so much. I can't believe the other Tico brought *gallo pinto*. I haven't had it since I left home. Oh, to finally spend an evening with people who are passionate!

GRACIE: I'm not passionate?

LUNA: Well, in a different way from a Latino. I can't remember when I laughed so much. That Eduardo. (*She laughs at the memory.*)

GRACIE: That joke he made about the Mexican prostitute...

LUNA: Why did you argue with him? It was just a joke!

GRACIE: Yes, about women being greedy and stupid.

LUNA: Now. Graciela, people in different cultures express themselves in different ways.

GRACIE: Eduardo expressed himself by feeling you up all night.

LUNA: Stop taking everything so seriously! You need to relax. Otherwise, you're gonna have a terrible time when we go to Costa Rica.

GRACIE: Are you attracted to Eduardo?

LUNA: Don't be ridiculous.

GRACIE: And he wasn't the only man you were flirting with. It was so degrading

LUNA: (*Tenderly mocking.*) Oh, Pajarito's feathers are all ruffled. She doesn't like how we Latin people play with each other.

GRACIE: And when I put my arm around you, you just walked away!

LUNA: That was very inappropriate, amorcito. That was not a gay party.

GRACIE: There were two gay people there.

LUNA: Who?

GRACIE: You and me!

LUNA: *Madre de dios*!

GRACIE: You know how I felt tonight?

LUNA: No. And I don't want to know.

GRACIE: Like a...gringo. Like a great big white blobby thing.

LUNA: You are too fucking complicated.

GRACIE: Well, I didn't feel complicated at the party. I felt like I didn't have a soul.

LUNA embraces GRACIE, a bit drunkenly

LUNA: Let's go home and I'll make beautiful love, Pajarito...

GRACIE pushes her away.

GRACIE: Don't give me that "Pajarito" shit. This little birdie was at the party.

LUNA: I suppose you remember every single moment of the evening.

GRACIE: It's engraved on my brain.

LUNA: I wish I could smash that fucking video camera inside your head.

GRACIE: Luna, let's go home. Tomorrow morning, when you're not drunk, we'll talk about what happened at the party.

LUNA: Talk talk talk talk talk talk. You make my stomach hurt with all your talk. I'm going back to Eduardo's. I'll spend the night there.

GRACIE: Good! I'm sure you'll be more comfortable with your compagneros than with your unpassionate gringo…roommate.

LUNA: I'm sure I will!

LUNA exits. GRACIE returns to the apartment, picks up her journal and starts to write in it. She flings her journal across the room, with a strangled howl of frustration and rage. Then she kicks over a chair. She sits in the other chair.

Lights cross-fade to indicate time passing.

LUNA enters. She is no longer high.

LUNA: Oh. It's six in the morning. I thought you'd be asleep.

GRACIE: I couldn't sleep.

LUNA: Neither could I.

GRACIE: Oh. Is that because you were fucking Eduardo?

Pause.

LUNA: No. It's because I was writing this letter to you. But I didn't have a stamp on me, so I decided to deliver it myself. Here.

She throws the letter on the table and starts to exit.

GRACIE: Wait!

LUNA stops. GRACIE hands the letter to her.

GRACIE: I want you to read it to me.

LUNA: (*Reading the letter, she is very uncomfortable. She tries to conceal* *her feelings, but she can't.*) This is a message in a bottle. But the bottle broke and the ocean poured out of it and it's drowning the cat, which is me, going down in a remolino.

GRACIE: What's a *remolino*?

LUNA: When the water goes around and around...

She makes a circling motion with her finger.

GRACIE: Ah, yes.

LUNA: Where was I...(*Reading.*)...the cat, which is me, going down in a remolino. I am the cat and I am the broken bottle. When I try to put myself back together, I cut my hands on the sharp glass. I got blood all over this paper. It's the blood of my soul, which is the color of everything and nothing. Can you see my soul? I showed it to you. For a few seconds precisely the other day. Maybe you weren't looking when I opened my raincoat and closed it again. You didn't understand that I never did that before, that you needed to pay attention. And me, I say I want to see your soul, but it's like trying to read five newspapers a day. It's too much and I put them all in the garbage without looking once. If only we could slowly slowly examine the soul of the other, let it in, let it wash over like a wave. I believe we both want to. But we are afraid. And so Gatito and Pajarito are snapping and clawing with their eyes closed, drawing soul blood from each other...

LUNA stops reading. She is crying. GRACIE goes to her, puts her arms around her.

GRACIE: Oh, amorcito, I've never seen you cry.

LUNA: I didn't finish the letter.

GRACIE: It's a beautiful letter.

LUNA: (*Harshly, repressing her tears.*) I never cry. I don't like it.

GRACIE: Your tears are very precious to me. Oh Gatito, we're trying so hard, aren't we?

LUNA: Yes. But I don't think it's working. If we break up, do you think we can be best friends for the rest of our lives?

GRACIE: Shhhh. No no no. Don't talk like that. Listen.

She looks at LUNA with great intensity.

I see you. I see your past and your fears. I see your soul. You just showed me. I could never bear to be parted from you after this.

She takes two steps away from LUNA.

Do you see me? Can you bear to read the five newspapers right now?

LUNA: (*Studying GRACIE.*) I see that you want to know everything and do everything and make everything better. And you also want to love me too much.

GRACIE: We'll work everything out. I promise.

Embracing LUNA, she helps her off with her jacket, with great tenderness.

Come on, let's go to bed.

LUNA: Yes. Let's go to bed. We're exhausted.

LUNA starts to unbutton her shirt.

GRACIE: No, let me do that.

LUNA: I'm so tired.

GRACIE: Because it's six in the morning, and because you cried.

They both take off their overshirts and their shoes and get into bed.

LUNA: Yes. Gatito and Pajarito are both very tired. Let's go to sleep.

GRACIE lies next to LUNA, and puts her hand between LUNA'S legs. She looks up.

GRACIE: I don't think so. You're very wet.

LUNA: (*Smiling innocently.*) Hmmm. Maybe we're not going to sleep right away.

GRACIE is on top of LUNA. Both actresses are fully clothed, but they are creating the illusion that GRACIE is slowly and rhythmically penetrating LUNA with her fingers. LUNA gives herself to GRACIE, responding fully with her voice and body.

GRACIE: And then I made love to you. It was the only time that you truly surrendered to me. When I possess you, I love you more than when I am possessed by you. Perhaps because when I make love to you, I see you. And you are so beautiful. You lay with your head turned to the side, holding my hand to your lips, kissing my hand, murmuring in Spanish.

They form this image.

GRACIE: (*whispers.*) Más?

LUNA: *Sí. Más.*

GRACIE: *Así?*

LUNA: *Así.*

> *LUNA slowly sits up, starts making love to GRACIE.*

GRACIE: When we make love, we speak in Spanish. The sounds of the words seem to blend with our sounds. Then you make love to me, for a very long time.

> *GRACIE's body arches in a final spasm. They lie down, entwined with each other.*

Finally, we lie still, our bodies pressed against each other. I cannot tell anymore where my body ends and yours begins. We breathe as one person, very softly, quietly. Slowly we drift off to sleep.

> *Lights fade to black.*

Scene Twelve

> *Lights come up as LUNA is pulling GRACIE onstage.*

LUNA: To celebrate the first day that we really see each other, I'm taking you here for a drink in my favorite bar in la Mision!

> *They enter a bar, which is the Downstage Center area. Lively Latino music is heard.*

Listen, amorcito, listen. They have absolutely the best music in town. Music that makes me want to fly!

> *GRACIE starts to take out her journal.*

GRACIE: I like that. "…music that makes me want to…"

LUNA: (*Warning her.*) Remember what you promised.

GRACIE: Oh, of course.

> *She puts her journal away.*

LUNA: Crazy gringo girlfriend. Can't you stop thinking for one minute?

GRACIE: No, I can't, amorcito. I can stop writing but I can't stop thinking.

LUNA: Just listen to the goddam fucking beautiful music, will you? It's enough. Sometimes life itself is enough.

GRACIE: Oh, that's good.

LUNA: Don't you dare!

GRACIE: Am I writing?

She innocently holds up her empty hands.

LUNA: And don't write it down later, either!

GRACIE: Your secret is safe with me. (*Whispering in LUNA'S ear.*) Sometimes life itself is enough!

LUNA: Come on, let's dance.

GRACIE: Are you sure? This isn't a gay bar.

LUNA: This bar is my country and it is the right place for us to dance together!

GRACIE: Look at you! Now you're a real big cat.

LUNA: I want to show everyone that you are my girlfriend, my lover, my soulmate, my Pajarito.

GRACIE: Okay, then. Teach me that dance you were doing last night at the party.

The music gets louder as they dance. LUNA leads GRACIE in some complicated steps. They are totally in sync with each other.

LUNA: Graciela, the bartender is smiling at us!

GRACIE: That's because we're such great dancers. *Pura vida!*

Their dancing becomes more free and joyful. LUNA twirls GRACIE and catches her. GRACIE returns the favor. Suddenly the music stops. GRACIE sees something and freezes with fear.

GRACIE: Oh shit. Luna.

LUNA: What?

GRACIE: Those two men. They're checking people's ID's. I think they're INS agents. Let's get out of here.

They walk toward the bar's entrance and then stop.

LUNA: Is that another one standing right outside the doorway?

GRACIE: Yes.

LUNA: Fuck. The bathrooms are back there. Maybe there's another door.

She starts to hurry out through the upstage portal.

GRACIE: Or even a window. Good, good. Don't run, for god's sake, don't run.

LUNA exits, walking very fast. She finally breaks into a run.

GRACIE: (*To the audience.*) There were four of them. One outside the front door and three in the bar.

Her eyes follow one of the men as he goes toward the bathrooms.

I watched one of them go in the back. Did he see Luna go there, or was he just checking? Everyone was totally silent as the two other agents checked people's IDs. Everyone in the bar had noticed Luna rushing out the back. I could feel all of them silently rooting for her. The agents checking IDs passed by me without so much as a look. Finally, they left the bar without finding anyone to arrest. The bartender came up to me and handed me a piece of paper with a phone number on it. He said, "I hope you don't need it, but this is a good lawyer. She helped me." That's when I realized the INS agent who had gone in the back had never reappeared. He had gone after her.

Lights fade to black.

Scene Thirteen

Lights come up on GRACIE in her apartment. She tries to write in her journal, but can't. She is restless, disturbed. She paces her apartment. The phone rings. LUNA appears holding her phone. GRACIE answers.

GRACIE: Hello?

LUNA: (*Very subdued.*) Hello, Graciela.

GRACIE: At last! Thank god! Are you alright? Where are you?

LUNA: I'm with my family. And how are you?

GRACIE: Now that I'm hearing your sweet voice, I'm wonderful. Oh Luna, I've been going crazy. It's been two weeks! I found out they put you on a plane to Costa Rica. I had no idea how to contact you. I've been waiting. I was just about to buy a ticket to fly there and…I don't know… walk the streets shouting your name. But now we can make a plan…

LUNA: I'm not coming back to Gringolandia. Ever.

GRACIE: Fine. I'm coming to live in Costa Rica.

LUNA: No. I never loved you! It was a fling. A very large one, I admit.

But still, just a fling.

GRACIE: You stop this right now! You love me, you stupid idiot.

Pause.

LUNA: You never called me a stupid idiot before.

GRACIE: Because you've never been a stupid idiot before.

LUNA: Amorcito…

GRACIE: Yes.

LUNA: I miss you.

GRACIE: That's why I'm coming to you.

LUNA: No. It wouldn't work. I could be happy in San Francisco not just because of you but because of San Francisco. It suited me.

GRACIE: Oh, amor, you belong here.

LUNA: But you here, in Costa Rica, no. I love my people. But it is still very macho here. It would be like you were living in Eduardo's party. Everyone would be telling jokes about Mexican prostitutes and you would be angry all the time. People would not like you.

GRACIE: I can change!

LUNA: You're used to living totally out. Are you willing to go back into the closet for me?

GRACIE: Of course! I'm a very flexible person.

LUNA: No, you're not. Graciela is not a flexible person who can fit in anywhere. And if you were, I would not be in love with you in the first place.

GRACIE: Let's both move back to Amsterdam! Women can get married there. You could get your old job back.

LUNA: They hired a replacement long ago. I would be illegal there, cleaning houses. I can't do that again.

GRACIE: We would be illegal together!

LUNA: In Amsterdam an illegal white Gringa is much more welcome than an illegal black Costa Rican. What if I got caught again? I couldn't face that.

GRACIE: Let's list all our options. Let me get a pen...

LUNA: You don't need a pen. We've gone as far as we can go.

GRACIE: We can't let the bastards get us down.

LUNA: They have done it. The bastards have got me down.

GRACIE: Never.

LUNA: Pajarito, for the first time since I arrived in San Francisco and that stupid customs jerk thought I had drugs on me—for the first time, I don't have a pain in my stomach. Not even a tiny little one..

GRACIE: You'll rest. We'll talk on the phone, write beautiful letters. In a few weeks, I'll come. Then we can see if Costa Rica and I are a good fit.

LUNA: Amorcito, you think I'm a big, strong cat. But Gatito is a little sick weak kitten right now.

GRACIE: (*Protesting.*) Then you need me...

LUNA: (*Angry.*) Listen! Let me talk! Alright?

Pause.

GRACIE: Alright.

LUNA: Thank you. (*Pause.*) Graciela, something happened to me when they grabbed me in the alley behind the bar.

GRACIE: Tell me.

LUNA: Amorcito, I always thought I was tough. Luna, the strong one. That's how my friends in Costa Rica see me. The one who moves to Holland for work, to Gringolandia for love! But when they put those handcuffs on me, I became...a little animal caught in the talons of a beast.

GRACIE: Oh, amorcito!

LUNA: I didn't know who I was anymore. I was just...fear. Have you ever been fear? Has that ever happened to you, Graciela?

GRACIE: No.

LUNA: Good. I hope it never does. I'm not well, Pajarito de mi alma. I have to find out who I am again.

GRACIE: I can help you...

LUNA: (*Ignoring what she said.*) How long has it been since we danced together? I don't even know.

GRACIE: Two weeks.

LUNA: Two weeks! My god…I haven't left my mother's house, until today. Mi madre has been very kind. She doesn't ask me questions… she feeds me…I just stayed in my room. I slept. Slept and thought.

GRACIE: What did you think about?

LUNA: You, us. (*Pause.*) Then, yesterday, for the first time, I heard the birds singing. We have so many birds here, but my ears had been plugged up with fear. I opened my window. I felt a breeze. A little sweet breeze. My country is so beautiful, amorcito. It breaks my heart that we will never see it together.

GRACIE: Don't say that, Gatito!

LUNA: (*As LUNA speaks, GRACIE says "Oh Gatito" again and again.*) All I want is to not be afraid, to never clean a stranger's house again, to have a happy stomach…

GRACIE: Oh, my Gatito, I want to hold you so close right now.

LUNA: …and to not be afraid.

GRACIE: You said, "not be afraid" twice.

LUNA: Did I? Please, let this little cat rest with her own people.

GRACIE: In a little while, you'll feel better. Oh, if only I could hold you.

LUNA: If you love me, you will let me go.

GRACIE: If I love you…?

LUNA: Please! If you love me, promise that you won't try to contact me.

GRACIE: Gatito…

LUNA: Please! I'm begging you.

Silence.

GRACIE: I promise I won't visit or phone. But I'll write you if I damn well feel like it. You can throw my letters in the trash if you don't want to read them.

LUNA: That's fair. Thank you. I think my stomach feels even better now.

GRACIE: Just remember I'm here, waiting. So whenever you're ready…

LUNA: No! Don't wait for me.

Silence.

GRACIE: (*Threatening.*) If I can't come to Costa Rica, I'm going to make you into a character! I'm going to write stories about you... I'll write a novel, a...a trilogy! I'll write down every single thing you said and then I'll make up all kinds of things that you never said and then I'll make up things you never would say in a million years and I'll write and write and write and then I'll send it to all the magazines and all the publishers. It'll be a best-seller and everyone will read it! Everyone! It'll be translated into all the languages, including Spanish, and...and Eskimo! And then they'll make a movie of it. And after that a TV series and...

LUNA: Good! I give you permission to make me into a character.

GRACIE: I don't need your permission!

LUNA: I'm giving it to you anyhow.

GRACIE: (*Pleading.*) Oh please, Lunacita, give me some hope!

LUNA: You and I will both have very happy lives. I know this. But not with each other.

GRACIE: NO!

LUNA: Pajarito de mi alma, you will always be fairly necessary to me. Adiós.

LUNA hangs up the phone and exits.

GRACIE: (*Into her phone.*) Luna...

GRACIE slowly hangs up the phone.

Lights cross-fade to suggest time passing as she crosses downstage. She speaks to the audience.

GRACIE (con't): It's been months since that phone call. I've written her so many letters. But I haven't tried to find out where to mail them. I priced plane tickets to Costa Rica. But I haven't bought one. How could I? She begged me...

Silence.

I guess she was right. We have gone as far as we can go.

Pause.

Last night I dreamed about Luna, for the first time. I was in her favorite bar in la Misión, the one with music that made her want to fly. The last place I ever saw her. I was dancing all by myself. And then I was flying! Dancing in the air, looking down on the tables and drinks and people. Suddenly Luna appeared… (*LUNA enters.*) …and she held me.

LUNA wraps her arms around GRACIE.

I was finally home after a long hard journey. We slowly, slowly drifted down to the floor. (*Pause.*) And then I woke up.

LUNA exits.

Amorcito, why can I only be with you in a dream?

Silence.

THE ENDING DOESN'T WORK!

Lights fade to black as GRACIE looks searchingly into the darkness before her.

End of Play

2003

WAITING FOR THE PODIATRIST

Dedicated to the memory of my adored sister Nancy, who shared the whole experience with me.

Premiere Information

Waiting For The Podiatrist was originally produced by Lilith Theater and Mary Alice Fry of Footloose Productions at Venue 9 in San Francisco. It opened on February 8, 2003.

Director .... Bobbi Ausubel
Set & Puppet Design .... Mari Kaestle
Musical Score .... Scrumbly Koldewyn
Lyrics .... David Hyman

CAST

ALEXANDRA ….....……………..……... Terry Baum
MOTHER .... A Puppet (Alexandra's Left Hand)
FATHER ....A Puppet (Alexandra's Right Hand)
NURSE and ACCOMPANIST......... Scrumbly Koldewyn

PRODUCTION HISTORY

In Fall 1999, I was working with another actress to create a short piece on Jewish women for the Women on the Way Festival in San Francisco. Suddenly, my father ended up comatose in Intensive Care in UCLA Hospital, and I was spending most of my time in Los Angeles. What to do about my commitment to the festival? I turned to my friend Paoli Lacy for advice. "You and your mother are Jewish women, aren't you? Do a scene about the two of you in the waiting room. If I know you, you always have to write about your life." But my acting partner refused, claiming the subject ws too heavy. I said, "To hell with you—I'll do it with a hand puppet!" And, with an actual oven mitt transformed into Mom by Mary Wings, I did it. With the support of Mary Alice Fry, the producer of W.O.W. I did a workshop of a longer version of *Podiatrist* in 2002. The play now had hilarious songs by David Hyman and Scrumbly Koldewyn and was directed by Paoli Lacy.

Then in 2003, a two-act version, with Mari Kaestle's gorgeous set and two fabulous puppets, and more songs, had its world premiere in San Francisco, directed by Bobbi Ausubel. It was almost two hours long and required that I play three-character scenes, sing three-character songs, and dance three-character dances. I felt like an Olympic athlete in a theatrical version of a triathlon. I was certain my mind-boggling achievement would strike all theater people in the audience with awe and reverence. But, as far as I know, only one theater person's mind was boggled. That's show biz!

Unfortunately, the play was too long. In fact, the second act, which explored Father's recovery, was a separate play, but I didn't realize that until I performed *Podiatrist* at my Antioch College reunion. Given a one-hour slot, I could only do the first act. Not only did it work as a complete play, but I had a much better time when I wasn't straining to win a theatrical gold medal. Performances in Ashland, Oregon and Amsterdam, Holland followed.

Fast forward to the 2016 San Francisco Fringe Festival. With director Velina Brown on board and J Althea as the Nurse/Accompanist, I expanded the part of the Nurse and, upon Carolyn's advice, added the climactic toenail-trimming scene. *Podiatrist* has finally achieved its ideal form. We won a Best of Fringe Award, and, with my crony Carolyn Myers directing, went on to be part of the 2017 National Queer Arts Festival.

CHARACTERS

ALEX: A middle-aged lesbian, displaced from her life in San Francisco to Los Angeles because her father is in Intensive Care.

MOTHER: ALEX'S mother, and a force to be reckoned with. She says whatever is on her mind.

FATHER: ALEX'S father, normally the host of the party, and a meaningful conversationalist, but now in a coma.

NURSE: Skilled and compassionate, but overworked and limited by hospital regulations.

TIME
The present.

PLACE
The Intensive Care Unit of a state-of-the-art hospital in Los Angeles, CA.

Prologue

AT RISE: Lights up on ACCOMPANIST/NURSE playing the overture on a keyboard Upstage Left. This area functions as the Nurse's Station. As the overture ends, a phone starts ringing. ALEX enters into a downstage spotlight, searching her many pockets for her cellphone. She is middle-aged with round, red glasses and short red hair. She is wearing pants, a man's shirt, jacket and shoes. She looks rather butch. She finds her cellphone in one of her pockets and answers it.

ALEX: Hi, Mom. (*Pause.*) I can't understand you. Try to speak a little slower…Daddy?…doctor…QUADRUPLE BYPASS SURGERY! Oh my g… Where are you now? Intensive care…I'll get there as soon as I can, Mom. There are lots of flights from San Francisco to L.A. I'll go straight to the hospital from the airport. Hold on, Mom. I'm coming.

She exits in a rush.

Scene One

SETTING: Lights up, with the moody music of the first song, "Intensive Care" fading in. The full stage is lit with a moody, dreamlike effect. The backdrop is painted as an abstract, cartoonish version of the machines in an intensive care ward in a big hospital, all in pastels. Upstage Right is a tri-fold screen in the same colors as the backdrop, folded up. Downstage Right there is a nightstand, with a chair next to it. On the nightstand sits a miniature hospital bed. Under the blankets, there is a lump, which is someone in the bed. All that can be seen is some wild white yarn hair sticking out above the blankets. Also on the nightstand is a basket of lemons. Downstage Left, in front of the keyboard/Nurse's station, are two hospital waiting room chairs, placed right next to each other. The rhythmic sounds of a ventilator and machines beeping are heard. These sounds continue throughout the song and during transitions between scenes.

NURSE: (*Singing.*)
                    Song: INTENSIVE CARE
Whoosh
Beep. Beep.
Whoosh.
Boop. Boop.

ALEX enters carrying a suitcase. She looks around warily. During the song, she explores this new world.

ALEX: (*Singing.*)
>Quiet halls …Acrid smells
>Nice clean walls …Private hells
>Pager calls…

NURSE: (*Speaking.*) Doctor Green, come at once, ICU nineteen!

ALEX & NURSE:
>It's so intense…Must be Intensive Care.

ALEX:
>People nod…People hug
>People plod…People shrug
>People sleep…

NURSE:
>And one finds…
>People weep…No one minds.

ALEX & NURSE:
>It feels so tense
>Must be Intensive Care.

ALEX:
>There are so many signs and warnings
>It almost takes away my breath

NURSE:
>And these are not just idle warnings
>Here "life or death" means life or death.

>*ALEX shivers as she hears these words.*

ALEX: (*Turning toward the backdrop of strange machines.*)
>Dials and pumps…Odd machines
>Groans and thumps…Behind screens
>Friends and kin…Young and old
>Hands on chin…Lives on hold

ALEX & NURSE:
>It makes no sense
>Must be Intensive Care.

>*ALEX sees the doll hospital bed, in which her FATHER lies. She crosses to him. The sight of her FATHER, hidden from the audience's view, horrifies her.*

ALEX:
>One great hose…Hides a face
>Up his nose…Taped in place
>Tubes for feeding… Tubes for air
>Tubes for bleeding…Tubes….down there.
>
>*She turns away, overwhelmed; then, with determination, slowly turns back to look at FATHER.*
>
>Don't act shocked…Don't look sad
>Keep in mind …He's your dad
>Eyes that were…Kind and wise
>Now just are…Empty eyes

ALEX & NURSE:
>Pain so intense…It's too immense to bear
>There's no defense…against Intensive Care.
>
>*Song ends and lights come up full. It's daytime in the ICU. ALEX crosses to the NURSE.*

ALEX: (*Still panicked by the sight of her Dad.*) Nurse, I'm Morris Bergman's daughter. He went to the doctor because he wasn't feeling well and suddenly he was having quadruple bypass surgery…

NURSE: (*In a soothing, professional voice.*) I'm sorry to tell you, but I'm afraid he's had a stroke on top of it.

ALEX: A stroke? A stroke! Does my mother know this?

NURSE: Yes, dear. Your mother's down the hall, in the visitors' lounge.

ALEX: Thanks.

>*ALEX rushes out Stage Right. A moment later, MOTHER appears peeking around the Stage Right curtain. MOTHER is a hand puppet in the shape of an oven mitt. She has bright fluffy red hair and wears earrings that are definitely too much. She is also adorned with a pearl necklace and a lovely scarf—in other words, a real lady. She has a high, squeaky voice like an elf, a gnome.*

MOTHER: Nurse, I'm expecting my daughter, Alexandra, from San Francisco. She's 56, she's got red hair like mine…

NURSE: I just sent her to the visitors lounge, Mrs. Bergman.

MOTHER: Thank you.

>*She disappears. Then, from offstage right, we hear her.*

Alexandra! There you are!

ALEX: (*From offstage.*) Ma!

> *MOTHER enters the ICU, of necessity, with ALEX. MOTHER, a hand puppet, cannot move without ALEX. But she is NOT a manifestation of ALEX's vision or imagination. She is a totally independent character.*

MOTHER: Thank goodness you're here. (*She looks away.*) I'm afraid to look at him.

ALEX: We'll look at him together, Ma.

MOTHER: Yes. We've got to stick together.

> *They look at each other, then take a deep breath together. They cross to FATHER. Pause, while MOTHER forces herself to look.*

Morrie, look who's here! Alexandra! You had to have a stroke and go into a coma to get her to come to Los Angeles to visit. But, whatever it takes. Right, Morrie?

ALEX: (*Tentatively.*) Dad, it's Alex here.

MOTHER: My poor baby. I can't stand to see him like this. How does he look to you?

ALEX: He looks…he looks… (*To audience.*) He looks like he's being tortured.

MOTHER: Do you think he's suffering?

ALEX: (*After studying FATHER.*) Yes.

MOTHER: (*Hysterical.*) That's horrible! We have to do something! Call the doctor! (*Shouting at NURSE.*) Call the authorities! Call the humane society!

ALEX: (*To herself.*) Why did I say he was suffering? (*To MOTHER.*) I take it back, Mom. He's not suffering. He's in a coma! He can't feel anything.

MOTHER: (*Immediately relieved.*) Oh. Good.

ALEX: (*To the audience, shrugging her shoulders.*) I can't do anything for my father, but I can help my mother delude herself.

MOTHER: What can we do to wake him up? Think of something!

ALEX: (*Pondering.*) They say the sense of smell is the last one to go.

MOTHER: I brought lemons!

ALEX sees a basket of lemons on the table where FATHER's bed sits. She picks up a lemon.

Look, Morrie! From the tree you planted yourself years ago! Here it is: the first Meyer lemons of 2018, the gourmet delight!

ALEX: (*Smelling the lemon, with great enthusiasm.*) It smells great. Doesn't it, Ma?

MOTHER: (*Smelling the lemon with exaggerated delight.*) Just delicious!

ALEX waves the lemon above where FATHER's nose must be, under the blanket.

ALEX: Can you smell it? Come on, Dad. Wake up and smell the lemon. (*There is no response from FATHER.*) Not working.

She puts the lemon back in the basket.

MOTHER: I've got another idea! Morrie, remember those awful earrings you gave me for my birthday? I told you I wouldn't be caught dead in them. Well, here they are! See? Just say the word and I'll wear them for the rest of my life.

MOTHER sings.

Song: PLEASE COME OUT OF YOUR COMA

(*Holding the first note for a looong time.*) Ohhhhhhh...
Please come out of your coma
So I can take you home-a
Oh home-a, oh home-a
Where you were meant to be
Oh home-a, oh home-a
With your Meyer lemon tree
Oh please come out of your coma
So I won't be all alone-a...

She speaks softly to FATHER.

My poor baby.

While MOTHER is hovering over FATHER, ALEX straightens the covers at the foot of the bed. She notices something disturbing.

ALEX: (*Very upset.*) Ma, look at Daddy's toenails!

As MOTHER looks at the toenails for the first time, the lights flicker and a few brief chords of horror music are heard. She draws back in shock. This routine—music/lights/revulsion—repeats every time anyone looks at the toenails. FATHER's bed is arranged so that the audience never sees his toenails—or anything else, other than his white yarn hair. They can only imagine the toenails.

MOTHER: (*Very alarmed.*) They are extremely long, aren't they?

ALEX: We'll get somebody in here to cut them. I don't want to do it.

MOTHER: (*Increasingly upset.*) We're in one of the finest hospitals in the world. We shouldn't have to cut Daddy's toenails ourselves!

ALEX: (*Soothing MOTHER.*) I'll take care of it, Ma. Don't you worry about anything.

ALEX and MOTHER exit.

Lights Fade to Black.

Scene Two

ALEX enters into downstage spotlight, speaks to audience.

ALEX: That was Day One of my new life. The days drag on and on. Every day, all day in the hospital, while my father continues to spiral downward. After fourteen days of this, I come in…

Lights up on whole stage. The sound effects of the ICU swell, with a new clicking sound added. ALEX does a double take as she hears the new machine. She locates it in the painted backdrop, looks at FATHER, and then runs to NURSE.

ALEX: Nurse, nurse!

NURSE: Yes, dear?

ALEX: What is this new machine connected to my father?

NURSE: (*Soothing as always.*) It's a dialysis machine, dear. His kidneys have failed.

ALEX: His kidneys! Does he have any organs left that are working?

NURSE: (*Checking her clipboard, cheerfully.*) His pancreas is doing wonderfully!

ALEX: What exactly does the pancreas do?

NURSE: Oh, all kinds of important things!

ALEX: (*With great urgency.*) The podiatrist is coming today, isn't he?

NURSE: (*Evasive.*) Well...

>*ALEX grabs NURSE, drags her downstage to FATHER's bed, lifts up the blanket.*

ALEX: Look at my father's toenails.

>*As the NURSE looks, lights flicker and toenail horror music swells briefly. NURSE shrinks from the dreadful sight.*

They keep growing and growing. You make him breathe, you regulate his heart rate, now you empty his kidneys. It seems to me you would be embarrassed to let his toenails get totally out of control! They've become weapons. My mother injured herself on them. She can tell you herself.

>*ALEX rushes offstage.*

NURSE: (*Calling after ALEX.*) There's no need, dear. I'll take your word for it.

>*Exasperated, NURSE addresses the audience.*

I don't have time for this. They don't understand. I understand that they don't understand. But they don't know that. They think I don't care. Once upon a time, I did have the time. But everything's changed. Now, I have too much to do.

>*NURSE returns to her station. ALEX re-enters with MOTHER.*

ALEX: (*To MOTHER.*) Tell the nurse how you scratched yourself on Daddy's toenails.

MOTHER: Oh, it was awful! And he's such a gentle man. All the men in his family are very gentle. I was shocked. (*She leans in toward NURSE, endearingly.*) Maybe you could cut them.

NURSE: I'm sorry, dear, but I'm not allowed to do that.

MOTHER: (*Turning on her considerable charm, coaxing NURSE.*) You could make an exception just this once. My husband would never allow his toenails to get like this. He's a dapper, civilized man. These are the toenails of a savage. You must be afraid of them too!

ALEX: Okay, you can't keep his kidneys working. Why not take care of his toenails?

MOTHER: (*Startled.*) What's wrong with his kidneys?

NURSE: (*With that damn soothing tone.*) They've failed, dear.

MOTHER: Oh, my poor baby.

NURSE: (*There's always a silver lining!*) But his pancreas is doing beautifully!

ALEX: Nurse, do you think there's any hope? Give us your honest opinion.

NURSE: Well…Just recently, in this very hospital, there was an 85-year-old man who came out of a coma after 54 days—and went home! So there's always hope. And now, I really must leave.

She tries to leave. MOTHER stops her.

MOTHER: Wait! Alex, give the nurse some lemons. We have so many, we don't know what to do with them.

ALEX retrieves the basket from the table next to the bed, and offers it to NURSE.

ALEX: From the tree my father planted.

NURSE takes the basket.

NURSE: That's very sweet of you.

She tries to leave again. This time, ALEX stops her.

ALEX: Could the 85-year-old man talk? Could he think?

NURSE: I'm not sure. I'm sorry, but I've got to…

She exits by sitting down at her keyboard/nurse's station and turning her back.

ALEX: (*Calling after NURSE, who ignores her.*) Did he have a good life?

MOTHER: He had a life! (*They sit in Downstage Left chairs.*) That's the only important thing.

ALEX: No it's not! I wonder what condition that 85-year-old guy was in, when he went home!

MOTHER: You know what I wonder? (*With feigned innocence.*) Who's going to help me take care of Daddy when he comes home? I'd hate to have some stranger in the house.

ALEX: (*Leaping to her feet.*) Wait a minute! Hold everything! I'm not falling for this! I've got a life of my own!

ALEX sings.

Song: DUTIFUL DAUGHTER RAG

ALEX dances as she sings. MOTHER responds with disgust and outrage at her daughter's assertion of independence.

> Doing the dutiful daughter dance
> You think I'll hop to it—Not a chance!
> This is not youthful rebellion
> I am a lesbian hellion!
> Sacrifice job, apartment, and friends
> Move here and help you change his Depends!
> Sorry it's out of my hands
> Just doesn't fit in my plans
> Doing that dutiful daughter
> Even if you say I oughtta
> I'm not doing that dutiful daughter dance!

MOTHER: (*Speaking.*) Sit down and listen to my side! (*They sit down.*)

> (*Singing.*) Doing the dutiful daughter rag
> You act as if it's a major drag
> Sacrifice? You? Please don't kid me
> You'd think I'd asked for a kidney
> You hate the dutiful daughter life?
> (*To audience.*) She should try being a dutiful wife!
> I know that I shouldn't nag.
> Caring just isn't your bag
> I guess you're just not a giver.
> Parents are only chopped liver.
> So don't do that dutiful daughter rag.

Dance break. MOTHER and ALEX battle it out in a sadistic tango. ALEX throws MOTHER around, but MOTHER ends up triumphant, with a grip on ALEX's neck, half-strangling her until she starts coughing. ALEX pulls MOTHER off her neck and sings.

ALEX:
> Maybe you're right and I'm wrong
> Maybe I should go along

MOTHER:
> Yes, you'll do the dutiful daughter...

ALEX:

Dutiful mother & daughter...

MOTHER:
We'll do the dutiful mother and daughter dance!

They end the dance with a cha-cha bounce and, exhausted, drop into the chairs downstage left.

MOTHER: (*Reminiscing.*) Yes, I was always the perfect dutiful daughter. Your grandma was lucky. Come to think of it, she was lucky in a lot of ways. She was in good health until she was eighty-two. Had some pains in her chest, the doctor put her in the hospital, a week later—bingo!—gone. In the old days, people were lucky. When their lives were over, they just died. Daddy was lucky until now. Had a good life. Enjoyed his work, made a nice living, had a lovely family. (*Pause. Then, with an enormous sigh of regret, she continues.*) Of course he did expect at least one grandchild to comfort him in his old age.

ALEX: I guess the worst thing that ever happened to Daddy, before the stroke, was me coming out as a lesbian.

MOTHER: Weeelllll ... (*She tells the audience the story with great relish.*) When he was a soldier in the Pacific in World War II, that was no picnic, believe you me. Once he was out on patrol with his squad, and everyone was killed except him. He had to crawl down a river for three days to get back to base camp! (*Pause. Then, addressing ALEX.*) But I think you're right. You coming out as a lesbian was worse.

ALEX: Know what I love about you, Ma? You have no subtext. I never waste a moment trying to figure out what you really mean, because everything is right there on the surface, smacking me in the face. (*She smacks her own face as she says this.*)

MOTHER: You're too sensitive.

ALEX: I admit I'm sensitive. Perhaps I'm very sensitive. But I'm not too sensitive. (*With pride.*) I'm just sensitive enough.

MOTHER: (*Screaming.*) No, you're too sensitive. I don't understand you. You live your life exactly as you please. And then you complain I don't approve of you. (*With great emphasis.*) Other people live for their parents' approval. Why not yoooooooou? (*This last word is a prolonged hoot.*)

ALEX (*To the audience, clearly "bugged."*) Thank goodness after seventeen years of therapy, she doesn't bug me anymore!

MOTHER: (*Having said everything she needed to say to drive her daughter crazy.*) I'm tired. I'm going to take a nap.

> *She lies down. That is, ALEX takes MOM off her hand and puts her down on a chair. Throughout the play, MOM will sleep and wake up when ALEX takes her off or puts her back on her hand. When ALEX has an aside to the audience, MOM disappears behind her back. ALEX crosses Downstage Center.*

ALEX: (*To the audience, at the end of her wits.*) You think this is a sweet little old lady? This is a force of nature!

> *Trying to calm herself down, she rummages in her suitcase until she finds small paperback book.*

Ah-ha! (*To the audience.*) I bought this in the airport.

> *She shows the book to the audience, and reads the title out loud.*

"It's Easier than You Think, the Buddhist Way to Happiness."

> *Feeling hopeful, she opens the book, and reads aloud from the beginning*

"Buddha's First Noble Truth: Pain is inevitable. Life is difficult."

> *A brief pause for contemplation. Suddenly the Great Revelation breaks through!*

Buddha is right! This whole big mess is just a part of life! There's nothing unfair about my father being in a coma or my mother having no respect for me. I'm not entitled to an easy life. No one is! Life is difficult! I accept it! I embrace all of life, even this! (*She takes a deep breath.*) I feel so much better! This'll help Mom too!

> *She runs over to her sleeping MOTHER.*

ALEX (con't): MOTHER!

MOTHER: (*Waking up irritated.*) What? What is it?

ALEX: I'm reading this book about Buddhism. And it says here that Buddha's First Noble Truth is that life is difficult.

MOTHER: (*Shocked.*) Difficult for everyone?

ALEX: Yes!

MOTHER: That's a depressing thought. I've never heard anything so depressing. Not everybody's life is difficult. (*With great satisfaction.*) I personally know several people who live without any difficulty at all.

ALEX: But…but…Buddha's first noble truth certainly applies to you and me, and it helps me…

MOTHER: Well, if that crap helps you, that's fine. But it doesn't do a damn thing for me. Why are you reading about Buddhism anyhow? Buddhist schmoodist. You're a Jew. You should read what the Jews say. (*Very sweetly.*) Do the Jews say life is difficult?

ALEX: (*After considering this possibility.*) Probably not. The Jews don't tell you how to think about life. They just tell you what to do.

MOTHER: (*Screeching.*) You should find out what the Jews say.

ALEX: (*Her nerves can't take much more.*) Your voice is like fingernails on the blackboard of my soul.

MOTHER: (*Hovering above ALEX, very loud.*) You're too sensitive! I bet the Jews don't say life is difficult!

> *Silence.*

ALEX: (*Shaking with frustration, she addresses the audience, while MOTHER still hovers above her.*) Here we are in Intensive Care. My father is lying there with his arm strapped down so he doesn't pull out the tube in his throat while he's in a coma. AND MY MOTHER REFUSES TO ACKNOWLEDGE THAT LIFE IS DIFFICULT!

> *ALEX stands, puts MOTHER behind her back, and crosses Downstage Center, speaks to herself.*

Why am I trying to change her? I want to help my mother, but introducing her to Buddhism is obviously not the answer. What can I do for her? Nothing. (*She looks at FATHER.*) And my father lies there, one organ failing after another. Mom!

> *MOTHER re-appears.*

MOTHER: What?

ALEX: We need to talk to someone.

MOTHER: About what?

ALEX: About organs! Toenails! Everything! I'm trying the social worker again. She oversees Daddy's whole case.

> *ALEX pulls out her cellphone. She searches on her phone for the number.*

MOTHER: Is she the one minding the store? That's what I want to know. Who's minding the store?

ALEX: (*As she makes the call.*) Don't worry, Ma. I'll find someone!

> *ALEX becomes increasingly frantic during the following phone calls. She never gets a person on the other end. She only gets voicemail.*

Hello, this is Morris Bergman's daughter, room 1343 in Intensive Care. I've left messages every day, but I've never talked to or seen you. My mother and I are very concerned because it's been two weeks, my father's still in a coma, his kidneys just failed and his toenails are going berserk. If you exist, can we talk? If you don't, could you please inform us as soon as possible? Thank you so very very much.

> *She ends the call.*

Never fear, Mother! I've got a lot of contacts here! Your intrepid daughter will discover who's minding the store!

> *She keeps talking to MOTHER as she calls second number.*

The heart surgeon! He's the most important. You know, Ma, once the surgeon operates on you, he owns your body...

> *ALEX gets voicemail and leaves a message.*

Hello, this is Alexandra Bergman. Again. We know you're busy busy busy, but we're flipping flipping flipping out about this coma thing. What does the future hold? What is the point of this modern medical purgatory? Kidneys...toenails...Room 1343. Thank you...lots.

> *She ends the call, and tries a third number.*

The head of Intensive Care.

> *ALEX gets voicemail and leaves a message.*

ALEX (con't): Intensive Care or intensive torture? Does anybody care? Room 1343, begging you. Thanks.

> *She ends the call and tries the fourth number.*

The hospital director.

> *Voicemail again.*

We demand to know who is minding the store! Father...daughter...coma...toenails failing...kidneys growing...1343. Thanks.

> *She ends the call, and tries the fifth number.*

My last contact!

> *And, alas, voicemail.*

We're desperate in 1343…the coma…barely hanging on…What did we do to deserve this? If there is a God, what is his problem? (*A cry from the bottom of her soul.*) Why didn't he make more podiatrists? Th…Th… Thank…

> *She ends the call, and collapses with all possible drama onto the downstage chairs.*

(*To MOTHER.*) That was the rabbi.

MOTHER: Alexandra, calm yourself!

ALEX: (*Bouncing back with renewed energy.*) The doctors do their rounds very early. Tomorrow, I'm getting here at dawn, so I can catch one of them!

MOTHER: Dawn! I can't get up that early!

ALEX: Then come later in a taxi.

MOTHER: I've never taken taxis.

ALEX: That's because you live in Los Angeles. It's a very common practice in other parts of the world.

> *She starts to exit.*

MOTHER: (*Stopping ALEX.*) What if I call a taxi and it never comes?

ALEX: Then. I'll. Come. Get. You.

MOTHER: Alright, alright.

> *They exit.*

> *Lights Fade to Black.*

Scene Three

> *As lights come up, ALEX enters with great energy and speaks to the audience.*

ALEX: The next day, there I was, bright and early. (*To NURSE.*) Hello, Nurse.

NURSE: Hello, dear.

ALEX: Have any of the doctors been in yet?

NURSE: Not yet.

ALEX: (*Disappointed.*) Oh. Okay. Thanks.

> *She goes over to FATHER.*

(*Speaking softly.*) Hey Dad, how're you doing?

> *ALEX sings and dances in a very sentimental and old-fashioned manner.*

Song: WAKE UP!

Observe how the night starts to draw to a close
The day is beginning to break
You've had several weeks of delightful repose
And now it is time that you wake.
The lark is a-twitter, the blossom a-bloom
Each creature is leaving its bed
And Father, my dear, if you don't wake up soon…
(*The sticky-sweet mood abruptly changes.*)
We're going to declare that you're dead.

> *ALEX sings the final verse with great intensity. She is really trying to awaken FATHER.*

Wake up, wake up, Father my dear
I really do want you to try.
Come on now, it's easy, just do it, we pray…
Wake up wake up wake up wake up
wake up wake up wake up wake up wake up!
Or die!

> *ALEX studies her hidden FATHER in the little bed, seeking signs of consciousness. Finding nothing, she slowly sits in the chair next to the bed. She decides to try another, softer approach to waking him up.*

ALEX: Dad, remember when I was a little kid and sometimes you'd get home from work and we'd go for a walk before dinner, just the two of us? And we'd talk about…life. We had real conversations. I was only nine or ten, but you listened to me with respect. (*Pause.*) Decades later, we had another real conversation when I told you I was a lesbian. And you told me that it made you nostalgic for the time you found out that I was living with my boyfriend. (*She laughs, then is again serious.*) You were also very upset and said some terrible things. But later you gave me one of your old jackets and all your bolo ties. I guess you wanted to help me build my new lesbian wardrobe. It was so sweet.

> *She leans in close to FATHER, examining him for any response, then sighs.*

Dad, I wish I had hope. If I had faith, I would have hope. I don't have faith in anything—in the doctors, in God. (*To the audience.*) How do you acquire faith when you don't have it? (*Pause.*) I'm sorry, Dad, but I think the best thing might be...

> *She cannot bring herself to say it. She sits in silence, struggling with her emotions. She crosses left, looks offstage.*

I wonder where the hell all the doctors are. (*Her phone rings.*) Maybe that's a doctor...(*She answers the phone.*) Hi, Mom. (*Pause.*) No, the doctors never showed up. (*Pause.*) Oh, you're in the lobby. (*Pause.*) Oh, you're right. I forgot to bring the lemons. I'm sorry. (*Pause. Very sarcastic.*) I'm sorry you had to carry that heavy basket of lemons from the house to the taxi. (*Pause. Feigning rational calm.*) Inconsiderate? No, Ma, I disagree. I'm evil. All lesbians are evil. The two traits go together. (*Exploding.*) I'm coming to the lobby right now to relieve you of the horrendous burden of the goddam fucking lesbians...I mean, lemons! (*To the audience, with wonder.*) Did I just say "goddam fucking lesbian lemons" to my mother?

> *She exits and returns with MOTHER and a basket of lemons.*

MOTHER: That taxi driver was so rude. He would not come into the driveway, so I had to walk all the way to the curb with that heavy basket of lemons.

ALEX: I'm sure he didn't mean to be rude. He just didn't know you have trouble walking.

MOTHER: I told you a cab was a terrible idea.

ALEX: Next time tell them you want the cab to come into the driveway!

MOTHER: There won't be a next time!

ALEX: (*In a fury.*) That is ridiculous!

> *She slams the basket of lemons down on the table with FATHER's bed.*

(*To the audience.*) Why am I arguing with my mother about the cabdriver? We have important things to discuss! (*To MOTHER.*) Ma.

MOTHER: What?

ALEX: (*With hesitation, softly.*) Do you have hope?

MOTHER: (*Crossing to look at FATHER.*) Hope? Remember the 85-year-old fart who woke up! And Daddy's only 83!

ALEX: (*Gently.*) I'm starting to wonder if there's any point in going on like this. (*Silence.*) Well, what are you thinking, Ma?

MOTHER: I'm thinking…about an article I read in the paper today that all the lesbians are having children now!

ALEX: Daddy is suffering, Ma.

MOTHER: You told me he wasn't!

ALEX: I just said that the first day to make you feel better. We could talk to the surgeon about…about ending his suffering. (*MOTHER looks away.*) What do you think about that, Ma?

MOTHER: (*Desperate to change the subject.*) I think…You're too old to have children the normal way. You're 56. But you could adopt! I could accept a little adopted grandchild. I'm very open-minded.

ALEX: I am not open-minded about having children, as you know!

MOM: (*Deflated.*) Oh. That's right.

ALEX: Now, about Daddy… (*Pausing for a moment, exhaling.*) Here's how I see it. If we don't take him off the ventilator, we're facing three possibilities. Number one: Daddy wakes up and he'll have to work really hard at rehabilitation.

MOTHER: Oh, he's too old for that. He'd hate it.

ALEX: I know. Number two: Daddy never wakes up. He dies… eventually. Who knows how long? A week? Another month? People can live hooked up to a ventilator for years.

MOTHER: (*Gasps.*) Don't even say that!

ALEX: I'm saying it. Number three: Daddy wakes up…and he's not Daddy.

MOTHER: What if he can't speak?

ALEX: What if he can't think?

MOTHER: What if he wishes he were dead?

ALEX: What if he doesn't have enough mind left to even know he's alive, but *we* wish he were dead? It's all supposed to be about him.

They've got all these machines to keep him going. What keeps *us* going?

MOTHER: (*She looks away.*) I don't know what to wish for.

ALEX: Mom, I don't think there's much chance of Daddy waking up and still being Daddy. Do you?

MOTHER: (*Pause.*) No.

ALEX: I'm terrified of the other possibilities. Daddy would be, too. He would want us to disconnect…

MOTHER: (*Interrupting, truly excited.*) I know what I wish! That you'd learn to play the ukulele! It's such a nice instrument. So portable. Everyone loves a ukulele player. You're old, but you could take lessons.

ALEX: (*Gentle but persistent.*) Ma, we need to talk about Daddy.

MOTHER: I'm so tired. Why? What do I do? Nothing. I'm tired all the time.

ALEX: I've abandoned my life in San Francisco just so I could be here with you right now…

MOTHER: (*Thoughtfully.*) You know, I'm glad you don't have children. You don't have anything important to keep you in San Francisco.

ALEX: Don't you think Daddy's suffered enough?

MOTHER: Please, Alex, I'm so tired. Let me take a nap.

MOTHER lies down on downstage chairs.

ALEX: Mom?

MOTHER is asleep.

(*To the audience.*) I can't even remember my life in San Francisco. Haven't I always been here, in this hospital room, with my mother, listening to the beep of the machines and whoosh of the ventilator? Who am I anymore?

ALEX crosses downstage to an invisible mirror. She studies her face, looking for something, perhaps the person she was.

She sings.

Song: NOT ME

Who is that reflected?
Not me.
Not what I expected.

Not me.
I don't understand.
Did I miss the band?
Is this what I planned to be?
Am I going soft? Have I lost my edge?
Am I dull, boring, cold?
Is this my face, or another?
Am I me? Am I my mother?
Am I getting old?
Not me! Not me!

ALEX walks away from the mirror, imagining herself back home.

There's someone who is needed in the City by the Bay.
Someone who is needed like the air.
Who's that person rare? Not me. Not there.
Who can know what right and wrong are?
Who can say if live or die?

ALEX crosses to FATHER's bed.

Who can save a life or ease a death, and who can say goodbye?
Not me.
(*To the audience.*) Where am I supposed to go?
Who am I supposed to be?
What am I to do? I don't know, do you?

She picks up her book, singing with bitterness.

Go and ask the Buddha. Not me.

Lights fade quickly to black as ALEX looks out at the audience.

Scene Four

ALEX and MOTHER are standing by FATHER's bed as lights come up. MOTHER is looking intently at FATHER, shaking her head sadly.

ALEX: (*To the audience.*) It's been three weeks now. Three weeks of calling all over Los Angeles, searching for a podiatrist who is willing to come to the hospital. Three weeks of his toenails growing.

She uncovers FATHER's feet. ALEX and MOTHER look at the toenails. Horror music swells, lights flicker.

MOTHER: (*With awe.*) I think they've gotten longer since this morning.

ALEX: (*Rising to the occasion.*) I'm going to cut them myself!

MOTHER: Are you sure?

ALEX: I feel I have no choice. I came prepared!

> *She pulls out super-sized nail clippers and holds them high.*

MOTHER: From my bathroom! Alright. If you're sure.

> *ALEX makes three increasingly desperate attempts to cut a toenail to the accompaniment of thrilling toenail-cutting music. Finally she gives up.*

ALEX: It's no good. They're too thick. (*She calls out in melodramatic despair.*) Is there no podiatrist in the whole city of Los Angeles who will cut my comatose father's toenails?

> *ALEX flings herself into a chair.*

MOTHER: You're always putting down Los Angeles. Of course there's a podiatrist. We'll find him sooner or later.

ALEX: Or her. It could be a woman podiatrist.

MOTHER: (*Scoffing.*) Next you'll be telling me there are lesbian podiatrists.

ALEX: One out of ten people is gay. So if there are more than ten female podiatrists in Los Angeles, then the likelihood is that at least one of them is a …

MOTHER: (*Unable to face this final indignity.*) I don't want a lesbian podiatrist to touch Daddy!

ALEX: I don't want anyone *but* a lesbian podiatrist to do it!

MOTHER: (*Shrieking.*) Over my dead body!

> *Silence. ALEX has ended up lying on her back on the chairs with MOTHER hovering menacingly over her. ALEX sits up. She attempts to calm them both.*

ALEX: Mother, Mother. Look at us. We're tearing each other apart. We're trapped in an endless nightmare. We've been fed into a huge machine that keeps Daddy alive because that's what the machine does, without any thought. We're spending all day every day in this little room with Daddy. We've got to get out away from these machines. Have some fun. Relax.

MOTHER: We can't leave Daddy!

ALEX: Just for a little while.

MOTHER: I can't walk a lot. It hurts.

ALEX: (*An inspiration!*) We'll park in the basement garage of the Hammer Museum, take the elevator up, look at some art and then have lunch in the courtyard.

MOTHER: That does sound nice.

ALEX: Let's go.

MOTHER: But what if Daddy needs us?

> *ALEX crosses upstage to the NURSE.*

ALEX: Nurse, you have my cellphone number. Will you call us if anything changes?

NURSE: Of course! You two just go and have a good time.

MOTHER: Promise you'll call?

NURSE: You can bet your sweet patootie on it, Mrs. Bergman.

ALEX: Come on.

MOTHER: I don't know...

ALEX: (*Tempting MOTHER.*) Portobello mushroom sandwich with Gruyere cheese...

MOTHER: Oh, alright.

> *They move toward the exit.*

And remember, when you're making a left turn, don't dawdle.

ALEX: But you're always telling me I drive too fast!

MOTHER: That's the problem! You're either too fast or too slow...

> *MOTHER and ALEX exit. Lights cross-fade to show time passing. ALEX and MOTHER re-enter.*

MOTHER: (*Relaxed and jolly from the lovely outing.*) Hello, Morrie! We're back. Did you miss us? Morrie, you can't imagine the things they call art nowadays! One artist did all these things with sticks. Some of them burned...

ALEX: Some covered in seaweed...

MOTHER: Some stuck in mud...

ALEX: They were beautiful, weren't they?

MOTHER: I loved them! Morrie, you cannot imagine burned sticks could be so nice. (*Pause.*) And the sandwich was delicious! (*MOTHER suddenly suffers an attack of Daughter Appreciation.*) Oh, Alex, I don't know what I'd do without you.

ALEX: Really?

MOTHER: You make me go to the museum. You call all over L.A. for a podiatrist. You sit here with me and Daddy. You go up the ladder to pick lemons. You're a good daughter.

ALEX: REALLY?

MOTHER: (*Clarifying.*) Not a *great* daughter. But a *good* daughter. Yes. (*To FATHER.*) She's a good daughter, right Morrie?

ALEX: Wow, Ma.

MOTHER: Even though you're a childless lesbian living a pointless life in San Francisco.

ALEX: Gee Ma. Thanks. I'll take it. (*She sits down, overwhelmed.*) Wow.

MOTHER: (*A bit of the shrillness creeping back.*) What are you making such a fuss? You act like I never say anything nice!

ALEX: (*Her joy overflowing.*) Ma, I love you.

MOTHER: Oh, my little Alexandra...

They hug. Then ALEX pulls back, her expression serious.

ALEX: Mom, let's talk.

MOTHER: About Daddy.

ALEX: It's been three weeks, as of today.

MOTHER: Twenty-one days. My poor baby.

ALEX: I want to call the surgeon. We have to put an end to Daddy's torment. (*Suddenly moved to make a political statement.*) We must stop being passive victims in this gigantic system of suffering!

MOTHER: (*Timidly.*) Can't we stop being passive victims a little later?

They cross to FATHER's bed.

ALEX: Mom, this is Daddy, toastmaster at every family gathering. He has a joke for every occasion. He got a sunburn from working in the garden too long. Do you really think Daddy wants the life he will have if he does out of this coma?

Silence while MOTHER thinks. She reaches a decision.

MOTHER: (*To FATHER, accusingly.*) Morrie, you know I was supposed to go first! I said you could hire a housekeeper, but I would never forgive you if you married her. Well, goddammit, I'll never forgive you for this, either! You were always so healthy! (*She speaks to ALEX, defeated.*) Call the surgeon.

ALEX: (*Making a call.*) What a relief to do something.

MOTHER: (*To herself.*) What will I do without him?

ALEX: (*Speaking into the phone.*) Hello…I…I… Is this a real person? (*Pause.*) I'm Morris Bergman's daughter. Can I speak with Dr. Sweetzer? (*Pause.*) Yes, I'll hold—for as long as it takes. (*To MOTHER.*) He's in, Ma. This is a sign. We're doing the right thing.

MOTHER (*To the audience.*) He was so strong. Only had one cavity—and he got that during World War II, when he couldn't brush his teeth every day. Always ate his vegetables. Now we're afraid he'll *be* a vegetable.

ALEX: (*To Dr. Sweetzer, on the phone, struggling to find the right words.*) Hello, Dr. Sweetzer. My mother and I are thinking…that there is something worse than my father dying. And that is his not dying. (*Pause.*) But it's been three weeks. Let me be frank. We are terrified of my father waking up to a totally miserable life. (*Pause.*) We're selfish? We're selfish? What about you? Who gets anything out of this situation besides you?

MOTHER: Alex, that's the surgeon, for god's sake!

ALEX: (*To Dr. Sweetzer, very hurt.*) Yes, my mother's life is important, too. So is mine. Who's going to change the diapers on my father, if that's what he needs? You? (*That anger starts to build.*) Let's face it, Dr. Sweetzer: Even if it was your own father, you wouldn't be changing the diapers, would you? Oh no! You're a man, you're a surgeon, you've got important things to do! I know who would end up with the job— (*Exploding.*) Your lesbian sister! (*Pause.*) How did I know you have a sister who's a lesbian? (*Triumphantly.*) Because we are everywhere!

ALEX slams down phone.

MOTHER: (*Totally outraged.*) How can you talk to the surgeon like that?!? He tried to save your father's life and you insulted him!

ALEX: So I insulted him! He'll live.

They abruptly turn their backs on each other.

Lights Fade to Black.

Scene Five

The lights bounce back on to reveal ALEX in the downstage spotlight. MOTHER puppet is concealed behind her back.

ALEX: (*To the audience.*) She could not get over the fact that I had insulted the surgeon. It was as if I'd burned down his house. Even the next day, when we were back at the hospital…

Lights up on full stage. MOTHER comes out from behind ALEX's back.

MOTHER: What you said! What you said! If you won't apologize, I will.

She tries to get the phone out of ALEX'S pocket.

ALEX: Alright, alright. I'll apologize just to make you feel better.

MOTHER: Good! I don't care whether you're sincere. Just do it.

ALEX phones Dr. Sweetzer. As she does this, MOTHER gets in her face. ALEX turns away. MOTHER moves to get in her face again. This pattern continues throughout ALEX's conversation with the doctor, as MOTHER vigilantly monitors what ALEX says.

ALEX: (*Speaking to the receptionist.*) Hello, this is Alex Bergman. Can I speak to Dr. Sweetzer please? (*Pause, then contrite.*) Hello, doctor. I got a little too excited yesterday. I want to apologize…(*Pause, then very surprised.*) Oh really?… I hope I didn't pressure you. (*Pause, then near tears.*) Yes, it is hard. (*Pause.*) You're right. I'll talk it over with her again and call you right back. (*She ends the phone call.*)

MOTHER: (*Finding the suspense unbearable.*) What? What? What? What?

ALEX and MOTHER sit.

ALEX: (*Quietly.*) Mom. Dr. Sweetzer agrees it's unlikely Daddy will have much quality of life if he does wake up. So if we're really sure we want to…disconnect the ventilator, he'll do it. Are you sure, Ma? (*MOTHER is silent.*) I know I've been pushing you. But if you have doubts, then let's not do it.

Silence.

MOTHER: Daddy wouldn't want to go on like this.

She rests her head on ALEX's shoulder, looking past her at FATHER.

Oh, my poor Morrie.

ALEX: (*Hugging MOTHER.*) Oh, Ma.

A calm and terrible sadness settles on both of them.

MOTHER: Call the surgeon.

ALEX: (*Makes the call. She speaks to the receptionist.*) Dr. Sweetzer, please. (*Pause. To Dr. Sweetzer.*) Hello, Doctor. Let's do it. (*Pause.*) Alright. Thanks for listening to us. (*Hangs up.*)

MOTHER: (*Still on ALEX's shoulder.*) When?

ALEX: Tomorrow morning.

MOTHER: (*Distraught.*) How will I live without Daddy?

ALEX: (*Embracing MOTHER, with a rush of feeling.*) I'll take care of you.

MOTHER: Yes, you'll move down here. I won't charge you rent. You'll save a lot of money.

ALEX: (*Cradling MOTHER in her arms, to the audience.*) She needs me. Could I really live in Los Angeles? (*To herself.*) Why did I say I would take care of her?

MOTHER: You wouldn't believe how tired I am.

ALEX: Try to take a nap, Ma.

MOTHER lies down on one of the chairs.

MOTHER: He only had one cavity...

MOTHER goes to sleep. ALEX watches her with great sympathy, then slowly removes her hand from puppet and picks up her book.

ALEX: What does Buddha have to say about convincing the surgeon to remove your father from a ventilator? (*As she reads aloud, her spirits revive.*) Life is difficult...the lessons we learn from pain, how it helps us to grow spiritually.

> *ALEX sings a very determined and cheery song about bouncing back from adversity. She guides the audience through the lesson.*

Song: LEMONADE

When life hands you lemons, make lemonade.
That is what we're regularly told.
When stuck in the muck as the river floods
That's the time to begin to pan for gold.
When life slaps you down, and flattens you out
And you're stomped by the whole entire parade
Take a breath, pull your socks up
And beat those frigging jocks up
And then go make lemonade!
The word from the Buddha is life is hard
And pain is the price that must be paid…

> *ALEX pauses, and her tone changes.*

But with all respect to Buddha
And I don't mean to be rude-uh
I'm not sure I like lemonade!

When I'm supposed to meditate I fidget.
So what if I remain a moral midget?
The Ten Commandments seem rather over-stated,
Perhaps the holy books are wholly over-rated.

If pain and travail are the way of things
I think I'd prefer another way.
For just as you're getting the lay of things
Bam! You're laid up and there you lay.

> *Tempo slows to doleful.*

Then in comes the chaplain to comfort your soul
And to tell you that for you he has prayed:
"Your condition well may worsen
(*Brightly*) But you're growing as a person!"
(*Furious*) Please don't hand me that charade!
I really loathe lemon…
Though he grows lemon..
I detest lemon…
Even the best lemon…
I hate lemonade!
I tell you I hate lemonade!

Lights Fade to Black.

Scene Six

Lights up. ALEX sits next to MOTHER, who is still sleeping.

MOTHER: (*Talking in her sleep.*) No! No! Help! Help! Save me!

ALEX: Mom! Wake up! You're having a nightmare. Wake up!

MOTHER: (*Awakening.*) What…Oh…I dreamt I was being pursued by an enormous toenail. It was horrible.

ALEX: Well, I guess it's too late now to get a podiatrist before Daddy … before he…

Pause as they look at each other.

MOTHER: Daddy dying is one thing. But with those toenails…That's something else. Oh no! He can't leave with those toenails! The shame, the disgrace. A man like your father…a gentleman…After such a nice, orderly life.

They run to FATHER. MOTHER is distraught.

Oh Morrie, I failed you. I vowed I would stand by you in sickness and in health. And that included keeping the toenails nice. I'll never get over this. (*She is moaning, almost keening.*) The toenails, the toenails…

NURSE appears from behind the station. SHE is wearing a tool belt and carrying a hard hat.

NURSE: Alright, ALRIGHT! I can't bear this anymore. (*To the audience.*) I became a nurse because even as a little girl, I had a great longing to alleviate the suffering I saw in the world. That's my calling, that's my reason for being on this planet. That's. My. Job. (*To MOTHER and ALEX.*) Mrs. Bergman, Alex…I am going to cut Mr. Bergman's toenails!

MOTHER: But it's against the rules.

NURSE: I know.

ALEX: What if you got caught?

NURSE: I have decided to take that risk.

MOTHER: You would do that for us?

NURSE: (*Taking a Superman stance.*) Yes!

MOTHER: Thank you!

ALEX: Thank you!

NURSE: You're very welcome. And now, let's go alleviate a little suffering! Ladies, better move back. This might get messy.

> *She takes the screen from Upstage Right and moves it around the bed, unfolding it to hide the actual toenail surgery from the eyes of FATHER's family and of the audience. NURSE puts on her hard hat. MOTHER and ALEX move off to the side.*

MOTHER: Isn't this exciting?

ALEX: Yes, but how is she going to do it???

> *NURSE brandishes a toy chainsaw and powers it up. The cry of the chainsaw is heard in the land.*

MOTHER & ALEX: (*In awe and admiration.*) Oooooooh!

NURSE: The battle begins!

> *NURSE disappears behind the screen, chainsaw raised. Chainsaw sounds can be heard throughout NURSE's epic battle, along with the grunts and groans of her struggle with FATHER's gnarly nails. MOTHER and ALEX watch from the sidelines, transfixed!*

ALEX: It's finally happening, Mom.

MOTHER: Oh, my poor baby.

ALEX: What a nurse! (*She's falling in love.*)

MOTHER: I hope she's not hurting him.

ALEX: So brave! So strong!

MOTHER: (*She looks down at the floor.*) It's too violent! I can't watch!

ALEX: (*To the audience.*) So decisive! What a woman!

> *Suddenly, the chainsaw's scream falls silent.*

NURSE: (*Triumphantly, from behind the screen.*) Ah-hah!

> *NURSE emerges victorious.*

The battle has been joined. And the left big toenail has been conquered!

> *She raises tongs holding a gynormous toenail high above her*

head. Celebratory trumpets are heard.

Now let's get this bad boy into the biohazard bin.

She exits to throw toenail away. ALEX and MOTHER run behind screen to look at FATHER. Hidden from the audience, ALEX now puts the FATHER puppet, which has been artfully concealed from the audience's eyes in his little bed, on her free hand. FATHER remains concealed under the blanket for the moment.

MOTHER: (*From behind the screen.*) It looks so much better.

ALEX: (*From behind the screen.*) That nurse does amazing work, doesn't she!

NURSE returns without toolbelt or hardhat. She wipes her face with a bandanna. She runs her fingers through her hair. She hikes up her scrubs. She makes the most of her moment.

NURSE: That took a lot out of me. I need a breather before the other ones.

She puts the screen away, revealing MOTHER and ALEX sitting behind FATHER'S bed. NURSE sits down at the Nurse's Station, fanning herself.

MOTHER: (*To NURSE.*) We're just so grateful. Take as long as you need to recover, dear.

ALEX: But not too long! Nine more big ones await! (*She cannot stop staring at NURSE.*)

MOTHER: (*Addressing FATHER.*) Morrie, I bet you feel lighter already.

MOTHER pulls back the blanket to reveal FATHER to the audience for the very first time. He is a giant sock puppet, with huge eyes that are able to open and close. At this moment, FATHER's eyes slowly open. Long pause, while MOTHER takes in what is happening.

Alex! Look at Daddy! His eyes are open!

ALEX: (*Staring in shock at FATHER, then turning to the audience.*) Did the chainsaw pedicure awaken my father from his coma?

MOTHER: (*Ecstatic.*) Morrie darling, hello!

FATHER's eyes stay open, but he does not move or look at

MOTHER directly.

ALEX: Wait a minute, Ma. Just because his eyes are open doesn't mean he's conscious. We don't know if he's actually seeing anything. Move your head back and forth. See if his eyes are following you.

MOTHER does so. FATHER sits up. His eyes follow the motion of her head. MOTHER and ALEX look at each other and nod their heads "Yes."

MOTHER: (*Just so very happy.*) Oh Morrie, it's so good to see you. So good to see you seeing me.

FATHER's eyes start to close. He groans.

He's fading! (*FATHER groans again.*) Alex, do something!

ALEX: Ma, the earrings, the earrings!

MOTHER: I forgot.

She turns her head from side to side, dangling the hated earrings in his face.

Morrie, here they are! Look, look! I'm wearing them!

FATHER: (*Slowly opening his eyes, speaking very feebly.*) Told you so… sweetie…

MOTHER: That's right, Morrie. You told me they're beautiful. Of course, you have no taste.

ALEX: (*Pointing to the basket of lemons next to FATHER's bed.*) Dad, look! The crop is in.

FATHER: (*Weakly, but with great pride.*) Gourmet delight!

MOTHER: Morrie, are you comfortable?

FATHER: (*He considers before speaking.*) Making a living.

MOTHER and ALEX look at each other with wonder and joy.

MOTHER: He made a joke! He's back!

ALEX: (*To the audience.*) It's really Daddy!

MOTHER: Oh, Morrie, you'll come home and see the whole lemon tree…

ALEX: (*Suddenly overwhelmed.*) Oh my god. I almost killed my father. I tried to kill him! And if he hadn't just woken up, I would have succeeded.

MOTHER: So what? You didn't kill him. Who cares if you tried?

ALEX: (*Anguished.*) I knew better than the doctors. I had to take charge. I had to make something happen.

MOTHER: You're too sensitive! Daddy's awake, and he's really Daddy. Nothing else matters.

> *She kisses FATHER.*

ALEX: (*Wallowing in the swamp of guilt.*) What kind of person am I?

NURSE: (*Having fixed FATHER, she must now fix the daughter.*) Alex, You're just a human being who loves her father.

ALEX: (*Sinking in the guilt swamp.*) How can I ever trust myself again?

NURSE: You made a decision, to the best of your ability. You couldn't see into the future. And now your dad's awake. Isn't this life amazing? You gotta love it.

> *FATHER looks down toward his uncovered feet. Toenail horror music swells and lights flicker.*

FATHER: (*Terrified.*) Augggh! What…what are those?

ALEX: Those are your nine remaining uncut toenails, Dad.

MOTHER: Morrie, this wonderful nurse here just cut off one of them. And thank goodness for that. I was worried we might be forced to have a lesbian do it.

NURSE: (*Smiling mischievously.*) Weeelllll…

> *ALEX slowly turns toward the NURSE and they make some very serious eye contact.*

MOTHER: And as soon as the nurse has recovered, she's going to cut all the rest of your toenails! Right, nurse?

NURSE: You can bet your sweet patootie on that!

MOTHER: So don't you worry.

> *NURSE returns to the piano and begins to play.*
>
> *MOTHER sings.*

Song: BETTER LATE THAN NEVER

MOTHER:
We've been waiting around
for the Podiatrist to come.

ALEX:
I've been dialing around
until my dialing finger's numb.

NURSE:
You've been nagging all the nurses;
you've been pestering the docs,

MOTHER:
Cause his feet are really ugly
when he isn't wearing socks!

NURSE: (*Interjects.*) It shocks!

MOTHER:
Oh we thought we'd have to wait forever,
But it's better late, better late than never.

ALEX:
I've known my mom for many a year;
But never thought I would
Hear her tell me loud and clear
That as a daughter I was good.

MOTHER: (*Interjects.*) Not great but good!

ALEX:
She may have thought it from time to time.
But never got stated.
It's tough to wait till you're as old as I'm
To be appreciated!
Yes I thought I'd have to wait forever.
But it's better late…

MOTHER: (*Interjects.*) Better late!

ALEX:
Better late than never!

NURSE:
You've been sitting and wond'ring
how this play was going to end.

FATHER: (*Speaking in rhythm.*) Will I live? Will I die?

NURSE:
And can we hit the bars by ten?

ALEX:
>But when the song is upbeat
>and we sing it right at you

ALEX & NURSE:
>Then it's pretty damn obvious
> the show is nearly through.

MOTHER & NURSE:
>Oh you thought you'd have to wait forever

FATHER: (*Speaking in rhythm.*)
>But it's better late, better late than never.

MOTHER: (*Interjects.*) Morrie, say it again. Are you comfortable?

FATHER: (*Interjects.*) Making a living!

MOTHER: (*Sings.*)
>Yes we thought we'd have to wait forever,
>But it's better late

FATHER: (*Interjects.*) Better late!

MOTHER: (*Sings.*) Better late than never.

(*She invites the audience to sing along.*) Everybody!

MOTHER & NURSE:
>Yes we thought we'd have to wait forever,
>But it's better late than never!

Quick Fade to Black.

End Of Play

2012

BUBBIE & HER BUTCH

FROM
CRONES FOR THE HOLIDAYS

Premiere information

Bubbie & Her Butch was part of *Crones for the Holidays*, a sketch comedy revue that opened on December 15, 2012 at Stage Werx in San Francisco. Bobbi Ausubel helped develop the script.

Director .... Joan Mankin
Producer .... The Crackpot Crones
Set Design .... Vola Ruben
Lighting Design .... Stephanie Johnson
Costme Design .... Val Von
Production Stage Manager ... Pam Higley

CAST

CHRIS .... Terry Baum
FRANNIE .... Carolyn Myers

PRODUCTION HISTORY

The first version of this primal battle between a butch lesbian and a pair of earrings was *Chanukah Butch*, which was commissioned by the City Lights Theater in San Jose, California, in 2000. City Lights wanted a very short, Jewish lesbian-themed play as an opener for their winter holiday show.

Chanukah Butch was a four-character, 10-minute play about a newly-minted lesbian in her 30s bringing her butch girlfriend home to meet her parents. It was later produced at a one-act festival in San Francisco. In December 2010, The Crackpot Crones (Carolyn and me) did a one-night holiday show at The Space in Oakland and attempted to include *Chanukah Butch* by playing the parents with the hand puppets from *Podiatrist*. What a disaster.

When the Crackpot Crones decided to do a full-length holiday revue with a three-week run in 2012, Carolyn demanded a scene for a lesbian couple of our own ages (64 and 61 at the time). She was very conscious that, even as I had aged, I still tended to create characters in their 30s.

So, instead of the new lesbian bringing her butch lover home to meet her parents, this time it's the new lesbian bringing her butch lover to the home of her very conservative adult daughter and grandchildren. The action now takes place when the two women are getting ready to leave for the Chanukah party. This eliminates all family members in the original script, leaving the total focus on Frannie and Chris.

I wanted to deepen the exploration of butchness which I began with *Immediate Family*. Chris defends her butch identify, her "people." For the patriarchy, The Butch is the most terrifying aspect of Woman. All the trappings of femininity are alien to her. She dresses and walks in a masculine way. She is a competitor with men for women's attention and a direct threat to male supremacy. The Butch's soft spot is her love for other women. The play revolves around such a love story. Two women struggle over the wearing of a pair of dangly earrings, and each discovers what she will and will not do for her lover.

CHARACTERS

CHRIS: In her 60s. She's the butch. She has been out as a lesbian for a long time. She has spent quite a lot of that time meeting the parents of her lovers and accommodating herself to them, eventually winning them over. She's had enough of it and cannot now believe she has to accommodate her lover's children.

FRANNIE: In her 60s. She is the Bubbie—that is, Jewish and a grandmother. She is very comfortable with both those identities and not so comfortable with her new one as the lover of another woman. Before meeting Chris, she had lived a traditional heterosexual life—dating boys, marrying a man, divorcing, dating men.

CHRIS and FRANNIE have been together a short time and are madly in love and in lust. They are both professors in the Department of Education at the state university.

TIME

The present. The first night of the Jewish holiday of Chanukah, when families get together to light candles and sing songs and eat potato pancakes, aka latkes.

PLACE

The sitting room in Frannie's house. It is located in a city big enough and progressive enough to have tolerated Chris being out as a lesbian for a few decades.

In the darkness, traditional Chanukah songs (Chanukah oh Chanukah, Dreidel Dreidel) are heard being played by a klezmer band.

SETTING: FRANNIE's sitting room. There is a large free-standing frame of a mirror Downstage Left. Upstage Right is an upholstered armchair and a small table sitting on a Persian rug. On the table is a very small gift-wrapped box with a large bow. All the furniture is antique and elegant and feminine.

AT RISE: FRANNIE and CHRIS are standing next to each other, looking at themselves in the mirror. Since the frame of the mirror is empty, the actors are totally visible to the audience.

Both women are in their 60s. They're getting ready to go to a party. They both enjoy dressing up and have the money to buy nice clothes. FRANNIE is wearing a swirly skirt, a shiny blouse, and low heels. Her hair is red and very curly, creating a halo around her head. CHRIS's brown hair is extremely short and her attire is masculine and fashionable, from shoes on up. CHRIS is putting on a man's tie. She is excited and happy. FRANNIE is excited and anxious. The music fades out.

CHRIS: (*As she finishes tying her tie.*) My very first Chanukah party, with my very first "nize Joosh goilfriend!" (*She says the last three words with an exaggerated Brooklyn accent.*)

FRANNIE: (*Holding up a tube of lipstick to inspect.*) What do you think of this color? It's called "Kiss Me, Silly."

CHRIS: Don't mind if I do!

She pulls FRANNIE to her. FRANNIE surrenders for a moment, and then disentangles herself. She turns back to the mirror, applying the lipstick.

FRANNIE: I don't want to be late!

CHRIS: If only my mother was still alive. Mama would be so happy. She always told me I should find a Jewish man to marry. She said, "Honey, those Jewish men are good to their families."

FRANNIE: Did she say anything about Jewish women?

CHRIS: I don't think she foresaw me falling in love with a Jewish woman.

They are jostling each other for space. They both continue to perfect their outfits as the scene continues.

CHRIS (con't): Babe, could you move over?

FRANNIE: No, I can't! You're not the only one who needs to look good.

CHRIS: You know, I think you need a second mirror in this room, now that you have a girlfriend.

FRANNIE: Oh you do, do you? I never needed it when I had boyfriends.

CHRIS: That's what I'm saying, babe. It's a whole new ballgame, ever since that night at the tavern!

FRANNIE: I haven't had time to get another mirror. It's only been… (*She pauses to figure it out.*) …two months and three days!

CHRIS: My, my. How time flies when you're madly in love.

She straightens the handkerchief peeking out of her jacket pocket, determined to get it just right.

I have got to look spiffy. Not only am I meeting my new girlfriend's family, I'm going to eat lopkes for the first time! It's an historic moment!

FRANNIE: Latkes, with a "t." It's just a potato pancake.

CHRIS: (*Very let down.*) A regular potato pancake? That's all?

FRANNIE: Yup.

FRANNIE runs offstage.

CHRIS: (*To FRANNIE offstage.*) I thought it was some exotic…I imagined a stew of vegetables I'd never heard of, with weird spices like tamarind and zagoot.

FRANNIE: (*From offstage.*) Zagoot??

CHRIS: (*To offstage.*) I just made that up. Really? Just a potato pancake like other potato pancakes?

FRANNIE: (*From offstage.*) Absolutely not. My daughter's latkes are to die for.

She re-enters with a pair of pantyhose and starts to put them on.

FRANNIE (con't): And why not? She learned to make them from me. They will throw all the potato pancakes of your life into deep shade.

CHRIS: (*Staring in amazement.*) Frannie, what are you doing?

FRANNIE: Isn't it obvious? I'm putting on pantyhose.

CHRIS: I've never seen you wear pantyhose!

FRANNIE: I never do. I want to look nice tonight.

CHRIS: Have I told you I love pantyhose?

FRANNIE: No.

She wrestles them up her legs with difficulty.

I hate them. Oh, we're going to be late.

CHRIS: Keep them on when we go to bed. I love taking them off.

FRANNIE: Are all lesbians as weird as you?

CHRIS: Actually, about half the lesbians are weirder than me. But then, half are less weird. I happen to be the exact median of lesbian sexual weirdness.

FRANNIE: Wow! Aren't I lucky to have found the median weird lesbian for my very first woman lover!

CHRIS: You have no idea how lucky you are. I'm going to rip those panty hose to shreds. Yumm…

FRANNIE: (*Examining her skirt.*) Oh no, my skirt's got a spot on it!

CHRIS: You in a skirt! And pantyhose! The hits just keep on coming.

FRANNIE: It's alright. It's just a shadow. I have to look perfect… (*Grandly throwing out her arms.*) …for my family debut as a lesbian!

CHRIS: And mine as your devoted paramour…

She caresses FRANNIE's arm.

FRANNIE: Listen, Chris… (*Pause.*) I haven't mentioned it…My daughter Sarah is very religious.

CHRIS's hands have gotten down to FRANNIE's legs.

CHRIS: Pantyhose, pantyhose…

FRANNIE: Chris, please stop feeling up my legs!

She bats CHRIS's hands away.

FRANNIE (con't): I'm trying to tell you something important!

CHRIS: Uh-oh.

She sits on the ottoman, giving FRANNIE her full attention.

FRANNIE: My daughter is an Orthodox Jew. That's why the Chanukah party is at her house. She keeps kosher, so she can't eat at anyone else's house.

CHRIS: As long as she's a good cook, I don't see the problem.

FRANNIE: Sarah's a very proper person. I don't know what she'll think about about us…about…you.

Silence.

CHRIS: You're worried.

FRANNIE: Yes.

CHRIS: Why didn't you tell me before?

FRANNIE: I'm embarrassed. And I'm embarrassed to be embarrassed.

CHRIS: Sarah does know about us. Right?

FRANNIE: Yes, she knows I'm bringing a woman I'm in love with…

CHRIS: That's good, that's good!

FRANNIE: But…

CHRIS: But what?

FRANNIE: But she doesn't know how butch you are!

Silence.

CHRIS: You're saying I'm too butch.

FRANNIE: Not for me, of course. But for Sarah…Yes. Probably too butch.

CHRIS: So she's not bothered that you're with a woman…

FRANNIE: She is! She is! She's already bothered by that!

CHRIS is very discreetly fondling her legs again. She bats away CHRIS's hands.

FRANNIE: Stop that. Sit down.

CHRIS sits in the armchair. FRANNIE stands next to her, takes her hands to make sure she knows where they are. She speaks with great earnestness.

FRANNIE (con't): I'm Sarah's mother and she has little children and that makes me a grandma, a Bubbie, do you understand? Bubbies are not supposed to have sex at all let alone with another woman let alone with a woman who looks so…so…

CHRIS: (*Looking up adoringly at FRANNIE.*) Wow, I am so in love with you. I'm trying to be insulted, and I just cannot find it anywhere in me. It's pathetic. Being in love is pathetic. Did you know that?

FRANNIE: Oh, you are impossible! Come here. I'll let you feel my pantyhose one more time, and then we are leaving. Deal?

CHRIS: Deal!

She strokes FRANNIE's legs.

Mmmmmm… Are you starting to like it?

FRANNIE: Mmmmm… A little…no, more than a little. Mmmmm… Alright, that's it!

She pulls CHRIS up, away from her legs.

Are you ready?

CHRIS: Yes, Frannie! I'm ready to meet your Orthodox daughter! I'm ready for lopkes with or without zagoot. Don't worry, Frannie. Sarah will love me. I'm cute! Don't you find me cute?

FRANNIE: No, you're much too sexy to be cute. (*Pause.*) In fact… you're so sexy, you deserve a present!

She gets the little present on the table and hands it to CHRIS.

Happy Chanukah!

CHRIS: (*Could it get any better?*) My very first Chanukah present from my nize Joosh goil!

She tears off the wrapping paper.

FRANNIE: (*Extremely nervous.*) I hope you like them.

CHRIS: It better not be a wedding ring, because I want you to understand right now that I'm the one in charge of any proposing that might be necessary in the future…

CHRIS takes two very large and elaborate dangly earrings out of the box and holds them up. She gazes at them in silence.

FRANNIE: (*Tentatively.*) What do you think?

CHRIS: Well…it's certainly something I don't already have! Thank you, baby.

She hugs FRANNIE in a perfunctory way, then slips the earrings into her jacket pocket.

Let's go!

She starts toward the door.

FRANNIE: Aren't you going to put them on?

CHRIS: You want me to wear them *now*?

FRANNIE: Yes!

CHRIS: (*Stunned.*) You really expect me to meet your daughter wearing these earrings?

FRANNIE: Why not? The earrings are beautiful, you're beautiful…

CHRIS: Perhaps. But the two of us beauties together…

She holds the earrings up to her ears.

Rather ridiculous, don't you agree?

FRANNIE: Not at all!

She's not really looking at CHRIS.

CHRIS: (*Still holding the earrings up.*) Frannie, look at me!

FRANNIE: (*Extremely upset, throwing herself in the armchair.*) I'm sorry, I'm just too old to become a lesbian. People don't want me to change. Sarah, she's so…so straight, in every way! I want her to like you. I want you to like Sarah. I want everybody to love everybody… Oh, I wish you were at least Jewish…

CHRIS: Would Sarah like me better if I was Jewish?

FRANNIE: (*Calming down.*) It would be absolutely huge if you were Jewish.

CHRIS: Okay! I'll convert! What the hell!

FRANNIE: (*Insulted.*) You can't convert just like that.

CHRIS: (*Placating FRANNIE.*) I don't mean "what the hell." I mean, I mean… (*Inventing.*) I always wanted to be Jewish, felt I really was Jewish, felt this tremendous connection…

FRANNIE: You would be willing to convert to Judaism in order to avoid wearing the earrings?

CHRIS holds up the offending jewels for scrutiny.

CHRIS: These earrings? Absolutely.

FRANNIE: (*Warning her.*) I'm telling you, it's a lot of work. It takes years.

CHRIS: Really? That's so different from the Christians! You confess that you're a horrible sinner, they throw a little water on you, and presto change-o— you're one of them!

FRANNIE: Months of classes with the rabbi. And at the end you take a ritual bath. Plus it really helps if you believe in God.

CHRIS: (*Sitting on the arm of the armchair.*) I had no idea. Let me think about this.

FRANNIE: Darling, you're perfectly free to think about converting to Judaism at any time.

> *She jumps up, grabs the earrings from CHRIS's pocket.*

But right now we have to leave for Sarah's Chanukah party.

> *She dangles the earrings before CHRIS's face. CHRIS stares at them fixedly.*

(*In a seductive sing-song.*) I think these would look beautiful on you.

CHRIS: Okay. I've decided. I'm going to convert. Let's go.

> *She grabs FRANNIE's arm to exit, but FRANNIE doesn't move.*

FRANNIE: Why are you doing this?

CHRIS: No, really. I'm only teaching half-time now. I could easily spend 10 hours a week converting. That would be enough, don't you think?

FRANNIE: You are mocking my religion!

CHRIS: Your religion! I didn't know you really believed!

FRANNIE: Okay, it's not really my religion, but it is my daughter's religion, and it is my ethnic background, my people, and you are mocking them!

CHRIS: And you are mocking *my* people!

FRANNIE: *Your* people! And what people would that be?

CHRIS: The Butch People! We're a people too!

FRANNIE: Come on.

CHRIS: We've been oppressed like the Jews, we hang out together like the Jews. We have our rituals, our beliefs just like the Jews.

FRANNIE: (*Mocking.*) Really? What beliefs do the Butch People have?

CHRIS: (*Thinking hard.*) Ummmmm… That we have to initiate the first kiss.

FRANNIE: That's not how I remember it.

CHRIS: You violated my beliefs, right from the start!

FRANNIE: You seemed to handle it very well.

CHRIS: I was in shock! I thought you were straight.

FRANNIE: I was—until I saw you.

CHRIS: There we were in the tavern, after the committee meeting…

FRANNIE: (*Staunchly, fist in the air.*) The Committee to Consider Restoration of the Women's Studies Program!

CHRIS: (*Lovingly.*) Your brilliant idea.

FRANNIE: (*Fiercely.*) Yes!

CHRIS: Did you ever find out why all those people agreed to be on the committee and then decided they didn't really want to restore the Women's Studies program?

FRANNIE: Yes I did, just yesterday! One of them admitted that the Dean had called them all in, and told them it was a bad career move.

CHRIS: What cowards!

FRANNIE: Just a momentary setback, sweetheart. Nobody stops Frannie Kaufman that easily! Anyhow, the culmination of that evening was ending up alone in a bar with you—something I'd been trying to manage for over a year! I can usually make things happen much more quickly.

CHRIS: You jumped my bones! If only you had confessed to me in a stumbling, awkward, adorable way, that you were attracted to me. That would have given me the opportunity to seduce you properly, something my people do very well.

FRANNIE: Sorry. I couldn't take any chances. If I couldn't get my women's studies that night, I was damn well going to get you.

CHRIS: And another thing about my people. We have a strict prohibition against wearing any kind of sparkly dangly jewelry.

FRANNIE: Is that so?

CHRIS: Yes, that is so.

FRANNIE: Is it really that big a deal?

Silence.

CHRIS: (*Patiently.*) You're asking me to deny who I am, to pretend. You're asking me to lie.

FRANNIE: (*With disbelief.*) Wearing these would be lying?

CHRIS: (*A little less patiently.*) I might as well just go back into the closet and pretend I'm your quote friend unquote.

FRANNIE: But I told you, Sarah already knows.

CHRIS: (*This is bringing up a lot of pain and CHRIS is getting angry.*) I spent a lot of my life being a quote friend unquote at my lover's family gatherings. I don't do that anymore.

FRANNIE: I'm not asking you to do that!

CHRIS: (*Very pissed off.*) You're right. You're asking me to pretend I'm some nice, feminine, unthreatening, well-mannered lesbian lady, when I'm an in-your-face proud butch dyke! I'm no lady and I don't wear lady earrings!

She throws the earrings on the table.

And if I did, you wouldn't have kissed me in the tavern in the first place!

FRANNIE: Look, I've taken this huge leap. I fell in love with you! I've come out as a lesbian! At great personal risk, I told my Orthodox daughter about you. I was worried she would refuse to invite you to the Chanukah party. I was worried she would refuse to invite *me*. But we're both invited! Isn't that wonderful? Isn't that gracious and open-minded of Sarah?

CHRIS: (*Exploding.*) Oh, yes. Amazing! I can't wait to get down on my knees to thank her for allowing me in her house, just as if I were a normal human being! Sarah's a fucking saint!

Silence.

FRANNIE: Can't you give just a little this one time and wear the damn earrings?

CHRIS checks the time on her wristwatch.

Why are you looking at your watch?

CHRIS: (*Cool.*) I was just wondering if there's still time for me to get into that poker game at JD's house. I've heard everyone there is very gracious and open-minded.

FRANNIE: (*Warning.*) Don't you dare leave.

CHRIS: (*Cold.*) Look, Frannie, maybe you're not ready to introduce me to your family. Then go by yourself. I have no problem with that.

FRANNIE: (*Despairing.*) Oh no! We're having our first fight!

CHRIS: (*Frozen, distant.*) I'm not mad.

FRANNIE: You're a million miles away.

CHRIS: Listen, if the full frontal Me is too much for your Chanukah party, so be it.

Silence.

FRANNIE: (*Desperate.*) I'll wear the pantyhose in bed tonight. I'll wear them every night for…for a week…for a month!

CHRIS: Really?

She sits in the armchair.

Hmmmm… (*She is very interested.*) That's a lot of pantyhose, you know, because I always destroy them.

FRANNIE: Damn the expense! I'll wear fishnet stockings, would you like that?

She puts one leg up on the ottoman, pulls her skirt up and runs her hands up and down her own legs in the most disconcerting way imaginable.

FRANNIE (con't): How about those old-fashioned ones with the seam down the back, hmmmm? Ooh, those are nice… Maybe real silk stockings…with a garter belt…

CHRIS: (*What a turn-off!*) I'm not into garter belts.

FRANNIE: Okay, no garter belt. How about those really, really high-heeled shoes? I bet you like those, don't you?

CHRIS, speechless, nods "yes." FRANNIE sits in CHRIS's lap.

The kind with the thin little straps?

CHRIS: So you think I'd sell my butchness for a mess of pantyhose?

FRANNIE: I'm trying to find out. So is it a deal?

CHRIS: What am I going to do with you?

FRANNIE: You're going to go to the Chanukah party wearing these.

She grabs the earrings from the table and holds them up. Silence.

CHRIS: I...I just can't.

FRANNIE: Really?

CHRIS: Really.

Silence.

FRANNIE: Okay. Fine.

She leaps out of CHRIS's lap, disgusted.

Go to your stupid card game at JD's.

She goes to get her coat. CHRIS didn't expect this.

I'm already late. Sarah doesn't like that. Actually, nobody in my family likes that. As a matter of fact, Jews as a people are always on time.

CHRIS: (*Conciliatory.*) I didn't know that.

FRANNIE: There are a lot of things you don't know about Jews. And you're not going to find anything out tonight, because...

Her coat on, she turns to CHRIS, taunting her.

FRANNIE (con't): You're not coming to the party!

CHRIS: (*Trying to find an opening.*) I was looking forward to the lopkes.

FRANNIE: (*Fed up, briskly.*) Too bad. Too bad. Maybe JD will serve lopkes at the poker game. Come on, move, move! I've got to leave.

She hands CHRIS her coat. CHRIS does not move.

CHRIS: You'd really wear them for a month?

FRANNIE: What are you talking about?

CHRIS: The pantyhose!

FRANNIE: Oh! For god's sake. (*Pause. Really thinking about this.*) Yes. I guess so. I said I would. (*Pause.*) And I'll make that special stew with zagoot for you.

CHRIS: Zagoot stew and a month of pantyhose. Hmmmm…

> *She holds out her hand for the earrings. FRANNIE gives them to her. CHRIS puts them on, looking in the mirror. She feels abashed, weak—like Samson after his haircut. FRANNIE wraps her arms around CHRIS, from the back, without seeing her face.*

FRANNIE: Oh, Chris, sweetie, thank you. You have no idea how much this means to me.

CHRIS: (*Still looking in the mirror.*) How do I look? Do I look okay?

FRANNIE: (*Glancing at CHRIS.*) Yes, of course. You look beautiful.

CHRIS: (*Scrutinizing herself in the mirror, trying to convince herself.*) This isn't so bad. Maybe I'll grow to like it. Maybe I'll try a little lipstick, some eye shadow. You just wait.

FRANNIE: (*Worried.*) You don't really mean that, do you?

CHRIS: No.

> *She starts to put her coat on and moves slowly to the exit.*

FRANNIE: (*Finally really looking at CHRIS.*) I don't like it.

CHRIS: What don't you like?

FRANNIE: I don't know what I was thinking. You do look ridiculous!

CHRIS: What the hell…?

FRANNIE: You're a butch. I love you as a butch. I love your people. I want your people to meet my people tonight at Sarah's Chanukah party. Let me have those earrings.

> *She takes them off CHRIS and throws them on the floor.*

CHRIS: You're a piece of work, do you know that?

FRANNIE: Let's go get us some lopkes!

> *She starts to exit. CHRIS follows her.*

CHRIS: And when we come home…Pantyhose!

FRANNIE: We'll see.

> *CHRIS stops.*

CHRIS: "We'll see"?!? "We'll see"!!! I was willing to wear those damned earrings…

FRANNIE: (*Brightly.*) Yes, but now you don't have to.

CHRIS: That's not the point. A deal's a deal.

FRANNIE: How about a week?

CHRIS: I'm entitled to a month.

FRANNIE: (*Really protesting.*) But you only wore them for a minute!

CHRIS: That was one of the worst minutes of my life! That was real suffering.

FRANNIE: We'll negotiate later tonight.

She starts to exit again, with CHRIS following.

CHRIS: There's nothing to negotiate!

FRANNIE: (*Scoffing.*) One month of pantyhose for one minute of earrings?

CHRIS: (*As they exit.*) That's what I'm talking about!

They continue to argue (" You're not being gracious and open-minded." "No, you're not being..." etc.) as the Chanukah music heard in the beginning of the scene is heard again. It gets louder, as the lights fade to black. Then the music fades away.

End Of Play

2013

BRIDE OF LESBOSTEIN

DEDICATED TO THE MEMORY OF
JOAN MANKIN, THE FIRST BRIDE

Premiere Information

BRIDE OF LESBOSTEIN was written by Terry Baum and Carolyn Myers. It was originally produced by The Crackpot Crones at The Garage, in San Francisco. It opened October 30, 2013, with the following cast and crew.

Production Stage Manager .... Pam Higley
Directing Consultant .... Joan Mankin
Set Design .... Vola Ruben & Mari Kaestle
Costume Design .... Val Von
Lighting Design .... Stephanie Johnson
Sound Design .... Pam Higley
Hair and Make-up .... LauRose Felicity

Lyrics for "The Perfect Bride," based on "The Modern Major General's Song" by Gilbert and Sullivan, written by David Hyman.

CAST

DR. GERTRUDE LESBOSTEIN .... Terry Baum

IGORINA .... Carolyn Myers

THE HIPSTER, THE WEREWOLF, THE BRIDE ... Joan Mankin

PRODUCTION HISTORY

Long ago in a city far away (Amsterdam), my friend Mary Wings and I sat drinking our morning coffee in her flat. Mary wrote murder mysteries and I wrote plays. We were amusing ourselves by thinking up funny titles for future plays and novels we might write. She came up with the title "Bride of Lesbostein." We laughed heartily and then went on about our day. Meanwhile, the tantalizing title was burrowing its way into my brain. I was absolutely certain that I would one day write the play that went with that title. But then, I'm absolutely certain I'll write a lot of plays that I never get around to.

Twenty-five years went by. Mary and I both moved back to San Francisco. She wrote more mysteries, I more plays. Carolyn and I became The Crackpot Crones. Then, in 2011, the Crones began doing plays about the holidays. The idea for *Lesbostein* came out of its burrow to become a play for Halloween. I did all the writing during sessions of our Friday morning writers group. So I'm deeply grateful for the encouragement of Carolyn, Calla and LauRose Felicity, and Bobbi

Ausubel. In preparing *Lesbostein* for publication, Carolyn added so much that we are rightly co-authors.

This is the only silly play I've written. Although my writing has usually been funny, I think perhaps I have scorned "silly." Why did I feel free to be silly with *Lesbostein*? Maybe it was just the spirit of Halloween, the night of inspired silliness for all of us. And maybe it's that aging phenomenon where you just don't give a damn what anybody thinks about you anymore— even what you think about yourself!

Lesbostein was only performed two times, and I remain dissatisfied with my own performance. I strayed into complicated emotional angst, which is always a temptation for actors. I started unconsciously angling for the audience's sympathy. I had truly lost my way as an actress. As a result, the audience actually felt compassion for this uncontrolled egomaniac! Didn't they realize she deserved her comeuppance? WHY WERE THEY SIGHING WITH PITY WHEN THEY SHOULD BE LAUGHING?!? I can't wait to get back into that lab coat and rainbow fright wig to do it right—accompanied by Carolyn's Igorina, of course.

Just in case anyone is wondering, I want to make it very clear that there is absolutely no resemblance between the character of Dr. Lesbostein and myself. I certainly have not been in love 34 times. Thirty-two, tops!

CHARACTERS

DR. GERTRUDE LESBOSTEIN: A classic mad scientist. She is old enough to have had 34 lovers, to have established herself as a mad scientist, and to have seen better days. She cuts an imposing, demanding, eccentric and completely self-obsessed figure.

IGORINA: Lesbostein's assistant. She is more goofball than creep. Like all Igors before her, she is utterly, slavishly, and worshipfully dedicated to her brilliant Mistress.

THE HIPSTER: A representative of the techie invaders of San Francisco in the 2010s.

THE WEREWOLF: A classic but clearly female Werewolf. She is extremely athletic and aggressive.

THE BRIDE: Brought to life during the play. Although dazed and confused at first, she is a quick learner, especially about getting what she desires.

The Hipster, Werewolf and The Bride can all be played by one actor.

TIME
Halloween, 2015, early evening.

PLACE
Dr. Lesbostein's laboratory, in a garage in the Mission District, San Francisco.

SETTING: *The action takes place entirely within the garage laboratory of DR. GERTRUDE LESBOSTEIN. There is a messy Do-It-Yourself quality to the lab, an air of genius and mania. The equipment and supplies are just as likely to have been knocked together from items found in a garage as they are to have been ordered from a scientific supply company.*

Upstage is dominated by a complicated and completely incomprehensible machine, with pipes and hoses, receptors, and exhausts. At the top of the machine, perched like a basketball hoop, is a huge funnel.

Stage Left of the machine is an electrical control panel, with knobs, a Geiger counter, and THE BIG LEVER. Stage Right of the machine, tacked to the wall, is a large poster of a naked woman, legs and arms akimbo, copied from Leonardo da Vinci's "Vitruvian Man." This is the Vitruvian Lesbian.

Center Stage is a rolling lab table, over-full of scientific equipment: test tubes, beakers, distilling columns, retorts bubbling with sinister chemicals, condensers, pipettes, poorly adjusted Bunsen burners, and those whatchamacallits that hook all of those things together.

Downstage Right is IGORINA's chintz-covered stool. A plastic pumpkin-head bucket with handle sits on the stool, filled with Halloween candy to distribute to trick-or-treaters.

Stage Left is a curtained doorway, leading to a hidden room. The light behind the curtain glows and pulses.

Stage Right is a window and a door to the outside.

AT RISE: *A classic haunted house soundtrack is heard, underscored by organ fugues. An ominous sunset orange shows through the window and there are flashes of lightning.*

The lights rise on the laboratory. DR. GERTRUDE LESBOSTEIN stands at her laboratory table, intently moving large pills from different jars into an oversize pill-sorter. She wears a stained lab coat and big purple-framed glasses. Her hair stands up in a spiked rainbow-hued Mohawk.

The music changes into a well-known song about female empowerment, its disco style morphing into weird distortions in rhythm and tempo. LESBOSTEIN sings along and dances awkwardly. She lets loose her mad scientist laugh, then checks her watch, and looks toward the door with irritation.

LESBOSTEIN: Igorina, that good-for-nothing, is late again. What a worthless assistant. Oh well, time to take my vitamins. I need all the strength I can get to forge ahead with my Top Secret Experiment. Bottom's up!

> *She is about to throw an enormous handful of pills into her mouth when IGORINA charges in.*

IGORINA: Dr. Lesbostein! Dr. Lesbostein!

LESBOSTEIN: What? What?

IGORINA: I've got them, I've got them!

> *IGORINA is moving fast. LESBOSTEIN spins around. They collide. The vitamins fly all over.*

LESBOSTEIN: Igorina, I was in the final steps of performing the very delicate procedure of taking the last of my vitamins. Now, your ill-timed interruption has screwed the whole thing up.

> *IGORINA completely forgets the news she had been so excited to share. She accepts all the blame for the collision.*

IGORINA: Oh dear!

> *She runs around the lab, picking up the huge pills, loudly counting down the seconds it takes her.*

5...4...3...2...1.

> *She stops abruptly when she reaches "1".*

LESBOSTEIN: There are more over here.

IGORINA: Oh no, Mistress. You can't take those.

LESBOSTEIN: Why not?

IGORINA: It's science, Mistress. The Five-Second rule. The little germs stand in wait, they count to five, then they jump on whatever has been dropped on the floor, contaminating it.

LESBOSTEIN: The five-second rule is a myth! It certainly does not count for laboratories kept up to pure scientific standards. Now give me the vitamins in your hand.

IGORINA does so.

And pick up the rest of them.

LESBOSTEIN downs the vitamins with the vividly colored liquid of whatever beaker is at hand.

You know very well that I, Dr. Gertrude Lesbostein, need my vitamins so that I can keep laboring over my Top Secret Project, The Beloved Bride , as I have done for years…

IGORINA: Years and years!

She continues to pick up vitamins, but hides them in her pocket.

LESBOSTEIN: …In a heroic attempt to create the perfect woman, so that finally, finally there will exist a woman so beautiful, so intelligent, so loving, so healthy, so athletic, so witty, such a fabulous cook, so damn GOOD that she *deserves to be my Beloved Bride!*

IGORINA stands, reverent, the task of picking up the vitamins permanently forgotten.

IGORINA: The Bride of Lesbostein!

LESBOSTEIN: But, in order to create the Beloved Bride, I needed to capture the finest qualities of all my 34 ex-girlfriends, each of whom was perfect in some way. In the years before I hired you, I worked night and day to invent a machine that could do the impossible: convert 34 different DNAs into one living breathing woman.

She indicates the huge machine.

Here it is, the fruit of my genius—a brilliant upgrade of the three dimensional printer—the Cerebellapoodle!

LESBOSTEIN hugs the Cerebellapoodle as much as it is possible to embrace a cumbersome machine.

LESBOSTEIN (con't): Seven years ago, I finally finished construction of the Cerebellapoodle, and I was ready to begin the final phase of this magnificent project—the creation of my Bride.

IGORINA: So, seven years ago, you put up an ad at Rainbow Grocery, Mistress. I'll never forget the day I walked in, thinking only that I would walk out with the ingredients for a spirulina smoothie. But I happened to glance at the bulletin board and saw your ad: "Assistant Wanted to Sneak Around San Francisco and Collect DNA Samples from 34 Lesbians Without their Knowledge. No experience necessary. Slavish adoration required." And my life changed forever.

LESBOSTEIN: (*Deeply puzzled.*) Strangely, you were the only one to answer my ad.

IGORINA: I never understood why no one except me tore off the little piece of paper with the phone number, Mistress.

> *She produces the little slip of paper from her bosom, kisses it, folds it up and replaces it.*

LESBOSTEIN: (*Tragically.*) I'm a misunderstood genius, a woman born before my time.

IGORINA: You are! You are! And ever since that day I have collected the DNA samples according to your instructions. No lesbian has been harmed in the process. I have performed your bidding, Mistress.

LESBOSTEIN: Yes, in your own bungling, incompetent way, you have. But you have failed to bring me a DNA sample from Number 13, the fingernail sample!

> *DR. LESBOSTEIN strides to the wall and points to the fingernails on the poster of "Vitruvian Lesbian." IGORINA watches, stricken and apologetic.*

And in order to extract from my poor overworked brain an alternative to having the actual fingernail clippings of number 13, which you failed time and time again to get, I need my vitamins!

IGORINA: But Mistress, I've got fingernail clippings from Number 13 right here!

> *She extends her arm, palm up, fist clenched around the vial she is holding.*

LESBOSTEIN: Fingernail clippings from Number 13?

IGORINA: Ha ha ha ha! Yes, mistress! Here they are, the precious fingernail clippings.

> *She opens her hand to reveal a large stoppered test tube, labeled, "Number 13, Fingernails."*

LESBOSTEIN: Ah-ha! Finally!

> *She grabs the stoppered test tube.*

The very last ingredient I need to create the Beloved Bride!

She unstoppers the test tube and, using a pickle picker, plucks out a fingernail.

My goal is so close, I can taste it.

She nibbles on a fingernail.

IGORINA: Mistress, stop biting your fingernails! Naughty naughty!

LESBOSTEIN: I'm not biting MINE, Igorina. I'm biting Number 13's!

She laughs maniacally.

IGORINA: The fingernails of Lena! And there you have it Mistress…

She strides to the poster to display it.

…all 34 samples of lesbian girlfriend DNA, collected at last.

LESBOSTEIN: Yes, I have done it!!! It is complete!!! We can bring my Bride to Life!

LESBOSTEIN joins IGORINA at the Vitruvian Lesbian Poster. The figure of the Vitruvian Lesbian is surrounded by 34 women's names. There is a line drawn from each name to a different part of the body. They sing a song of celebration, modeled on "I Am the Very Model of a Modern Major-General" from Gilbert and Sullivan's comic opera "The Pirates of Penzance." DR. LESBOSTEIN indicates each name as they sing it, with a pointer.

Song: THE PERFECT BRIDE

LESBOSTEIN:
The perfect bride will have the disposition of Lucretia
The tiny feet of Lizzie and the bosom of Laetitia

IGORINA:
The heart of Lanny, Lily's eyes, and Leah's practicality
The mind of Luna, nose of Lee, and Laura's punctuality

LESBOSTEIN:
She'd smell a bit like Lucy and have Laurie's love of trivia

IGORINA:
Lucille's hair, Leilani's voice, the ruthlessness of Livia

LESBOSTEIN:
Linetta's sense of humor and the laughter of Listeria

And it wouldn't hurt if she could have Leonora's sweet interior

IGORINA:
It wouldn't hurt if she could have Leonora's sweet interior

LESBOSTEIN:
It wouldn't hurt if she could have Leonora's sweet interior

TOGETHER:
It wouldn't hurt if she could have Leonora's spicy sweet interior

Breaking from the song, LESBOSTEIN speaks.

LESBOSTEIN: (*Speaking.*) Leonora really does have superb genitals.

IGORINA: (*Speaking.*) Ah, the gentles, the gentles! I remember getting the DNA swab for that. Very delicate job, Mistress.

LESBOSTEIN: (*Speaking.*) I have to admit, Igorina, despite your spectacular inadequacy, sometimes you carry out an errand perfectly.

IGORINA: Oh, Mistress, thank you!

Song resumes.

LESBOSTEIN:
She'll have the charm of Letty and have Lulubella's wittiness
And certainly she'll have to have the lovely Lacy's prettiness

IGORINA:
If she has all these qualities and wears a wedding dress so fine

LESBOSTEIN:
Then possibly she will deserve to be The Bride of Lesbostein.

TOGETHER: THE BRIDE OF LESBOSTEIN!

They dance a jig of triumph. LESBOSTEIN struts a la Mick Jagger, while IGORINA applauds adoringly. There is a final "Oh yeah" with jazz hands.

End of song.

LESBOSTEIN: Now I will prepare the fingernail clippings, so that the Cerebellapoodle can extract the DNA from them. And that will give me the final piece of this enormous jigsaw puzzle. Drum roll, please!

IGORINA turns over two "hazardous waste" buckets, sits on one and drums on the other. LESBOSTEIN returns to the lab table and puts the clippings into a large jar filled with purple baking

soda. When she adds white vinegar, the whole thing bubbles up.

IGORINA: It wasn't easy to get the fingernail clippings, oh no. It was very very late, past midnight. I had to open the window ever so gently. Then I had to climb in ever so quietly. There they were, fast asleep in bed.

LESBOSTEIN stops gazing at the fingernails, turns to IGORINA.

LESBOSTEIN: She wasn't alone?

IGORINA: No, Mistress.

LESBOSTEIN: Who was with her?

IGORINA: In fact, there were two who were with her!

LESBOSTEIN: Two! Oh, that slut…oh, my heart.

IGORINA: Yes, three altogether.

LESBOSTEIN: Go ahead. Stab me again, Igorina.

IGORINA: Very beautiful, all three, entwined. Lena in the middle.

LESBOSTEIN: In the middle??? Worse and worse. How did you recognize her?

IGORINA: By your description, Mistress. You told me she used far too much mousse in her hair.

LESBOSTEIN: Her tragic flaw.

IGORINA stands and begins to re-enact her story.

IGORINA: So I ever so cautiously and gently pried her fingers away from the other one…

LESBOSTEIN: And you didn't forget the nail clippers this time.

Silence.

I said you didn't…

Silence.

IGORINA: I'm sorry, Mistress, I'm sorry! I'll never make that mistake again! I promise.

She resumes acting out her story.

So I very quietly sneaked back to the window. I very carefully lowered myself to the ground, then I ran very quickly to the 24 hour Walgreens…

LESBOSTEIN: Shut up, shut up, you blockhead! I send you to get nail clippings, and you don't bring the clippers! I send you to get a swab of saliva from a cheek and you forget the Petri dish to put it in! I send you to get a lock of hair and you somehow neglect to bring scissors with you...

IGORINA: Sometimes I forget...

LESBOSTEIN: (*At the top of her lungs.*) MAKE A LIST!

IGORINA: (*A great revelation.*) A list! Yes, Mistress, yes! Of course! A list!

> *She gets a pipette and filter paper from table, stabs her finger and, using the pipette as a pen, writes in blood.*

My list.

> *She considers carefully, then writes.*

Number One: Make list...

LESBOSTEIN: I'm paying you by the hour! Do you have any idea what the minimum wage is in San Francisco?

IGORINA: You've told me many times, Mistress.

LESBOSTEIN: Ten fifty-five an hour.

IGORINA: Actually, Mistress, minimum wage in San Francisco is now fourteen—

LESBOSTEIN: Ten dollars and fifty-five cents! And I have to pay you to sneak in the window not once but twice! Not to mention what I pay for health insurance. I can't afford it. That's it. I've had it. I've got to get a new assistant. I'm putting an ad on CraigsList right now. No more Rainbow Bulletin board for me! I'm going to find somebody competent!

> *LESBOSTEIN produces her computer, which is, of course, made up of many DIY PC parts, some of which drag along the ground.*

IGORINA: No, Mistress, no! Anything but that!

> *LESBOSTEIN sits on one overturned "hazardous waste" bucket and puts her computer on the other.*

LESBOSTEIN: Or maybe I should put it on my LinkedIn profile...

IGORINA: Mistress, I would die if you forced me to leave you!

LESBOSTEIN: Let me check my Facebook...Oh, look! Draculetta has posted a photo of the latest neck she's bitten! Maybe I should post one of the fingernail clippings...

IGORINA: Mistress, Mistress, stop it!

She slaps LESBOSTEIN and grabs the computer.

You're being lured by the evil spirit of the social media again!

IGORINA puts computer away.

LESBOSTEIN: (*Coming to her senses.*) Thank you, Igorina. Thank you.

Doorbell rings.

IGORINA: Oh goody!

LESBOSTEIN: Don't answer that!

IGORINA: Oh but I must, Mistress! It's Halloween! The favorite holiday of all little kiddies!

She rushes to get her plastic pumpkin full of treats.

LESBOSTEIN: A curse upon your love of little kiddies!

IGORINA opens the door to reveal the HIPSTER. He wears the standard hipster uniform of the times—tight jeans, close-fitted plaid shirt, square-framed glasses, and a narrow-brimmed fedora.

IGORINA: Happy Halloween! How cute! Look, Dr. Lesbostein, a Hipster costume! Like all the new neighbors wear.

HIPSTER: Oh, r-i-i-i-ght! I fucking love Halloween and all that shit. What ya got?

LESBOSTEIN: That's no little kiddie!

IGORINA: It's a sweet little kiddie. And here's your Reese's peanut butter cup.

HIPSTER: A real Reese's peanut butter cup still in the package?

IGORINA: Yes!

HIPSTER: Hey, I'm going to take a selfie with my Reese's peanut butter cup and post it on Instagram.

He does so.

LESBOSTEIN: No photos! No photos of the Cerebellapoodle!

She jumps up and throws herself spread-eagled against the Cerebellapoodle, to try to hide it from the HIPSTER's view.

HIPSTER: Hey, man, actually I stopped by to take a look around— see, I've rented a closet in the apartment upstairs for $2500 a month, and it's cool, right? But it's kind of tight in there with my customized bike and my electric swagboard—I thought maybe I could rent this garage—

LESBOSTEIN: Shut the door on him, Igorina, I'm begging you!

HIPSTER: Just trying to be neighborly.

IGORINA: Good night, little kiddie. Happy Halloween.

> *IGORINA closes the door. LESBOSTEIN leans on the lab table, greatly weakened.*

LESBOSTEIN: My vitamins, I need my vitamins…

IGORINA: Maybe this will help, Mistress.

> *IGORINA sympathetically unwraps a peanut butter cup and hands it to her boss. LESBOSTEIN takes a bite and is magically restored to her former greatness by just one bite of the power of the candy.*

LESBOSTEIN: Ah, that's better.

> *She looks at the candy critically.*

LESBOSTEIN (con't): You know, I've talked to all the other mad scientists, and their assistants hand out jelly beans. One bean per person. But *you*—Reese's Peanut Butter Cups!

> *She disdainfully puts the rest of the candy on the lab table.*

IGORINA: (*Defensively.*) I buy them out of my own salary!

LESBOSTEIN: Now I can't remember what I was doing before the doorbell rang!

IGORINA: You were about to extract the DNA from the fingernail clippings of Lena so the Cerebellapoodle could replicate it to recreate her hands, to add to The Beloved Bride you are reproducing under the sheet!

LESBOSTEIN: Those hands, those hands. Have you ever been made love to by a conga drummer?

IGORINA: Never, Mistress.

LESBOSTEIN: It's indescribable, Igorina. The sensation of those fingers drumming everywhere… and I mean *everywhere*!

IGORINA: (*Overcome with embarrassment.*) Mistress, please! I'm blushing.

LESBOSTEIN: Oh, Igorina, don't act the innocent with me! You've played around.

IGORINA: Never, Mistress, never. I have never loved anyone but you.

LESBOSTEIN: I don't believe it. A good-looking butch like you.

IGORINA: (*Eagerly.*) Do you find me attractive, Mistress?

LESBOSTEIN: How many times do I have to tell you you're not my type?!?

IGORINA: A thousand! A million! A trillion! I'm in love with you, Mistress!

LESBOSTEIN: (*Mocking.*) In love! In love! And how many times have you been in love?

IGORINA: You know the answer to that, my darling Mistress.

LESBOSTEIN: Do you know how many times I've been in love?

IGORINA: Thirty-four times, Mistress.

LESBOSTEIN: And you've only been in love once! I scoff at your puny once! Ha ha!

IGORINA: Yes, thank you, Mistress.

LESBOSTEIN: Thirty-four times. Thirty-four women who deceived me into believing that they and only they possessed the secret to my happiness. Yes, Igorina, I have always been the victim of lies, misrepresentations, manipulations.

IGORINA: Not to put too fine a point on it, but perhaps you should have noticed something wrong when Number 29 punched you in the nose.

LESBOSTEIN: How was I to know she did that whenever anyone licked her ear? In all other ways, she was perfection itself! I begged her to get help to reverse this appalling condition of otolingual phobia. But she refused! She said I should just stop licking her ear!

IGORINA: Perhaps you could have refrained, Mistress, her being so perfect and all that.

LESBOSTEIN: How could I, Igorina, when Number 29's earwax was so aromatic, so fragrant! I couldn't imagine life without it!

IGORINA: And you don't have to, Mistress, since I retrieved a blob of earwax with a Q-tip last New Year's Eve, after slipping a mickey into her drink to knock her unconscious.

> *She finds the large earwax-covered Q-tip specimen in a test tube on the lab table and offers it to LESBOSTEIN to smell. LESBOSTEIN swoons in ecstasy.*

LESBOSTEIN: I, Dr. Gertrude Lesbostein, can never settle for anything less than perfection, even when it comes to earwax. After all, it's only what I deserve.

IGORINA: No doubt, Mistress, no doubt.

LESBOSTEIN: And then there was the one that got away.

IGORINA: Ah yes, Number 23.

LESBOSTEIN: Number 23—Lillian! (*With exagerrated innocence.*) Where's my phone?

> *She starts looking for it.*

I'm going to give Lillian a call.

> *IGORINA grabs the phone from the lab table when LESBOSTEIN isnt looking. Its case has been burned by acid, dyed by chemicals, and swollen by dampness. She hides it behind her back.*

IGORINA: I don't think that's a good idea, Mistress.

> *LESBOSTEIN feels in all her pockets.*

LESBOSTEIN: My phone, my phone. She must have gotten that fruitcake by now.

IGORINA: (*Very nervously.*) Not necessarily.

> *LESBOSTEIN acts out the next paragraph as she imagines it to have occurred.*

LESBOSTEIN: A mysterious package arrives. Lillian tears off the wrapping to discover— a fruitcake! Now, everyone knows that Lillian despises fruitcake. However, her boyfriend—who she left me for—is a renowned fruitcake connoisseur, and can't resist sampling a morsel. Mmm, the flavors explode in his mouth. The best fruitcake he's ever had in his life! He grabs a hunk and gobbles it down, then another and another, stuffing himself until he falls down dead.

> *LESBOSTEIN enacts a horrifying choking death.*

Yes, it's the classic poison fruitcake ploy!

She resumes looking for the phone.

Where the hell can that phone be? I know, with her boyfriend dead, I can win back Lillian's love. She will be my back-up just in case The Beloved Bride fails! *(Frustrated, at the top of her lungs.)* WHERE'S MY GODDAMN PHONE?

Behind IGORINA'S back, the phone starts to ring. IGORINA tries, and fails, to turn it off. Apologetically, she hands it, still ringing, to LESBOSTEIN.

Who can this be?

LESBOSTEIN answers the phone.

Hello?... The Werewolf Little Cubbie Fund?... No! I do not wish to donate! I don't like Werewolves and I hate Little Cubbies!

She hangs up.

LESBOSTEIN (con't): You give them a dollar ONE time, and they never... Now, who was I calling?

Avoiding LESBOSTEIN, IGORINA busies herself putting away the earwax Q-tip.

Earwax, that's right! I was smelling the ear...Lillian! Oh, yes, I was calling Lillian.

She dials, and speaks into the phone, in a very over-the-top jovial manner.

Hello, Lillian... Yes! It's me again! How are you... Oh good! And how's your hubby-bubby?... Oh, really? So his health is still holding up... Oh, by the way, have you received any mysterious packages in the mail lately?... No? That's very strange... So glad to hear that you're still in love!

She slams down phone.

So glad to hear it—NOT!

She stifles a sob, then turns to glare at IGORINA and begins to stalk her.

IGORINA: *(Backing up.)* Sometimes fruitcakes get lost in the mail.

LESBOSTEIN: *(Ominously.)* But this one didn't, did it?

IGORINA: I'm sorry, Mistress. I just couldn't do it.

LESBOSTEIN: I would never kill a woman—but a man! What's the big deal, Igorina? Men kill women and each other all the time! The world would be better off with one less.

IGORINA: He was once a little kiddie, Mistress!

LESBOSTEIN: What did you do with the poison fruitcake?

IGORINA: I hid it.

LESBOSTEIN: Where?

IGORINA grabs the pumpkin bucket and hugs it tight to her chest.

IGORINA: I'm not telling! Oh Mistress, Mistress, why don't you just give up on Number 23?

LESBOSTEIN: I have no backup now, because of you, you treasonous traitor, you double-crossing dimwit. I'll just have to succeed in bringing Number 35 to life!

She stands tall, a triumphant arm stretched to the sky.

IGORINA: That's what I like to hear from Mistress!

The doorbell rings.

Oh goody!

She turns to open the door. LESBOSTEIN stops her.

LESBOSTEIN: Word has spread on Instagram about your confounded Reese's Peanut Butter Cups, you profligate idiot. Now we'll never have a moment's peace! I'm going to take care of this problem myself, right now!

She rushes to the door.

IGORINA: Don't hurt the little kiddies, Mistress! No!

Miserably, IGORINA sits on her little chair, throws her apron over her face, and buries her face in her hands. LESBOSTEIN flings the door open.

LESBOSTEIN: No Reese's Peanut Butter Cup for you, you greedy little monster.

Pause.

Auggghhhh!

LESBOSTEIN backs into the room. A large WEREWOLF is

choking her. She clutches a "Werewolf Cubbie Fund" sign-up sheet on a clipboard; which she shoves in LESBOSTEIN'S face.

O.K. I'll donate! I'll donate!

LESBOSTEIN attempts to grab the clipboard. WEREWOLF does not release it. Back and forth, they struggle in a tug of war over the clipboard.

Look, I don't hate Little Wolf Cubbies any more than I hate all Little Kiddies.

The WEREWOLF throws the clipboard aside and returns to choking LESBOSTEIN. The combatants circle around the room, LESBOSTEIN choking and tearing at her throat, WEREWOLF growling, gnashing her teeth, never letting go. IGORINA stays covered in her apron, doesn't notice them. LESBOSTEIN and WEREWOLF exit. Sounds of their fighting continue outside.

IGORINA takes the apron off from over her head and pulls herself together. She begins rearranging and worrying over her candy treats.

IGORINA: Oh, I do hope I have enough cups for all the little kiddies. I spent my whole salary, but maybe it is not enough!

LESBOSTEIN: (*From offstage.*) Help! Help!

IGORINA: Ohhhh, it sounds like Mistress is having fun with the kiddies!

LESBOSTEIN: (*Still offstage.*) No, let me go!

IGORINA: I hear them playing together.

LESBOSTEIN runs in, spins around and holds the door closed. WEREWOLF is outside the door, pounding, then running and throwing herself against the door. There is a sudden pause. Silence. LESBOSTEIN and IGORINA regard each other. The doorbell rings.

IGORINA: Oh, goody!

LESBOSTEIN blocks the door.

LESBOSTEIN: No, Igorina, no!

Nothing will stop IGORINA from handing out Halloween candy. She easily throws LESBOSTEIN off the door and opens it.

IGORINA: Just a minute, little kiddies.

She turns away to get her pumpkin bucket full of goodies. WEREWOLF rushes in, looking for LESBOSTEIN. who hides behind the rolling lab table. IGORINA, failing to notice WEREWOLF, exits through the open door with her pumpkin bucket.

Little kiddies, little kiddies, Reese's Peanut Butter Cups for you-hoo!

WEREWOLF becomes more and more frantic looking for LESBOSTEIN. She growls and snarls, leaps, shows her teeth and claws, works herself into a frenzy. Each time WEREWOLF gets close, LESBOSTEIN, crouching, skillfully rotates the table so that she remains hidden behind it.

LESBOSTEIN: (*In a stage whisper.*) Oh rats, I'm feeling faint. If only I'd taken those vitamins. Oh no, now my hypoglycemia is kicking in! Where's the rest of that peanut butter cup?

Without daring to look, LESBOSTEIN sticks one arm up to feel around for the candy. WEREWOLF, who had been just about to give up, sees her hand and pounces. The fight is about to begin again, when WEREWOLF notices the lights glowing from behind the curtained entrance on Stage Left, and, entranced, lets go of LESBOSTEIN, goes to the curtain and is about to draw it open.

Not The Bride!

LESBOSTEIN staggers up. She heroically creates a distraction, calling to WEREWOLF.

Yoo-hoo, Foxy Lady!

WEREWOLF is startled, and turns.

Catch me now, you Big Bad Wolf!

LESBOSTEIN waves, turns and runs out through the open door, WEREWOLF in pursuit.

Pause. IGORINA re-enters.

IGORINA: I wonder where Mistress has gone with all the little kiddies…maybe to the playground…maybe Mistress is having so much fun in the playground that her heart is overflowing with joy…maybe she is learning to love little kiddies…

IGORINA becomes completely engrossed in rearranging the candy in the pumpkin head.

WEREWOLF and LESBOSTEIN re-enter in part-fight, part-Tango mode; although still combatants, we can see that they have sexual chemistry. WEREWOLF twirls LESBOSTEIN, who goes spinning off towards Stage Left. WEREWOLF sneaks up behind IGORINA and tries to reach over to get some candy. LESBOSTEIN picks up clipboard with "Werewolf Cubbie Fund" on it, and sneaks up behind WEREWOLF. She raises it overhead to bash WEREWOLF's head in. WEREWOLF reaches up, grabs clipboard. They face each other. The tug of war with the clipboard from the first encounter resumes, but this time, the clipboard is rotated: at first, from length to width, so that they are closer together, and then flipped so that it is flat between them; finally WEREWOLF tucks it into her armpit so that they are pressed together with nothing between them. The Tango resumes. The sexual tension is uncomfortably high. They exit, dancing and fighting.

IGORINA notices nothing of this fight and dance.

And…and…maybe Mistress will return and say to me, "Igorina, let's have a little kiddie together." Lesborina or Igorastein. Or, or, both! Lesborina *and* Igorastein. Twins. The "Little Kiddies of the Night."

LESBOSTEIN enters alone, completely battered and disheveled.

LESBOSTEIN: Igorina, there are real wolves living around here!

She closes the door, and collapses onto a hazardous waste bucket.

IGORINA: Yes, Mistress. The Mission is a very diverse neighborhood.

She regards LESBOSTEIN disapprovingly.

No, no, Mistress. Now is not the time to rest.

LESBOSTEIN sighs.

Let's get back to work.

LESBOSTEIN: (*Still dazed.*) Work?

IGORINA: Creating The Beloved Bride!

LESBOSTEIN pulls herself together.

LESBOSTEIN: Alright! (*Muttering.*) If only I had taken my vitamins…

With IGORINA's assistance, she stands, crosses to the lab table, and picks up the test tube filled with fingernails.

I, Dr. Gertrude Lesbostein, will now insert the final ingredient,

Lena's nail clippings, which I have carefully prepared, into the Cerebellapoodle! The marvelous machine will extract Number 13's DNA and insert it into the protoplasm. Then I will bring my Bride to life! Once I've done that, I'll patent my invention and be able to support both of us!

IGORINA: All THREE of us, Mistress! You, your Beloved Bride, and ME!

LESBOSTEIN: What? Oh, right. I'll support all THREE of us.

Rolls her eyes.

Into the Cerebellapoodle with the fingernail clippings!

Before she can throw them in, doorbell rings.

Don't answer it. You have no idea who it is, you dithering blockhead!

IGORINA: Oh, Mistress! Oh, your endearments are music to my ears! But I must, I must. It's Halloween!

She opens the door. An arm in a khaki shirt hands her an envelope. Expecting WEREWOLF, LESBOSTEIN ducks behind the lab table, grumbling to herself.

LESBOSTEIN: I've got to find a new slave…I mean assistant.

IGORINA closes the door.

IGORINA: Mistress, it wasn't an adorable little kiddie wanting candy. It was a lady. She handed me this envelope to give to you.

LESBOSTEIN stands up from behind the table.

LESBOSTEIN: What did the lady look like?

IGORINA: She had a beautiful shiny badge.

LESBOSTEIN: A badge? Oh no!

IGORINA: And a uniform…It was a kind of a gray-green…or maybe a tan…no, not tan. Beige. Well, not really a beige either. Khaki! Yes! It was khaki.

LESBOSTEIN: The sheriff! Good god! Did anyone see you sneak in Number 13's window?

IGORINA: I don't think so.

LESBOSTEIN: You didn't look around to check?

IGORINA: (*Shamefaced.*) The first time I did, but the second time

I was so excited to have the nail clippers that I bought at the 24 hour Walgreens—Mistress, what would I have done if it was closed! —I was so excited that I forgot to look around.

LESBOSTEIN: Don't you realize that every single errand I send you on is illegal?

IGORINA: Even when you send me out to buy toilet paper?

LESBOSTEIN: I mean the errands for our Top Secret Project, the creation of The Beloved Bride! No one understands the greatness of my mind, Igorina.

IGORINA: I do, Mistress.

LESBOSTEIN: Yes, well, unfortunately, you don't count. They don't see me as a woman before my time. They see me as a criminal!

IGORINA: No!

LESBOSTEIN: The Republicans don't want another lesbian added to the world. The gay establishment won't let me in the Pride Parade because I'm not a corporation. And who knows what the Trans community will do to me once they discover that all my DNA samples are from biological women! We have no friends, Igorina, no allies. If the law has caught up with us, we're toast.

IGORINA: (*With great staunchness.*) I will fight to the death to defend you, Mistress! I'll keep them busy so that you can get away!

LESBOSTEIN: (*Thoughtfully.*) Yes, that's a good plan.

> IGORINA hands the letter to LESBOSTEIN. She opens the letter and reads it silently.

IGORINA: What does the letter say, Mistress? Tell me, tell me!

LESBOSTEIN: It's an eviction notice. Apparently this is the 17th notice they've sent. What happened to all the others? (*Silence.*) WHAT DID YOU DO WITH EVICTION NOTICES NUMBER ONE THROUGH 16?

IGORINA: I didn't want to upset you, Mistress, so I threw them away.

LESBOSTEIN: You threw them away???!!!

IGORINA: No! I meant, I *recycled* them. I *recycled* them.

LESBOSTEIN: We have to be out by tomorrow morning. Someone has bought the building. They're going to convert this basement into a garage for their BMW and that hipster idiot's bicycle.

IGORINA: But why do they need a garage, Mistress?

LESBOSTEIN gives her a piercing stare.

IGORINA (con't): No, no! Is it the Parking Curse being visited upon us? Not the Parking Curse! Anything but that, Mistress!

LESBOSTEIN: I thought we had protected ourselves from the Parking Curse, by never having a car. But now I see that the Parking Curse can strike anyone at any time.

IGORINA: What are we going to do, Mistress?

LESBOSTEIN: What are we going to do! What are we going to do.... what...what...All my equipment...the delicate wiring...

IGORINA: The fragile glass tubes and vials...

LESBOSTEIN: I'll never be able to set it up anywhere else.

IGORINA: It's taken you years.

LESBOSTEIN: Tonight's the night! It's all we've got.

IGORINA: We have no more time to waste. We've got the 34 DNA samples.

LESBOSTEIN: And gay marriage is finally legal—and who knows how long that's going to last, with this Supreme Court! After all, what's a Beloved Bride without a marriage license? Now the moment has come! I must bring my Bride to life before we're evicted!

IGORINA: Yes, Mistress, let's do it!

LESBOSTEIN: (*Singing.*)

> Song: THE PERFECT BRIDE (short reprise)

The only woman that can earn my ultimate affection is the woman who's assembled by the ultimate perfectionist
But even with recombinant genetic ovum hatchery
I don't believe she'll have Lorena's talent for back-scratchery.

Speaking.

Ahh, Lorena...She always knew exactly where my back itched. Oooh, just thinking about her makes me itchy... Igorina, scratch my back...

IGORINA: Of course, Mistress!

IGORINA scratches LESBOSTEIN's back.

LESBOSTEIN: No, up a little…To the right…No, that's too far… Left… no, down…

IGORINA is frantically trying to get it right.

LESBOSTEIN (con't): Damn it, just bring me the backscratcher!

IGORINA: Please, Mistress, let me try a little longer!

LESBOSTEIN: What's the point? You can never find the spot, you ham-handed ninny. Lorena went right to it, without me saying a word! What a woman…

IGORINA gives her the back-scratcher. LESBOSTEIN finds the spot. As she scratches, her foot moves like a dog being scratched.

Ahh… That's good.

IGORINA: Hand it over.

Takes back-scratcher from LESBOSTEIN.

Now, back to work.

She brings the clippings to LESBOSTEIN.

LESBOSTEIN: Alright, alright.

She regards the clippings in her hand. She seems immobilized.

IGORINA: This is not the time to give up, Mistress. No!

LESBOSTEIN: I feel so weak! If only I had the rest of my vitamins. Wait! Where are the ones you picked up off the floor?

IGORINA: In my pocket, Mistress.

LESBOSTEIN: Hand them over.

IGORINA: But Mistress, the Five-Second Rule.

LESBOSTEIN: That is a myth! Hand them over, you twit.

IGORINA pulls out some vitamins, covered with pocket lint, and hands them over. LESBOSTEIN regards them dubiously, pulls off some pocket lint, and downs them with the colorful contents of another beaker. LESBOSTEIN immediately begins sneezing and continues to sneeze.

IGORINA: You see, you see! Contaminated!

LESBOSTEIN: (*Still sneezing.*) What else is in your pocket?

IGORINA pulls a huge ball of pocket lint from her pocket, and using big scientific tweezers, begins to dissect it. LESBOSTEIN, with growing horror, sneezes compulsively after each allergen is listed.

IGORINA: Let's see, grasses and pollens, my special perfumed hankie, cat hair—oh, Mistress, I found some little abandoned kitties and carried them all day in my pocket until I found some little girls to take them home—and a lot of pepper!

She accidentally blows some pepper right in LESBOSTEIN's face.

LESBOSTEIN: You numbskull! You set off all my allergies by putting my precious vitamins in your cursed pocket! (*Still sneezing.*)

IGORINA takes LESBOSTEIN by the shoulders, sits her up, looks her straight in the eyes and shouts right into her face.

IGORINA: GESUNDHEIT!

LESBOSTEIN abruptly stops sneezing.

OK, Mistress, now, let's throw the fingernails in together.

LESBOSTEIN, too overwhelmed to even get angry, nods "Yes" in agreement.

TOGETHER: Into the Cerebellapoodle with the fingernail clippings!

Together, they throw the fingernails into the large funnel at the top of the machine. Immediately there is a loud splash, followed by sucking and gurgling sounds.

LESBOSTEIN: I hear the DNA flowing into the protoplasm.

They listen as burps and gurgles and bubble popping sounds occur, and various parts of the Cerebellapoodle light up. Finally, there is a huge flushing noise, the machine vibrates and then is still.

That's it. Everything is complete.

She doesn't seem as excited as one would imagine.

IGORINA: Now I will bring out The Bride.

She starts to exit toward the glowing curtain stage left. LESBOSTEIN stops her.

LESBOSTEIN: Igorina, what was your favorite part of the Top Secret Project?

IGORINA: I believe my favorite exploit was catching Number 21's laugh. Now I will bring out The Bride…

LESBOSTEIN: (*Stopping her.*) You've never told me how you got Listeria to laugh so hard that she snorted milk out her nose.

IGORINA: First, I gave her a glass of milk. And then I told her I wanted to capture the DNA of her laughter for you, so you could create your ideal bride. And she couldn't stop laughing…

LESBOSTEIN: Oh, really…

IGORINA: She didn't believe I was serious. But when I convinced her I was, THAT'S when Listeria experienced hysteria and snorted the milk through her nose! And I caught some of it in a test tube!

LESBOSTEIN: Let's move on.

IGORINA: I caught it! I caught it!

LESBOSTEIN: Enough!

IGORINA: She was cute.

LESBOSTEIN: Yes, especially when she snorted milk. She never took my ideas seriously.

IGORINA: Mistress, quit whining. You're stalling. Now I will bring out The Bride—and don't try to stop me!

LESBOSTEIN: It's true. I'm afraid to take the final step.

> *IGORINA exits Stage Left—behind the glowing curtain. She returns with THE BRIDE, strapped to a dolly. The dolly is decorated to look like a small shrine, complete with twinkling Holiday Lights. THE BRIDE is covered with a sheet. An expanding exhaust hose trails from the dolly and a big Jacob's Ladder (a high voltage arcing device that looks like a rabbit-ear antenna with an electrical arc between the poles) is attached to an upside down colander, indicating that it is sitting on THE BRIDE'S head. IGORINA sets the dolly upright and nods approvingly.*

IGORINA: You've got everything you need now.

LESBOSTEIN: This protoplasm, which I have so carefully crafted from information I Googled…what if it doesn't come to life? What if it does come to life, but doesn't have the attributes I have so meticulously implanted in the germs of every cell? What if everything goes right and she's still not good enough for me?

IGORINA: Take courage, Mistress! You will succeed!

LESBOSTEIN: Do you really think so, Igorina?

IGORINA: I know it, Mistress.

LESBOSTEIN: Alright. Let's get this baby on the road!

IGORINA: Oh Mistress, it's finally happening!

> *LESBOSTEIN pulls The Big Lever. There are sparks and explosions inside the lab. Outside, lightning flashes and thunder booms as if Halloween night itself supports the experiment. There are sounds of an engine revving up, and the sheet begins to move. But then the engine sounds sputter and everything dies away. LESBOSTEIN pulls The Big Lever again. Same as before. Once more LESBOSTEIN pulls The Big Lever. And… Success!*

> *THE BRIDE pulls the sheet away. She is costumed to look exactly like LESBOSTEIN, with a rainbow Mohawk, big purple framed glasses, and a white lab coat. However, her lab coat is fitted and covered with all the lace and decorations befitting a bridal gown. She opens her eyes and looks around in confusion.*

LESBOSTEIN: She's—She's—She's ALIVE!!!!!

IGORINA: Oh Mistress, she's so beautiful!

LESBOSTEIN: Come to me, my sweet Number 35!

IGORINA: Oh Mistress, I've never seen anyone so wonderful…so magical…so magnificent!

LESBOSTEIN: Of course she's magnificent, you nincompoop. She's my creation.

IGORINA: Oh no, Mistress. She's more than your creation. She's… She's HERSELF!

LESBOSTEIN: (*To THE BRIDE*) Come to Mama!

> *THE BRIDE remains frozen.*

Alright, then Mama will come to you, Thirty-Five!

> *She embraces THE BRIDE vigorously. THE BRIDE stands rigid. IGORINA gently picks up THE BRIDE'S hand, stroking it worshipfully.*

IGORINA: So lovely…the little cutiecles…Beauteeeful cutiecles…

> *THE BRIDE squirms out of LESBOSTEIN's embrace, pushes her away.*

LESBOSTEIN: What the hell?

> *THE BRIDE looks at IGORINA, makes garbled sounds of love. She can speak only in gibberish, which IGORINA understands. She kisses IGORINA.*

You've got to be kidding.

IGORINA: (*To THE BRIDE.*) No, no, you've made a terrible mistake. That's Mistress over there. You're going to marry her. She's a famous misunderstood genius. I'm just her lowly assistant. I'm not worthy.

> *THE BRIDE puts her finger to IGORINA's lips to stop her from speaking. She kisses her sweetly.*

THE BRIDE: (*Loving, sexy gibberish.*)

IGORINA: (*Translating for LESBOSTEIN.*) She says she feels like I've already touched every part of her. Which, when you stop and think about it, is absolutely true.

> *As THE BRIDE begins touching her again.*

Oooooh!

LESBOSTEIN: (*To THE BRIDE.*) Are you nuts? *I'm* your creator!

> *THE BRIDE drums her fingers over IGORINA'S body.*

IGORINA: Oh, Mistress, I see what you mean about the conga drummer!

> *LESBOSTEIN tries to untwine THE BRIDE from IGORINA. THE BRIDE bares her teeth at LESBOSTEIN, hisses to drive her away.*

IGORINA: (*To LESBOSTEIN.*) Mistress, I'm so sorry. There's nothing I can do.

THE BRIDE: (*A proposal in gibberish.*)

IGORINA: (*To THE BRIDE.*) Really?

LESBOSTEIN: What did she say? What did she say?

BRIDE: (*An increasingly ardent proposal in gibberish.*)

IGORINA: (*To THE BRIDE.*) But we just met!

LESBOSTEIN: What's she saying?

BRIDE: (*A desperate proposal in gibberish.*)

IGORINA: (*To THE BRIDE.*) Let's think about if for a while.

LESBOSTEIN: WHAT'S SHE SAYING??!!

IGORINA: (*To LESBOSTEIN.*) She thinks I'm a real catch and she's worried someone else will grab me. She wants to get married right away.

LESBOSTEIN: But that's *my* dream!

> *THE BRIDE describes the white picket fence and the two perfect children dream in gibberish, using illustrative gestures.*

IGORINA: (*To THE BRIDE.*) You want to have little kiddies too?!? You'll be my number one!

> *THE BRIDE howls in protest.*

I mean, my one and only.

> *They smooch.*

> *LESBOSTEIN is desperate to figure out how she can please THE BRIDE.*

LESBOSTEIN: It's the white coat! You're right. It's not a good color for me. Look, I'll never wear white again!

> *She takes off the coat.*

Or maybe I'm too butch.

> *Rummaging through a pile of detritus, she finds a scarf to put on and poses as a temptress. Through all her changes of costume, the two lovebirds continue to smooch and playfully tickle each other, oblivious to LESBOSTEIN.*

No, I went too far to the femme side. A hipster?

> *She gets the fedora that THE HIPSTER must have dropped on his way out. She poses as a hipster, and still gets no response.*

LESBOSTEIN (con't): Just really really butch.

> *She finds a toolbelt in another pile of stuff on the floor, and wraps it around herself. Now wearing a scarf, a fedora, and a tool belt, LESBOSTEIN takes a final pose.*

Ta-dah! (*They ignore her.*) What can I do to make you love me?

THE BRIDE: (*Speaking to LESBOSTEIN in very kind gibberish.*)

IGORINA: (*Translating for LESBOSTEIN.*) It's not you. It's her.

THE BRIDE: (*Continuing to speak to LESBOSTEIN, in slow explanatory gibberish.*)

IGORINA: (*Translating for LESBOSTEIN.*) You're just not her type.

LESBOSTEIN: And *you* are???

THE BRIDE: (*To IGORINA, in firm decisive gibberish.*)

IGORINA: (*Translating for LESBOSTEIN.*) Mistress, we're going now to City Hall to get married. Can we have your blessing?

LESBOSTEIN: My blessing? After all this you expect my blessing? Forget it!

> *THE BRIDE stomps around in a fury. She advances menacingly on LESBOSTEIN.*

IGORINA: Please, Mistress. It would mean so much to both of us.

LESBOSTEIN: Alright, alright. You have my blessing. Just get out of here. I never want to see either of you again.

BRIDE: (*Polite, questioning gibberish.*)

IGORINA: No, darling. She doesn't want to be a witness at our wedding.

> *IGORINA throws her arms around LESBOSTEIN.*

Goodbye, Mistress. Thanks for everything. And I do mean EVERYTHING!

> *IGORINA and THE BRIDE exit.*

LESBOSTEIN: Maybe Igorina was right. Maybe I SHOULD have stopped licking Number 29's ear. Igorina... Igorina... (*Light starts to dawn.*) ...How could I have been so stupid? She really loved me, for myself. Oh, Igorina, if only I hadn't been obsessed with The Beloved Bride. If I had realized that it was you, you, always you, and you alone— then we could have gotten married, you would have been my wife— and I wouldn't have had to pay you San Francisco minimum wage... I wouldn't have had to pay you ANYTHING at all for your devotion. ...But it's too late. No bride, no slave, no place to live. I can't bear the thought of looking for a cheap apartment in San Francisco. I'd rather die. Life, you win! I give up. I can't go on. Now, where did Igorina hide that poison fruitcake?

> *She looks around wildly.*

I'll find it eventually. In the meantime, I might as well rot my teeth with another peanut butter cup.

> *She picks up the pumpkin bucket.*

Oh, Igorina, what a fool I was. But it's too late, too late.

> *She reaches in to get candy.*

But wait, what's this?

> *She pulls out the fruitcake, which is wrapped in a dirty seeping rag and looks disgusting and poisonous.*

Ahhh! Here's the fruitcake!

> *She unwraps it and takes a chunk in her hand.*

Goodbye, cruel world!

> *LESBOSTEIN takes a big bite, but does not swallow. Reconsidering, she is about to spit it out, when the doorbell rings, startling her. She accidently swallows. The fruitcake gets stuck in her throat. She begins to choke. She cannot speak. She tries to make it to the door, where the doorbell ringing continues, but she cannot make it that far. She repeats the entire dying process she earlier imagined for Lillian's boyfriend. The doorbell rings again, then knocking commences; which gets louder and louder. LESBOSTEIN reaches helplessly toward the door, and then collapses. The WEREWOLF hurls herself against the door and bursts in. She quickly sums up the situation, grabs LESBOSTEIN, and performs the Heimlich maneuver. The piece of poison fruitcake comes shooting out. LESBOSTEIN is dazed but smiling.*

LESBOSTEIN (con't): You saved my life. No one has ever done that for me before, not even Igorina.

> *LESBOSTEIN extends her hand.*

Alright, let bygones be bygones.

> *WEREWOLF grabs LESBOSTEIN'S hand, then continues grabbing hand over hand up her arm and tries to embrace her.*

Not so fast!

> *LESBOSTEIN struggles. WEREWOLF gets her in a hammer-lock and kisses her. LESBOSTEIN surrenders, speaks in a shaky voice.*

Wow! You're…different!

> *WEREWOLF puts her arm around LESBOSTEIN, tips her chin up, growls softly, and gives her a kiss.*

I've never felt like this before.

> *WEREWOLF sits on bucket, gestures for LESBOSTEIN to sit in her lap. LESBOSTEIN does so.*

You're pretty cute.

> *She takes out a Reese's Peanut Butter Cup from IGORINA's pumpkin bucket.*

Want to share one?

> *WEREWOLF takes scary big bite and wolfs it down. They playfully feed each other. They giggle, LESBOSTEIN like a human, WEREWOLF like a wolf. LESBOSTEIN suddenly remembers her eviction and is overcome with despair.*

Oh, what difference does anything make now? I'll soon be homeless. I have nowhere to live and no way to pay two month's rent plus security for a new apartment! I'm destined for Sunset Scavenger's compost heap.

> *WEREWOLF carefully rises, and lovingly seats LESBOSTEIN on the bucket. She mimes that LESBOSTEIN should wait, then she runs out the door and re-enters with a little wagon that says "U-Haul" on it. She begins loading the lab up in the wagon.*

LESBOSTEIN (con't): But this is only our first date! It's not time for the U-Haul.

> *WEREWOLF growls in disagreement, shakes head "no" and re-enacts wrestling with LESBOSTEIN, tango with LESBOSTEIN, hammerlock kiss with LESBOSTEIN.*

Oh, so you're counting the fight as our first date?

> *WEREWOLF growls and nods "Yes!"*

Then it's a lesbian second date, and that means it IS time for the U-Haul!

> *WEREWOLF nods "Yes!", and returns to loading wagon.*

What's your name?

> *WEREWOLF shrugs unhappily, She has no name.*

I'll call you Lupe! Do you like it?

WEREWOLF, very pleased, growls and nods "Yes!"

Do you mind if I sometimes call you Number 36?

WEREWOLF shakes head "No!"

Lupe 36…Could I…could I ask you to scratch my back?

WEREWOLF enthusiastically starts to do so.

That's it! That's it! You went right to the spot!

LESBOSTEIN starts to move her foot like a dog getting scratched. She howls. WEREWOLF begins to howl along with her. Still howling, they finish loading the wagon, and walk towards the door.

WEREWOLF picks up the poisonous fruitcake on the way out and tosses it into the funnel on the top of The Cerebellapoodle, just before they leave.

There is a loud splash which LESBOSTEIN and WEREWOLF don't hear as they exit howling. The Cerebellapoodle comes to life— it makes all its gurgling and drainage sounds. There is the loud flush and all is still for a moment. The lights start to dim. But then there is the sounds of a toilet getting clogging up and spilling over, pipes bursting, a geyser erupting. The Cerebellapoodle's lights go up and down spasmodically. There is loud thunder and lightning outside, a huge explosion and BLACKOUT.

End Of Play

2014

HICK:
A LOVE STORY

**BASED ON ELEANOR ROOSEVELT'S
LETTERS TO LORENA HICKOK**

Premiere Information

HICK: A Love Story was written by Terry Baum and Pat Bond with additional writing by Lorena Hickok, and Eleanor Roosevelt. Originally subtitled *The Romance of Lorena Hickok and Eleanor Roosevelt*, it opened on July 10, 2014 at the Eureka Theater in San Francisco. It was produced by The Crackpot Crones and Theater Rhinoceros.

Director .... Carolyn Myers
Set Design .... Vola Ruben
Lighting Design .... Stephanie Johnson
Sound Design .... Audrey Howard
Costume Design .... Val Von
Production Stage Manager ... Pam Higley

CAST

LORENA HICKOK................................Terry Baum
Voice of ELEANOR ROOSEVELT (recorded)...Paula Barish

PLEASE NOTE: Selections from Eleanor Roosevelt's 2336 letters to Lorena Hickok are used with the permission of Mrs. Roosevelt's estate.

PRODUCTION HISTORY

In May 1978, the writer Doris Faber visited the Franklin D. Roosevelt Presidential Library in Hyde Park, New York. She was researching a biography of Eleanor Roosevelt for young adults. She found 18 filing boxes willed to the library by Lorena Hickok, a close confidante of Eleanor's, with the instructions, "Not to be opened until ten years after my death." Hick had died ten years and three days earlier. Inside the boxes, Faber found 2,336 letters from Mrs. Roosevelt to Lorena Hickok, dating from the 1930's right up to Eleanor's death in 1962. These letters documented a passionate love affair between the two women. Faber tried to convince the head of the library to burn the letters, but he refused. Having failed to get the evidence destroyed, she decided to write Hickok's biography. In 1980 Faber published *The Life of Lorena Hickok: E.R.'s Friend*, wherein the author strenuously denied the sexual aspect of the relationship she was writing about. But the evidence was there for all to see, and the reviewers all noted it.

Pat Bond, lesbian monologist and my close friend, had a life-long crush on Eleanor Roosevelt. Imagine her delight when she discovered that the great First Lady had actually had a lesbian lover! Pat's solo play, *Eleanor Roosevelt and Lorena Hickok, A Love Story*, opened in San Francisco in 1984. She toured the play throughout the country.

After I performed a short scene from Pat's play in 2012, Carolyn felt strongly that I should write my own play about Hick and Eleanor. Several books had been published since 1984 that shed more light on this remarkable story. Also, Pat's play only concerned the love affair. Carolyn and I were both excited by Hick's work as a journalist and felt that too should be known. The most famous "gal reporter" of her day, she went on to travel the country, documenting the Great Depression.

HICK: A Love Story first had a workshop production, directed by Bobbi Ausubel, as part of the 2013 National Queer Arts Festival. This early version, following Pat Bond's play, did not have a scene of the two lovers in bed. One of the audience members asked me, "So, what's the deal? Did they have sex or not?" Here I was, going to all the trouble to "out" Eleanor Roosevelt, and I had neglected to put the two women in bed together! Oops! Talk about internalized homophobia! I corrected this egregious political and artistic error for the official opening of *HICK: A Love Story*.

After the opening in July 2014 in San Francisco, *HICK* went on to be part of the 2015 New York International Fringe Festival, where it won a Fringe Fave Award and was selected for an extended run off-Broadway as part of Fringe Encore. It has been produced at the Berkeley City Club, the Baltimore Theatre Project, and 1st Stage in Virginia. In all these productions, I played Hick. The New York production was directed by Adele Prandini, and the Baltimore production by Velina Brown. Carolyn Myers directed the Berkeley and Virginia productions. I've performed *HICK* as a concert reading all over the U.S. and in Mexico and Morocco.

In the course of my performances, I've met two audience members who were told by older relatives, who had lived in the D.C. area, that Eleanor Roosevelt was a lesbian. One older relative was a right-wing grandma who wanted to prove to her granddaughter that all Democrats were evil. The other older relative was a loving aunt who wanted to reassure her niece, who had just come out to her, that some great women were lesbians. I also read an interview with Armistead Maupin who, when he first arrived in San Francisco, "lived in a building that used to be a hotel where it was rumored that Eleanor Roosevelt stayed with her lesbian lover." This, in fact, is the hotel in North Beach that Hick and ER fled to, after their disastrous vacation in Yosemite. All these stories convinced me that Hick and Eleanor's sexual relationship was common knowledge and the subject of gossip.

CHARACTERS

This is a true story. Any resemblance between the characters in the play and actual historical people is intentional. In fact, the purpose of the play is to bring to light a love story minimized, overlooked, and often denied by many historians: the love affair of Lorena Hickok and Eleanor Roosevelt.

HICK (LORENA HICKOK) (1893-1968) was born into desperate poverty in rural Wisconsin. When she was 14, her mother died and her father threw her out of the house. She worked as a hired girl, completing high school with the help of her aunt. Her career in journalism began in 1913, writing for the women's page of the *Battle Creek Journal* in Michigan. At the *Minneapolis Tribune*, starting in 1917, Hick blossomed into a successful journalist, known for the humor and humanity of her writing. She eventually became a top reporter for the Associated Press in New York City. By 1932, she was the nation's best-known woman journalist. Starting in 1934, she worked for the federal government, documenting the Great Depression and the New Deal throughout the country. Her reports are considered by scholars to be the most complete record of that period.

The bulk of the play takes place from 1932, when Hick is 39, to 1934. Born butch, she strikes everyone as "masculine." Her gestures, the way she talks—everything expresses this butch persona. Hick wears her hair short, sports a very male watch, and approximates men's clothing as much as she dares. She's one of the boys. She smokes cigars and drinks the other reporters under the table. She struggles with the great contradiction that afflicted many butch women: Despite the choices she's made to appear masculine, she is fearful of exposure as a lesbian and ashamed of her difference.

Hick lives for her work. She is proud of being the highest-paid woman reporter in the U.S. She is full of energy, passion, and ideas.

The first and last scenes frame the play. They take place in 1968, when Hick is 75 years old. She is an old 75. She walks slowly, wears thick glasses, is a little hunched over, but her spirit is undimmed.

In this one-woman show, only Hick is actually present onstage.

ELEANOR ROOSEVELT (1884-1962) was born into the American aristocracy, in a family ravaged by alcoholism. After a difficult and lonely childhood, Eleanor came into her own at Allenwood, an English boarding school for daughters of the elite. There, she was the favorite of the headmistress, Marie Souvestre, who taught the young women to use their privilege to change the world. Returning to the U.S., Eleanor fully immersed herself in public service, fighting injustice and advancing civil rights for African-Americans and women. She married distant cousin Franklin Delano Roosevelt in 1905. She raised five children and continued her work as an activist, while her husband pursued his calling in electoral politics. After FDR was stricken with polio, Eleanor became his eyes and ears, reporting back to him about a world he could not fully explore because of his disability.

When Eleanor meets Hick in 1932, she is 48 years old. Eleanor is adventurous, with a tremendous appetite for experience. After a life of progressive activism, she is very depressed at the thought of transforming herself into a meek and proper First Lady.

Eleanor Roosevelt is represented by voice-overs quoting from the letters she wrote to Lorena Hickok. When Eleanor appears in scenes with Hick she is invisible to the audience but is the focus of Hick's attention.

TIME and PLACE

The Times: Hick and Eleanor met in the depths of the Great Depression, a tumultuous time in our country's history. The crash of the economy had left millions destitute, without any kind of a safety net. Banks had run out of cash. Many feared that democracy itself was coming to an end, and that violent revolution was inevitable. FDR's presidency changed all that, creating gigantic programs that gave people jobs, relief and hope.

ACT ONE

Scene 1: 1968, Hick's Apartment
Scenes 2-8: 1932-1933, Various locations

ACT TWO

As Act Two begins, no time has passed
Scenes 1- 5: 1933-1934, Various locations
Scene 6: 1968, Hick's Apartment

SETTING: The stage has four defined areas:

Stage Left has a raised platform that is the living room of HICK's apartment in New York City. It is furnished in a cozy and comfortable way, in a 1930s Art Deco style.

The Center Stage is occupied by two green leather armchairs. A tall ornate lamp stands behind the two chairs. This area serves as four locations: ELEANOR's train compartment, a restaurant, a public room in the White House, and a hotel room.

Both the Apartment and the Center Stage are backed by flats painted with greatly enlarged copies of actual hand-written letters from ELEANOR to HICK. The letters are so magnified that the audience can read some of the phrases.

Stage Right is an office with a small desk and typewriter. The Office serves for all the locations where HICK does her work: the Associated Press offices in New York City and Washington D.C., and all the places where she writes when she's on the road. The Office is backed by flats painted with the headline banners of some of the newspapers that carried AP reports by HICK.

Downstage is used for outdoor settings.

ACT ONE

Scene 1: The Letters 1968

AT RISE: Lights come up on HICK's apartment in New York City, a slightly raised platform Upstage Left. It is cozy, furnished with a wingback chair, end table, footstool, and coatrack in Art Deco style, with a Persian carpet. Everything is tasteful, comfortable. On the end table sit a telephone and a fancy cigar box.

HICK enters, holding an envelope. She is 75 years old, and wears thick glasses, an old-fashioned men's dressing gown, and slippers. Her movements are slow. She is a bit stooped. She is a very old 75. She comes downstage to talk to the audience.

HICK: Look what came in the mail today...

She shows the envelope to the audience.

A letter from the Franklin Delano Roosevelt Presidential Library!

She takes out the letter.

It's from the director. Oh, I'll bet I know what this is about. (*She reads aloud.*)"January 10, 1968. Dear Miss Hickok: I'm writing because I know you were a good friend of Eleanor Roosevelt for many years and that you had a lively and extensive correspondence with her…"(*To the audience.*) "Extensive" doesn't begin to describe it. I have a whole closet filled with letters from my Dear One. Way more than a thousand… (*Reading.*) "Mrs. Roosevelt's life was the stuff of history." (*To the audience.*) He got that right! (*Reading.*) "Letters to friends and family are greatly valued by researchers. I would love to talk with you about donating the correspondence between you and Mrs. Roosevelt to the National Archive."

> *HICK settles herself in the armchair. She has never talked about her relationship to Eleanor Roosevelt. This letter confronts her with the possibility of making their love affair public. She makes the audience her confidante. She decides to spill the beans.*

I always knew this letter would arrive one day. Of course he knows that we were close. We went everywhere together in the beginning. Hell, the press used to call me First Friend! But he has no idea *how* close Eleanor and I were. And he hasn't a clue that the letters prove just how close.

> *She takes three letters out of the cigar box on the table.*

I keep some of my favorites right here.

> *She reads a letter to herself. Throughout the play, whenever HICK reads a letter from ELEANOR, we hear ELEANOR'S VOICE speaking the words. These letters are historical, quoted from ELEANOR's actual letters to HICK. HICK remains silent while we hear ELEANOR'S VOICE.*

ELEANOR'S VOICE: I miss you so much and I love you so much. The nicest time of day is when I write to you.

HICK: (*To the audience.*) This is a letter from Eleanor Roosevelt to me!

> *She reads a second letter.*

ELEANOR'S VOICE: Oh, how I want to put my arms around you in reality instead of in spirit. Please keep most of your heart in Washington as long as I'm here, for most of mine is with you!

HICK: Oh, we were so in love.

> *HICK presses the letter briefly to her heart. We see this gesture throughout the play—not every time she reads a letter, but frequently.*

I've got boxes and boxes of letters from my darling. Starting in 1933 and going all the way until she died. That was six years ago. In 1962. Now it's 1968 and the Director of the FDR Library wants me to donate these letters to the National Archive. Letters where the greatest First Lady in history talks about longing to put her arms around me! Oh, she didn't just write me love letters. She wrote me about all the little details of her life—her political work, her family problems.

> *She picks up a third letter.*

This one's about one of her special projects.

ELEANOR'S VOICE: My dearest one, I looked at all the new models in the furniture factory...

HICK: She actually was a partner in a furniture factory! The number of projects that woman took up!

ELEANOR'S VOICE: One corner cupboard I long to have for our camp or cottage or house. Which is it to be? I've always thought of it as in the country but I don't think we ever decided on the variety of abode nor the furniture. We probably won't argue!

HICK: "Probably won't," huh? We had a plan! Oh, we loved our plan: When FDR was finished being President, my darling and I would run away to a little cabin in the woods and read poetry to each other. No one could imagine he would run for president four times—and win! We never did get that corner cupboard...or any other furniture.

> *HICK holds up the letter.*

This is my inheritance from my Dear One: The letters. (*Pause.*) To donate them to the archive...or not to donate them...That is the question...

I always thought I'd end up an old woman with a closet full of newspaper clippings, not letters! I was a reporter, and a damned good one.

> *HICK stands, speaks with great pride.*

The highest paid gal reporter in the land! That's right. Until Eleanor Roosevelt came along and turned my life upside down in 1932!

HICK exits as lights fade to black.

Scene 2: The Associated Press Office 1932

Lights up on Stage Right, the office of the Associated Press in New York City. This is a small area with a typewriter table and chair. On the table, besides the typewriter, sit a phone and some files. HICK is typing. She is 39 years old. She wears a man-tailored shirt with the sleeves rolled up, a vest, a skirt, a big watch, and sensible shoes.

HICK: (*Reading aloud as she types.*) Dateline July 10, 1932. New York City. Byline: Lorena A. Hickok! The Democratic candidate for President, Franklin Delano Roosevelt, described his plan to lead us out of the horrific economic crisis that plagues this great land…

She stops typing.

"Plagues…" Maybe "engulfs" is better…

She makes the correction.

Gotta get this damn story finished and in!

HICK crosses downstage to speak to the audience.

And then…and then…I'm off! Covering the Presidential candidate on his campaign train! Oh, I like Governor Roosevelt. All the reporters do. At the press conference this morning he said, "Just call me FDR, boys. It takes too long to say 'Franklin Delano Roosevelt.' We haven't got the time. We've got a country to turn around, boys." And then he looked at me and said, "And when I say boys, I mean you too, Hick."

Everybody calls me Hick. My name's Lorena Hickok. You remember that. I have a byline on every story I write. (*She looks up, seeing her name as a banner in the sky.*) Lorena A. Hickok. Worked hard for that byline. Started out at the Battle Creek Evening News covering ice cream socials in Michigan and wrote my way up to the Associated Press in New York City. You know the A.P. Supplies copy to all the newspapers, big and small.

The phone on her desk rings once. She grabs the receiver. She knows who's calling.

Hello, Boss. Don't you have anything better to do than plague this poor newshound when she's trying to finish the job?

Pause.

Well, of course I knew it was you. I'm past deadline! I'll have the copy to you by six tonight.

> *She talks to her editor, the Boss, in a familiar, jocular tone. As a top reporter, she considers herself his equal—at least. HICK starts to put the phone down, then remembers something.*

Boss, don't hang up! I've got a great idea. It'll put the A.P. out in front of the other wire services! Just listen: You have to hire a gal reporter to cover Mrs. Roosevelt. She's not your typical candidate's wife. The Republicans call her a goddam Communist for trying to put an end to child labor. Tell me that's not a story: "Candidate's wife called a Commie." This Roosevelt dame has enormous dignity. She's… she's a person! You put a reporter on her, and you'll have every paper in the country begging to run those stories! Everyone's covering the candidate, but the Associated Press will be the only one covering his wife!

> *Pause.*

Aw, you won't regret it! So who's the lucky gal who gets to cover Mrs. R?

> *Pause.*

Me! That's funny. That's a good one.

> *HICK laughs her booming, hoarse laugh—a true guffaw.*

What do you mean you're not joking? I'm covering the candidate! Not his goddam wife!

> *Pause.*

I'm glad I convinced you she's worth some ink, but you need me in the middle of the action! I'm the first woman to get a goddam byline on the front page of the goddam New York Times. Remember? And how did I get that story? I used my goddam feminine wiles, that's how!

> *She guffaws.*

Of course I'm joking. Just like you!

> *Pause.*

Now listen, you son of a bitch, the candidate belongs to me…

> *Pause.*

Boss? Hello?

> *She taps the phone, the button. The Boss has hung up.*

I just talked myself out of the best assignment I ever had! Jesus Christ!

She returns to her typewriter.

Better finish that story so I can go pack. Campaign train leaves at dawn tomorrow. I can't believe what I just did. Oh Jeez…

HICK laughs as she continues to type.

Lights fade to black. We hear a train whistle mingled with FDR's campaign song. Whistle and music fade.

Scene 3: The Campaign Train 1932

Lights up on HICK still typing. She is now on FDR's campaign train.

HICK: (*Reading aloud as she types. She is happy.*) Dateline: July 20, 1932. Byline: Lorena A. Hickok. With FDR's campaign song still ringing in my ears, I'm writing you from the campaign train traveling across the whole country. Eleanor Roosevelt, her secretary, and yours truly are the only women on this train…

She springs out of her chair.

(*To the audience.*) Today was unbelievable! Mrs. R turned from stone into butter, and invited me to have coffee with her alone in her compartment. She told me she had always been afraid of reporters because a lady never gets her name in the paper, but for three times: when she's born, when she marries, and when she dies. So of course she'd been terrified to have me following her around. Then, she turned to me, and said, "I was wrong. I want to get to know you, Hick." (*Pause.*) And then she looked me straight in the eye.

Well, I damn near dropped dead and I had this funny feeling. I haven't felt it for so long—a kind of excitement, a kind of uneasiness. I knew what it was, but I didn't want to admit it, even to myself.

HICK paces.

But I sure as hell wired ahead to get a hotel room so I could clean up! Got to look good!

She stops abruptly.

Careful now, Hick. Don't be a complete idiot. This woman is straight as a string, married to—for all you know—the next President of the United States! Get a hold of yourself! You're 40 years old! Mrs. R must be ten years older! Have some sense! Want to get drummed out of the AP? Or, God forbid, land in jail?!? Just keep it up, old girl.

She shakes her head.

It's no good. I can't help myself. (*Ashamed.*) OK, OK, I'm a monster… But I was born like this. I can't stop—I'm falling. Jesus, am I ever.

HICK sits in one of two Art Deco leather chairs in the Center Stage. This space will serve as many locations. Now it is ELEANOR's train compartment. The invisible ELEANOR is in the other chair. HICK will sit often in this chair, with ELEANOR sitting next to her.

She started asking me to come back to her compartment all the time! Would I like to join her for tea? Why, certainly! Can we take her little Scots terrier for a walk? You bet!! Could I help her with some ideas she has? (*Slyly.*) Well, I wondered if she could help me with some of *my* ideas!

One afternoon, over coffee in her compartment, she told me she didn't want to be the First Lady, never had. She's got better things to do with her time than host tea parties for diplomats. She actually said, "If I were selfish, I would wish for him to lose." Now wouldn't that have made a headline! But she was speaking to me as a friend, you understand, not a reporter. Then she said, "If Franklin is elected, I want to be of use. But doing what?"

HICK paces, thinking.

Why, Mrs. Roosevelt, There are so many things you can… (*She gets an idea.*) Hey, hey, hey! You can hold press conferences for gal reporters only! I see gal reporters getting fired every day. There's a Depression going on! Now if you hold press conferences for them alone, they'll keep their jobs! And you will be the first First Lady to hold a press conference! (*Pause.*) Well, sure, it's a scandalous idea. The press conference itself will be news!

(*To the audience.*) She looked a bit cross, and said, "I don't think I'd be any good at it."

(*To ELEANOR.*) Well, I'll help you do it!

(*To the audience.*) And then she smiled. (*HICK sighs blissfully.*)

Lights cross-fade to indicate time passing as HICK goes to the

Office to make a phone call.

(*Into phone.*) Hey, Margery, how's it going at the old Associated Press?

Pause.

Oh, I'm having a grand time. Mrs. Roosevelt—she's something. Are you ready?

HICK reads from the paper she's holding.

Dateline: August 23, 1932—Hickok writing, from the Roosevelt campaign train, in Maine. These down-home Yankees always believed they would rather starve than ask for help. But now they are starving—and they're asking. (*Pause.*) Got that? Good. (*Reading.*) The candidate stops everywhere, shaking hands, being everybody's father, and he's good at it. Mrs. R is the perfect helpmate, always there to talk with the women about their kids, their future, and the future of women. I can see the compassion in her wonderful blue eyes. (*Pause.*) Wait a minute! Cut "wonderful blue." Just "compassion in her eyes."

HICK gives a sigh of relief. She caught that slip in time.

HICK crosses into a silvery light downstage. She acts out this scene with the invisible ELEANOR.

Getting off the train one morning just the two of us, all alone in a silver morning, a silver pearl morning, I could not stop myself. I took her lovely, graceful hand and held it, sort of swinging it like girls do. My stomach was doing flip-flops, my heart was pounding.

Her head whips around.

I thought I heard someone coming! I tried to pull my hand away, But she wouldn't let go! She held on and tight!

She looks around, vigilant.

No, there was no one. (*To herself.*) Oh lady, my lady, for that's what you are, whether you know it or not… Do you have any idea what a homosexual is?

(*To the audience.*) I never wanted to get back on that train. All I wanted was to be frozen in eternity with her, holding hands.

The train whistle sounds, breaking the spell. HICK returns to ELEANOR's train compartment.

One night, we stayed up late talking. She told me about her childhood. Oh, you'd think a person like that, born with a silver spoon in her mouth, just glided through life. But her mother died when she was young—just like mine! And her father drank! She didn't get thrown out of the house at the age of 14, like I did. But still, we had so much in common. And we both had grown up to make something of ourselves in the world. I felt like she could see my soul.

Oh, She was my kind of gal, alright! I edged closer, just to touch her shoulder. And I would brush casually across her as I reached for the salt. *You* know. I must have looked pretty silly, like a love-starved cocker spaniel. I noticed every once in awhile *she* was sneaking a look at *me*!

HICK leaps up, dancing a jig.

Oh, yeah!

Lights crossfade. HICK walks downstage.

We were outside the train walking...

She looks around, making sure no one is watching.

I slipped my arm around her waist! I expected to be struck dead—or at least slapped! I could feel her breathing. (*To herself*). Oh my lady love if you only knew, all I want in the world is to hold you, be with you...My Lady...

(*To the audience.*) I was really stepping it up! Fresh shirts at every stop, even if I had to buy 'em! (*She mimes polishing her shoes.*) Polish up the old Abercrombie and Fitches every day. I'd even taken to buffing my nails! I was really acting like an ass, because now she, the most beautiful lady in the world was, in my mind, my girl!

(*Silence.*) God forgive me taking my unnatural love to her, but I could not stop myself. And if I burn in hell for it, so be it.

She stands silent for a moment, then starts pacing briskly.

I had to make a serious pass soon or forget about it. I had to say what I felt right out loud to her. It was all I could think about night and day on that crummy train, hearing that damned campaign song...and talking softly with her.

The train whistle blows as lights fade.

Scene 4: The Proposal 1932

Lights up on the Apartment. HICK strides in.

HICK: Home at last! My sweet little New York apartment... GODDAMMIT! I was waiting for the perfect moment to tell her how

I felt, and suddenly, the trip was over! Why didn't I spill the beans last night? I'll never be alone with her again! Oh hell, she's probably kissing her countless children and embracing her innumberable friends right now. She's already forgotten about the silver pearl morning. I was nothing but a…a campaign train fling to her…

The phone rings. HICK answers glumly.

Hello?

Pause.

Why, hello, you!

Pause.

I miss *you*, Mrs. Roosevelt.

Pause.

It has so been a long time. Almost…

Checking her watch.

One hour and 45 minutes.

Pause.

It makes me happy too, to hear your voice. Say, I'm not busy right now. I can go anywhere. I can do anything. I'm completely free… Are you busy?

Pause.

No? Can I take you out for lunch?

Pause.

Really? I'll pick you up in a cab in thirty minutes.

HICK slowly hangs up the phone.

She said she was laughing because she was so happy to hear my voice! Could it be that I am *not* insane?

HICK dashes to the coatrack, grabbing the suit jacket hanging there. She stands before an invisible mirror, smoothes her hair, straightens her clothes. To the mirror.

Oh, Hick, you're a mess. How could she possibly want you? This woman is so far beyond me. She's going to say no. She is. Can I get out of this? It's too late. She's expecting me.

HICK pulls herself together and sweeps out of the Apartment.

Lights rise on the two chairs Center Stage, now the famous Russian Tea Room. An undercurrent of balalaika music is heard throughout this scene.

I took her to my favorite New York restaurant, the Russian Tea Room—balalaikas and all! She'd never been there before.

With a flourish, she ushers ELEANOR to her seat, then seats herself. She looks at ELEANOR, looks down, shifts nervously in her chair.

(*To herself.*) Now is now. It's the only now I've got.

She turns to ELEANOR.

I have to say this. I have to. Don't hate me…But if you do, you do. Eleanor Roosevelt, I love you! Now don't say anything, just listen. I love you, and not like a sister or a friend but…well…like a lover.

To the audience, as the balalaikas gets louder…

And then she said it, THE MIRACLE! "Hick, darling, don't you know I love you, too?"

…and the balalaikas get even louder…

And I said, "What?" The goddamned balalaikas were drowning her out! So she had to say it again: "I love you, Hick."

The balalaikas calm down.

(*Joyfully.*) There we were, in public, holding hands under the table and it dawned on me like the sun rising, like day breaking: She loves me. We're in love, not just me—we. All I wanted was to hold her in my arms. (*To ELEANOR.*) For God's sake, Mrs. Roosevelt, let's go home.

HICK leads ELEANOR back to her Apartment. The balalaikas play loud and wild and then fade out, as lights cross fade.

I took her back to my apartment and I took her in my arms, right here. I did.

HICK embraces ELEANOR.

I kissed her and kissed her. She told me that she'd been in love with me for a long time—ever since that silver morning we stepped off the train. I thought I was going to pass out. I didn't.

I got out the one valuable thing I owned, a beautiful ring, a diamond and sapphire band. I slipped it on her finger.

> HICK kneels, holding ELEANOR's hand.

Will you be mine? I can't ask you to marry me because you're already married but…Will you be mine?

And then we were both crying. There she was in my arms, erasing every hurt I ever had—touching my hair, kissing my eyelids, my neck and I heard myself saying, finally saying everything I had ever felt: "Jesus how I love you…You are my beauty… So good…

And she saying, "I thought I would never find you. All these years, love has only been about serving others and now—Oh Hick, Hick!"

(*To ELEANOR, carefully.*) Darling, I want to touch you… everywhere. I know you've never been with a woman, so I'll go very slowly and…

> She stops, startled.

(*To the audience.*) She put her hand on my mouth to stop me— and laughed! She told me that she'd gone to an English boarding school where all the girls were jumping in and out of each other's beds! Although Eleanor herself never partook, everyone considered it completely normal! And now her best friends are four women who are…two couples!! (*Pause.*) She said…"So, let's get on with it!"

(*Softly.*) And we got on with it.

> She utters a low, soft moan as she slowly sits on the footstool. They are now in bed.

Afterwards, she lay in my arms. Our skin had dissolved and our blood, our very souls were flowing back and forth between us.

She said, "It's October 8, just a month before the election. I have a lot of things to do." I said, "I know." She said, "I should at least phone to say I won't be doing them." I said, "Yes, you should." She said, "But to use the phone, I'd have to get out of bed." (*Smiling.*) I said, "Yes, you would."

She went to the phone, dialed. "Hello, this is Mrs. Roosevelt. Please cancel my appointments…for the rest of the day! I've got some very… urgent personal business to attend to. Thank you." Back in bed, she snuggled into me. We fell into a blissful sleep, never moving, not once, perfectly still.

> The lights fade slowly, leaving HICK momentarily silhouetted in blue light.

Scene 5: ELECTED! 1932

Lights come up quickly, FDR's campaign song plays loudly. HICK is in high spirits.

HICK: (*Shouting from the rooftops.*) It's November 8, 1932. Today, Franklin Delano Roosevelt was elected President of the United States! Thank god! (*Pause, normal voice.*) And…I convinced the Associated Press to let me keep covering Eleanor until the inauguration. After that, I'm back to covering whatever comes down the pike. But for the next few months, it's my job to follow around the great love of my life!

She guffaws at this great cosmic joke, as she crosses to the Apartment.

She started spending nights with me—in my apartment! My Dear One just scoffed at my worries. "Oh Hick, no one cares where I am—except for you."

Pause.

One morning over breakfast, she told me about the time fifteen years ago, when she discovered that her husband was having a serious affair with her own secretary. She was devastated, offered to give him a divorce. In the end, they decided to stay together—with Eleanor's proviso that their intimate relations were over.

I cannot tell you how overjoyed I was to hear that! (*Pause.*) But the truth is, I like FDR. And I'm so damn grateful to him for getting himself elected President. And yet here I am, sleeping with his wife…I've never committed adultery before. This is my very first adultery… and it's with THE WIFE OF THE COMMANDER-IN-CHIEF OF THE ARMED FORCES! It's a tad…daunting. Last night, I had a nightmare that FDR found out about Eleanor and me…and ordered the Air Force to bomb my apartment! I woke up feeling daunted, I can tell you.

Lights fade to black.

Scene 6: Inauguration 1933

"Hail to the Chief" is heard as lights come up on the AP office, where HICK is found pacing.

HICK: FDR's Inauguration is tomorrow! It's after midnight but I couldn't sleep if my life depended on it, so I came back to the office.

She sits. She stands. She sits. She stands.

The country's on the edge of exploding. Riots, civil war. FDR has to pull us all together. He has to. People are shaking in their shoes, waiting to hear the new President speak.

And just one hour ago, Eleanor read to me FDR's inaugural address. He's done it!

She is aflame.

He talked about putting people to work with government jobs—Jesus, how we need a president who believes in that…He's going to end the goddam greed and lies of the banks by regulating them. It's a good idea, isn't it? He says people need to make a living, but they need more than money. They need some joy and goddam meaning in their lives. He says we all need each other, and we'll work hard and sacrifice and turn the country around! He says, "The only thing we have to fear is fear itself." This speech is the beginning of hope for the country!

HICK rushes to her typewriter and types out the words.

"The only thing we have to fear is fear itself." In a few hours I've got to go cover the inauguration and pretend I'm hearing that speech for the first time.

A new, and very big, idea strikes her.

I can write that story for the A.P. now! Just type it up and hand it in…This Inauguration is the biggest story in the entire world!

She sees that banner in the sky.

Huge headlines everywhere: "Nothing to fear but fear itself." Byline: Lorena A. Hickok. The greatest scoop of my life!

Long pause.

But that would betray Eleanor's trust. Impossible. Impossible. (*To the audience.*) My boss has been hounding me for inside dope on the Roosevelts…Damn pest…He can go to hell…

HICK tears the paper out of the typewriter, balls it up, and hurls it into the wastebasket.

I'm ashamed to admit that I've been letting FDR's advisor approve my stories about Eleanor, before I hand them in. If the A.P. knew, they'd fire me. And they'd be right. It's unforgivable. That's not journalism. That's public relations, flacking for a client. I…I have already…betrayed the A.P.'s trust.

> *HICK grasps her typewriter like a life raft.*

I can't quit! How will I make a living? Who am I without my byline?

But she needs me. How many times has she told me the prospect of living in the White House would be unbearable if she didn't have me? (*Pause.*) "A reporter should never get too close to her sources." How many times have I heard that?! (*Pause.*) I'm not just close to the center of power. I'm sleeping with Power's wife.

> *HICK, deeply troubled, walks away from her typewriter as lights fade to black.*

Scene 7: Bathroom Interview 1933

> *Lights up on the Center Stage, now a public room at the White House. HICK rushes in. She is again in her element, as a journalist.*

HICK: The next morning, immediately after the Inauguration, I rushed to the White House to interview Eleanor—a first for First Ladies and for journalists! The White House was a madhouse of people running around, moving things in, setting things up.

> *HICK sits in one of the leather chairs.*

Eleanor and I sat there in the middle of it all, pretending that I was a reporter and she was First Lady. We were both vibrating with exhaustion…and energy! All we wanted was to hold each other. Suddenly Eleanor stood up and announced in a very loud voice that everyone was interrupting this very important interview, when we needed quiet and privacy. "We will be forced," she said, "to move the interview into one of the bathrooms and lock the door, so please don't anyone bother us." (*To the audience.*) And then she turned on her heel and marched off!

> *HICK follows ELEANOR upstage.*

Madam, what are you doing? We can't just…This is crazy…

> *HICK is pulled offstage by ELEANOR. The door slams behind her. Wild balalaika music is heard. After a noticeable amount of time has passed, HICK pokes her head out from behind the flats.*

We were very naughty. Oh my goodness…

> *HICK enters, her hair mussed, her shirt half-unbuttoned.*

We had a damn good time! It was a crazy thing to do. Everyone saw us go in there!

She looks around.

But they're all acting as if First Ladies get interviewed in locked bathrooms every day of the year!

HICK buttons her shirt, smoothes her hair, as she crosses downstage.

And then later that afternoon at the White House: The very first press conference ever held by a First Lady, with thirty-five gal reporters attending! When it started, my Dear One was so nervous, I was afraid she would faint. But she's a trouper. She pulled it off beautifully. What a woman!

HICK crosses to the Office.

And then I skedaddled back to the A.P. office to write my last story on Anna Eleanor Roosevelt, a woman possessed of many talents and the most magnificent blue eyes. And that was the end of the assignment.

Lights fade to black.

Scene 8: The Letters Begin 1933

Lights up on the Apartment. HICK is distraught.

HICK: I'm back in New York. It's over. Four days after the inauguration, and it's over. The White House changed everything. Two days ago, we were supposed to have tea before I left for New York. I show up at the White House gate—and they won't let me in! There's a list and she forgot to put my name on it! I stood there over two hours until they finally got word from Eleanor and... (*Sarcastically.*) I was permitted to enter. Hallelujah!

When I find my darling, she says to me (*Very briskly.*), "I'm very sorry, Hick, but I won't have time to see you today." And then her secretary whisks her away! She knew I had to get back to New York for an assignment that afternoon. She knew. She forgot to put my name on the list. And, when I finally got in, she couldn't give me the time of day.

HICK throws herself in the armchair.

She's finished with me...How could she have fallen in love with me in the first place? A pervert...I can't believe I ever had the nerve... She's come to her senses...Oh good lord. I called in sick today...I can't work…I'm not sure I can live…

The sound of a mailbox flap opening and closing is heard.

(*Glumly.*) The mail.

HICK drags herself offstage, re-enters holding a letter.

It's a letter from Eleanor! Oh god. This is it…She's ending it…

HICK opens the letter, reads it. We hear ELEANOR's voice speaking the words.

ELEANOR'S VOICE: The White House. March 5, 1933. Hick, my dearest, I cannot go to bed tonight without a word to you. I felt a little as though a part of me was leaving when you left. You have grown to be so much a part of my life that it is empty without you, even though I am busy every minute.

Oh! Darling, I felt I had brought you so much discomfort and hardship today and almost more heartache than you could bear and I don't want to make you unhappy. All my love and I shall be saying to you over thought waves in a few minutes—

> Good night my dear one
> Angels guard thee
> God protect thee
> My love enfold thee
> All the night through.

Always yours, E.R.

HICK: Oh, I am the luckiest gal in the world!

HICK presses the letter to her heart as lights fade to black.

INTERMISSION

ACT TWO

Scene 1: The Letters Begin 1933 (continued)

The beginning of this scene repeats the last few moments of Act One. No time has passed. HICK is reading the letter.

ELEANOR'S VOICE:

Good night my dear one
Angels guard thee
God protect thee
My love enfold thee
All the night through.
Always yours, E.R.

HICK: Oh, I am the luckiest gal in the world!

HICK presses the letter to her heart, the exact same gesture that ended Act One. The sound of the mailbox flap is heard again. HICK rushes off. She returns with several letters, opening the first one.

March sixth!

ELEANOR'S VOICE: My pictures are nearly all up and I have you in my sitting room. I can't kiss you in person, so I kiss your picture good night and good morning. (*HICK laughs.*) Don't laugh!

HICK: And I kiss your letter!

She does so. She opens another letter.

March seventh!

ELEANOR'S VOICE: My dear, when we meet may I forget there are other reporters present or must I behave? I shall want to hug you to death.

HICK: You must behave! (*To the audience.*) This woman is incorrigible.

She opens another letter.

March eighth!

ELEANOR'S VOICE: Oh! I want to put my arms around you, I ache to hold you close. Your ring is a great comfort. I look at it and think she does love me, or I wouldn't be wearing it.

HICK: She wore my ring to the Inauguration! (*Pause. With concern.*) I wonder if anyone noticed. Even if they did, they would never know it was a gift from me! Eleanor's been in the White House three weeks, and she's writing me every day! She calls me too. One night, we talked for hours, and right after we hung up, she wrote me this letter…

HICK makes herself comfortable on the footstool to read this latest letter.

ELEANOR'S VOICE: Hick darling, Oh! How good it was to hear your voice tonight. Words are so inadequate to tell you what it meant. My son Jimmy was near and I couldn't say, "*Je t'aime et je t'adore*" as I longed to do but always remember I am saying it. I go to sleep thinking of you and repeating our little saying— "*Je t'aime et je t'adore*" No one is like you, Hick. I love you and good night. E.R.

HICK: I knew that "*je t'aime*" meant "I love you" in French. But "*Je t'adore?*" It sounded like "shut the door" to me. So the first time Eleanor said "*Je t'aime et je t'adore*," I thought she was saying "I love you and shut the door." Well. The door happened to be open and her word was my command, so I shut the damn door!

She laughs that braying guffaw.

She can always cheer me up when I'm down by whispering tenderly in my ear, "Hick darling, shut the door."

The phone rings.

I'll bet that's my Dear One now!

She answers the phone with her sexiest voice.

Hello…(*Surprised.*) Oh hi, Boss.

Pause.

Yeah! I read about the Perkins appointment. Frances Perkins! Secretary of Labor! First woman in history appointed to the Cabinet. FDR done a good thing, huh, Boss?

Pause.

Of course I noticed it was a United Press story, not an A.P. story. Hey, sometimes we scoop the enemy, sometimes they scoop us!

Pause.

I know Perkins is a close friend of Mrs. Roosevelt.

Pause.

It's none of your damn business what Mrs. Roosevelt says to me. As you well know, I'm not covering the First Lady anymore. She's a friend, not a source. That's my personal life. Got that?

Pause.

Remember? I'm not covering the White House. I'm here in New York, covering the garbage strike. Now, if the UPI scoops us on the garbage strike, then you've got something to complain about.

Pause. HICK explodes.

Christ, I am so sick of you badgering me about the White House, the White House, the White House. I've had it. You can go to hell. I quit!

Pause.

Good riddance to you too and everyone else at the A.P.!

HICK slams down the phone.

What a RELIEF!

She sits down. Slowly, relief turns to shock and distress.

Jesus! What have I done?

Frantic, she grabs the phone, dials.

Margery, it's Hick. I gotta speak to the Boss right away! It's urgent.

Pause.

Sure, sure, I'll hold.

While HICK is on hold, ELEANOR's letters, sitting on the little table, catch her eye. She picks them up, then looks at the phone she's holding. She slowly puts the phone back in its cradle. We hear a collage of ELEANOR's words, with soft music under them, as HICK presses the letters to her heart.

ELEANOR'S VOICE: Empty without you…Angels guard thee…Kiss your picture…Must I behave?…Ache to hold you close…

HICK tenderly puts the letters in the cigar box on the table. ELEANOR's voice flows on.

Je t'adore…je t'adore…je t'adore…

Lights fade to black.

Scene 2: The Great Depression 1933

Lights up on HICK, downstage.

HICK: Just got back from my honeymoon! Honeymoon's more important than getting married, everyone knows that. My Dear One and I spent three weeks motoring up to Nova Scotia and back. Alone! Oh, the Secret Service demanded to go with us. But, as FDR once advised me, "Hick, don't argue with the Missus. She always wins."

It was delightful. Almost no one recognized her. She said, "Hick, don't you know that's because they're all Republicans up here." We stayed in little hotels and tourist cabins. Saw gorgeous scenery. Read poetry to each other late at night. (*Pause.*) Oh, we're as different as chalk and cheese. But when we're alone, we're like…we're like…We're like two violin strings vibrating in unison.

> *She pauses to savor the feeling.*

Now it's time to go to work!

> *HICK crosses to the coatrack in her Apartment, dons the trench coat hanging there and picks up the briefcase standing next to the coatrack.*

It's been six months since I quit the A.P., and I got a new job! I'm Chief Investigator of the Federal Relief Administration. My new boss is Harry Hopkins. I'm part of FDR's New Deal—a huge government program to create jobs for everyone who can work—and relief for those who can't.

I'm traveling all over the country, talking with preachers, teachers, factory workers, farmers, the unemployed—anyone and everyone. Folks are in trouble. They need a break, a hand up!

> *HICK enters the Office, which now represents wherever she stays in her travels.*

Mr. Hopkins said to me, "Don't pull your punches!" He's got to know where the New Deal isn't working, not just where it is. So I guess I'm still a reporter. But this time, instead of Eleanor Roosevelt, I'm covering the American people through the Depression. That's a helluva big subject, even for yours truly, Lorena Hickok. I worry that I'm not up to the task.

> *She picks up a letter from ELEANOR lying on her desk.*

ELEANOR'S VOICE: I know you are going to do a swell job and please let me share it, for I have an interest in what you are doing and then twice as much interest and pride in the way you are doing it.

HICK: She's proud of me!

> *She carefully files this first "on the road" letter, and all the others to come.*

My work takes me away from my Dear One for long stretches. But I need this job. I need the money. I'm taking buses and trains around the country…Hotels in little towns—oh, I've slept in some doozies!

> *She sits at her typewriter.*

I'm meeting meeting meeting with all kinds of people.

She types rapidly, stops.

What has happened to this country? People are suffering. They're desperate. And why? Because the banks and the wealthy played with the economic system until they broke it!

HICK reads aloud as she types.

October 10, 1933. Pittsburgh, Pennsylvania. Dear One: Today, I met with a group of relief clients for an hour. They begged me to come back this evening to hear more. I made the mistake of telling them I was tired. They said, "We're tired too, lady. And we're living on 90 cents a week!" So I came back and listened. For hours.

I feel like a great big sponge all filled with water, soaking up other people's ideas and complaints and hopes and dreams. I seem to have lost all my individuality. And it is the most interesting thing that has happened to me in my life.

ELEANOR'S VOICE: What a book you'll be able to write on 'how we live.' I can see what you have seen and feel as you felt, just reading your letters. How small one's worries seem in comparison to what so many human beings have been through.

HICK: (*To the audience.*) That's what keeps me going: Letters from my Dear One. I send her copies of all my reports. My readership is rather limited. Lorena Hickok, who was read by millions! Now it's Eleanor, Mr. Hopkins, and FDR. Oh, and sometimes those pig-headed Republicans who refuse to understand how desperate people are. FDR gives them copies. The New Deal says everyone counts. If they need help, they should get it. We're in this together!

Of course, I'm working all on my lonesome. I miss the newsroom, the hurly-burly…my pals, the gang. I even miss my boss yelling when I'm late. (*Pause.*) That life is finished.

HICK reads aloud as she types.

Nov 1, 1933, Minot, North Dakota. Dear Mr. Hopkins: Into the relief office came today a little middle-aged farmer—skin like leather, heavily calloused, grimy hands—incongruously attired in a worn white flannel suit of collegiate cut, flashy blue sweater, belted tan topcoat and cap to match. He explained. He said, "These clothes I got on, they belong to my oldest boy. They're all we've got now. We take turns wearing 'em."

(*Fiercely.*) Mr. Hopkins, These people have got to have clothing—right away! They've had their first snow up here. Snow is forecast for tomorrow. It's cold. I'm talking about North Dakota!

She picks up another letter from ELEANOR.

ELEANOR'S VOICE: The letter from North Dakota came, and I read parts of it to FDR, and he said he hoped clothes and blankets could be got out in a few days.

HICK: Thank god!

ELEANOR'S VOICE: How do they live through it? You are doing a grand job, my dear. I used your stories yesterday, and shall again today.

HICK: (*To herself.*) She's using my stories in her column! (*To the audience.*) Eleanor writes a column, "My Day," that's carried in papers all over the country—six days a week! "My Day" was my idea.

ELEANOR'S VOICE: I look at you long as I write. The photograph has an expression I love, so you and a bit whimsical. But then I adore every expression.

HICK: (*Typing.*) December 5, 1933. Bemidji, Minnesota. My Dear One: I've been trying today to bring back your face—to remember just *how* you look. Most clearly I remember your eyes, with a kind of teasing smile in them, and the feeling of that soft spot just northeast of the corner of your mouth against my lips.

ELEANOR'S VOICE: Though I can remember just how you look, I shall want to look long and very lovingly at you, when we meet again. Your return is getting nearer and nearer and I am half afraid to be too happy.

HICK: (*Typing.*) I want to put my arms around you and kiss you at the corner of your mouth.

ELEANOR'S VOICE: Every day that passes brings you nearer.

HICK: (*Typing.*) I wonder what we'll do when we meet—what we'll say.

ELEANOR'S VOICE: I don't know just how I shall behave!

HICK: (*Typing.*) It's been so long since I've seen you.

ELEANOR'S VOICE: Never are you out of my heart….

HICK: (*Typing.*) A week from now—right this minute—I'll be with you!

ELEANOR'S VOICE: I'll hold my breath till you arrive! We'll have tea in my room as soon as you get here Friday.

HICK packs her briefcase and tidies the office, preparing to leave.

HICK: I'm going home to the White House for Christmas! That's where I live when I'm not on the road. I have a little bed in the dressing room off Eleanor's bedroom. (*She winks at the audience.*)

I've been on the road for five months—from California to Maine, from North Dakota to Alabama—and too many chicken-fried steaks in-between to count. I bet I've talked with more desperate people than anyone on earth. Eleanor will fuss over me and read to me, and make everything alright. Joy to the world, indeed!

Christmas music plays as HICK leaves the Office with a jolly...

Ho ho ho!

Lights cross-fade.

Scene 3: Christmas 1933

Lights up on the Apartment. The Christmas music fades as HICK walks in, drops her briefcase with a thud and tears off her trench coat.

HICK: (*To the audience, heavily mocking.*) Ho ho ho.

The phone rings.

Hello?

Pause.

(*Sarcastically.*) Well, if it isn't "Dear One!"

Pause.

I'm fine now that I'm back in New York and not sitting alone in your goddam sitting room. What was it you wrote? Tea when I arrive? Yes, I did have tea when I arrived—by myself. You popped in for five minutes that evening to tell me how very much you adored me. And then Saturday, our "special" day was especially...lonely.

Pause.

I don't give a damn if you're daughter's getting divorced! She's got a father and brothers and friends, not to mention her extremely attentive lover. I only have you, Madam. And I was just home for a few days! I'm not some Christmas gift you can toss in a corner and unwrap when you happen to have a moment to spare. I'm an exhausted, overwrought human being, and I'm in love with you! (*Fighting back tears.*) I can't talk anymore. Goodbye, Mrs. Roosevelt.

HICK hangs up. The phone starts to ring almost immediately. HICK tries to ignore it. But after many rings, she gives in.

(*Harshly.*) Yes, Mrs. Roosevelt?

As she realizes how distraught ELEANOR is, her anger melts away.

Alright, alright. Calm down, darling.

Pause.

Of course I forgive you.

Pause.

Yes! That is what we need! Our own vacation, far from everyone! Yes, darling, let's do it—a second honeymoon!

Pause.

Darling, you know I....I...love you too. (*Teasingly.*) Shut the door.

HICK hangs up the phone, smiling. She exits, humming a Christmas carol.

Lights fade. We hear ELEANOR's letter in the darkness.

ELEANOR'S VOICE: December 23, 1933, the White House. Hick dearest, I went to sleep saying a little prayer, "God give me depth enough not to hurt Hick again."

Dearest one, forgive me and believe me you've brought me more and meant more to me than you know and I will be thankful Christmas Eve and Christmas Day and every day for your mere being in the world. Goodnight, sleep well, a world of love—ER

Scene 4: Rumpled 1934

As the lights come up, HICK can be heard offstage, counting "One-two-three-four, Two-two-three-four..." She enters, doing calisthenics, waving her arms in the air and lifting her knees high.

HICK: three-two-three-four... four-two...

She collapses in the armchair.

Three... (*She pants.*) ...Four....

She fans herself.

Oh lordy, I'll get into shape or die in the attempt. I need to be fit because Eleanor and I are going on vacation! Yosemite National Park! A little cabin, long walks through the silent forest, just the two of us... Giant sequoia trees! The oldest, biggest living things on the planet! I've always wanted to see them.

But I've got to get in shape or I'll be wheezing and grunting, just like I was yesterday, trying to keep up with her. She was crossing a field to inspect a crop—as is her wont—those long legs just swinging so gracefully. Oh, I love to see it, but I'm always behind. Puffing, panting, perspiring. My beloved never breaks a sweat. Never. Nobody can keep up with her! Let alone...let alone...

She grabs a TIME magazine from the table, finds the offending article.

Let alone quote "rumpled, fat and masculine" end quote ME.

She brandishes the TIME.

How would you like it if TIME Magazine described you as "rumpled, fat and masculine"?

Doesn't even have my name here. Just some anonymous rumpled, fat and masculine woman trundling after the First Lady...as...as...comic relief, I suppose.

Anyone would get rumpled trying to keep up with Eleanor Roosevelt! Nobody else is trying to do it at the moment. That's all. Just fat and masculine me. That woman is unrumple-able! I'd like to see that TIME reporter follow her across a field without a goddam rumple. What is this stupid bastard's name?

She searches the article.

Nothing! No byline!

Silence.

(*Softly.*) I had a byline.

HICK turns her back as lights fade.

Scene 5: Yosemite 1934

Lights up. HICK walks downstage enraptured.

HICK: Ah, Yosemite! Beneath the majestic sequoias, my love and I, alone!

Pause.

Fat chance. We were immediately set upon by a dozen rangers absolutely determined to put us on packhorses and take us on a goddam safari. Oh, Eleanor was tickled pink to climb mountains, swim in freezing lakes, and plunge down ravines and across rivers on the back of a horse with those cute little rangers. I, on the other hand, huffed and puffed up the slightest incline—and actually fell off my horse into the river! The poor animal was trying to take a bath, and who can blame her? Camping makes you filthy. Oh, not that Dear One cared. She was actually flirting with the rangers!

I don't know whose vacation this was, but it certainly wasn't mine!

> HICK crosses to the two chairs Center Stage, now a suite in the Yosemite hotel.

At long last, we were safely deposited in the beautiful Ahwahnee Hotel—ensconced in the Presidential Suite. Oh, my beloved was irked. She so longed to be treated like an ordinary person—probably because she's never been treated like one. As for myself, I found luxury quite easy to adjust to. And I had my Dear One to myself for the first time on this vacation!

Now's the moment for my special request. (*To ELEANOR.*) Darling, at the Inaugural Ball, you waltzed so beautifully. I was dying to ask you to dance, but of course I couldn't. Ever since then, I've been longing to do it.

> HICK bows deeply to ELEANOR, as a gentleman would.

Why, Mrs. Roosevelt, you're looking particularly lovely tonight! Would you do me the honor of this dance?

> She extends her hand to ELEANOR, who accepts.

I'll just have to supply the music myself.

> A waltz begins. They dance, gracefully. HICK sings along with the music. They whirl and twirl offstage as music and lights fade. Lights up. HICK re-enters.

Early the next morning, Eleanor put her arm through mine and we walked to the grove.

> They walk downstage. HICK looks around.

We were alone. I wrapped my arms around her. There we were, the happy lovers, with only the sequoias to witness us. The sequoias! Those majestic towering...beings! The presence of God...The absence of rangers...Just the two of us....

Suddenly, I heard a shout: "There she is!" The crowd surged toward us snapping photos. Did they see her in my arms? Did they take a picture? We were surrounded by tourists, shoving their goddam cameras in her face. They were crushing Eleanor!

HICK shouts at the crowd.

Back off! Give her some room! Don't you sons of bitches have anything better to do than ruin our vacation?

She explodes with rage, rushing at them.

Jesus Christ! Leave us alone!

The tourists flee.

Hah!

Triumphantly, HICK turns to ELEANOR, who is furious.

The look on Eleanor's face...I'd never seen it before...She was fed up...She dragged me back to the hotel room.

HICK sits in the Center Stage chair, terrified. ELEANOR stands implacable before her.

Darling, I just wanted you to myself for a little while...Everyone wants you...the rangers, the tourists...Oh, I'm bad, my dear, but I love you so...

(*To the audience.*) She said, "Hick, I'm going back to those poor tourists to apologize for your disgraceful behavior. You stay here."

HICK's eyes follow ELEANOR as she leaves.

There was no excuse...I've never blown up in public before...I crossed a line...

HICK sits, desolate, as lights fade. In the darkness, we hear ELEANOR's voice.

ELEANOR'S VOICE: Dear One: I'm afraid you and I are always going to have times when we ache for each other and yet we are not always going to be happy when we are together. Somehow we must find the things which we can do and do them so that what time we have together is as happy as it can be in an imperfect world!

Scene 6: The Decision 1968

> *Lights slowly fade up on HICK's apartment. We are back in 1968. HICK, now 75 as in the first scene and wearing her dressing gown, sits in her armchair, surrounded by three large cardboard boxes full of old letters, and a wastebasket full of torn-up letters. She is reading a letter.*

HICK: This one's alright.

> *She puts the letter in the "Yes" box to her right. She picks another letter from the center box, reads it.*

This one's no good.

> *She tears it up and throws the pieces in the "No" box on the left. The phone rings.*

Oh hell.

> *She answers, speaking immediately.*

Hello, Gerald.

> *Pause.*

I knew it was you because the phone ring has a certain yapping frustrated quality when you call.

> *Pause.*

Yes. I know today's the deadline.

> *Pause.*

No. I haven't made a decision yet.

> *Pause.*

Don't push me, Gerald. Do you want me to burn all the letters? Maybe then you'll stop bothering me!

> *She slams the phone down.*

(*To the audience.*) That was the director of the FDR Library. Oh yes, we're on a first-name basis. I made the mistake of admitting that I had… more than a few letters from Eleanor, and now he is relentless, pestering me to donate all of them to the archive. I told him I'd make a decision by today. Of course Gerald's foaming at the mouth to get these letters. But he has no idea what he would be getting.

She grabs a letter from the "No" box.

Listen to this...

ELEANOR'S VOICE: Oh dear one, it is all the little things, tones in your voice, the feel of your hair, gestures—these are the things I think about and long for.

HICK: "The feel of your hair..." If Gerald ever read this he would know she was in love with me! And so would anyone with half a brain. I intend to give him all of the letters where she only talks about her work and family. So first, I've got to find every single letter where she talks about loving me...and get rid of it. Good god!

Pause.

She didn't stay in love. It was never the same after Yosemite. She felt she couldn't trust me around other people. And she was right! She couldn't! She still loved me. We talked on the phone all the time. Wrote books together. I lived in the White House all of World War II, so she would have a friend nearby. Sometimes we even had a precious day alone. And of course, letters—as you can see. But her passion for me— gone. Not mine. Not mine. It's 1968. My Dear One's been gone six years, and I'm still in love. Once you've been had by Eleanor Roosevelt, you stay had.

She rereads the letter.

"The feel of your hair..." Oh, my lady...I never did understand what she found so special...

She runs her fingers through her hair.

It's just hair...

She picks up another letter.

Look at this letter...

ELEANOR'S VOICE: In just one week, I'll be holding you!

HICK: (*Finding another one.*)...And this one...When her daughter's divorce became a huge scandal...

ELEANOR'S VOICE: One cannot hide things in this world, can one? How lucky you are not a man!

HICK: "How lucky you are not a man!" If that's not a smoking gun I don't know what is! And this... (*Holding out another letter.*)

ELEANOR'S VOICE: Dear One, so you think they gossip about us. Well, they must at least think we stand separation rather well!

HICK: "Gossip about us!" They all knew. Everyone around us. Used to scare the bejesus out of me. She said, "Hick, darling, what we are doing is just too far beyond the pale to speak about, except behind closed doors."

HICK looks up, addressing ELEANOR in heaven.

And you were right, Madame. You were right about so many things. FDR *didn't* give a damn.

(*To the audience.*) He had his own secrets. How I loved that man. What he did for the country, for the world…And am I now going to reveal to the world that I had an affair with his wife?

HICK rummages in the center box, which holds the unread letters. She looks up at the audience.

I've burned quite a few letters already. The worst ones…They were the best ones. She could be a very naughty girl, you know. You don't know, do you? I'm the only one who knows that. I've never spoken about it…ever… And now I've been erased.

(*To ELEANOR above.*) You know, Dear One, people write books about you. You've become a goddam cottage industry. They interview the cook, they interview the gardener, they interview the goddam dogcatcher. (*To the audience.*) But they never interview old Hickey. I guess they know there's something…funny about me. I've been erased. Only one bothering old Hickey is Gerald. And he wants all the letters…

HICK picks a letter at random from the center box, reads.

ELEANOR'S VOICE: My dear, I feel more of an old lady than at 50. I have more limitations but I know them and accept them! I'm going to be no leader of thought or action but a homebody in the near future.

HICK: (*Laughing uproariously.*) A homebody! Oh, lordy lordy. What's the date on this? September 1, 1945. After FDR died and right before Truman appointed you to the United Nations. (*To ELEANOR above.*) "No leader in thought or action" indeed, Madame! Then who took the lead in crafting the Universal Declaration of Human Rights and then cajoled all those countries into signing it? It was you, Madame. Nobody else could have done it! My dear… homebody. First Lady of the World. That's what they called you.

She sees the final banner in the sky.

Huge headlines everywhere: "First Lady of the World Has Died."

Everyone knew who that was.

> *HICK sits, thinking, remembering.*

(*To the audience.*) People think being loved by millions is enough. But she needed to be loved by *one*. My Eleanor, who gave and gave and gave. Millions wouldn't do. She needed one to hold her up. And I was that One. Always.

> *HICK looks at the letter she holds.*

This goes in the "good" box. I've already sorted through these.

> *HICK puts it in the box with a sense of accomplishment. She picks a letter at random out of the "good" box. She reads it, enjoying it greatly.*

Oh, that picnic! Oh, didn't we have a good time… (*Pause. With alarm.*) Wait a minute! It's a bad one. How did I miss it? I thought I already sorted through this box! I don't understand. How did it get in here?

> *HICK tears up the letter, throws it on the floor.*

(*To the audience in despair.*) Do you know how many boxes of letters from Eleanor I have in the closet? Neither do I! Boxes and boxes. I will never find all the…special letters. I won't live long enough! That leaves me with two choices: Give everything to the archive…or destroy everything.

> *The phone rings. HICK yells at it without answering.*

You can't wait, can you Gerald, to get your grubby little paws into my boxes of letters? Jesus, shut up. Shut up! Shut up!

> *She keeps yelling "Shut up!" until the phone stops ringing.*

Thank you.

> *Hick grabs two handfuls of letters from the box. She holds them up to ELEANOR.*

Madame, what am I to do with all the letters you wrote me? Why did you leave this to me? You could have asked for your letters back. I would have given them to you. You could have told me to burn them all. I would have done it. I would have cried like a baby, but I would have done it.

> *She throws the letters back into the box. She is calmer now. She looks up at ELEANOR.*

Madame, my beauty, my love...Are you ashamed of who I am? You loved me. I must not be so awful. How can it be shameful, what we did together, what we felt for each other?

Pause.

Dear One, are you up for being mocked and despised as a pervert?

HICK grabs a random envelope, holding it high.

Because I'm seriously considering giving all the letters to the...

She feels something in the envelope.

What's this?

As HICK takes the letter out of the envelope, dried rose petals cascade to the floor.

Rose petals...

HICK looks up at ELEANOR, smiles. She reads the letter, inhaling the fragrance of the rose petals..

ELEANOR'S VOICE: June 3, 1934. Val-Kill Cottage.
Hick darling: I wonder if any of the sweetness of this little favorite rose of mine will linger by the time it reaches you? My garden at the cottage was a lovely sight in full bloom and unconsciously I wanted you to see it with me. Always yours, ER.

HICK holds the letter to her heart.

HICK: (*To herself.*) I was loved by Eleanor Roosevelt. (*To the audience with great force.*) I was loved by Eleanor Roosevelt! She was my lady. I was her knight, her refuge. We were violin strings vibrating in unison, to the end. Thirty years of love! I'm proud of that. People will never understand, but I don't give a damn!

Pause.

I cannot destroy these letters. They're all that remains.

She turns in a circle, her arms outstretched.

I'm giving the letters—all of them—ALL OF THEM—to the archive. I want people to know.

Pause.

(*To the audience.*) I want *you* to know.

HICK surveys the audience with a searching gaze. She stands in a pool of light, holding the final letter, inhaling the fragrance of the rose petals.

The surrounding light fades until there is only a pinpoint of light on HICK's face. That light slowly fades to black.

End Of Play

NOTES:

- A shorter version of *HICK*, about 1½ hours with no intermission, is available.
- A concert reading version of *HICK* is available. This can be done in any space with three actors. One plays Hick, one reads the letters, and one reads stage directions, replacing all technical aspects of the production.
- An audio file of Eleanor's letters, read by Paula Barish, is available.

FROM THE PLAYWRIGHT

The Responsibility Of Writing About A Real Person

This is my only biographical play. Very little was invented by me, but I'm a playwright, not a biographer obliged to stick to the verifiable facts. So I have taken the liberty to imagine what was not recorded. A good example is the outrageous "interview" in the White House bathroom. I didn't make this up. Hick wrote about it, and one of the White House servants wrote a memoir where she remarked with great disapproval on the event. But Hick maintained that she and Eleanor merely performed a journalistic exercise in that locked bathroom. I take the position that two people do not go into a bathroom and lock the door merely to talk to each other.

I did have to conjure an inciting incident from thin air, to create the scene where Hick receives her first letter. That first letter is dated March 5, 1933. In it Eleanor, clearly in love, spends most of her time apologizing for hurting Hick's feelings—without ever revealing the tiniest scrap of what happened! I greatly enjoyed inventing something probable to fill out the details missing in the historical record.

I have tried to be true to the characters of Lorena Hickok and Eleanor Roosevelt. The First Lady was a risk-taker. She was perfectly happy to walk the edge of appropriate public behavior with Hick, knowing that her position made her vulnerable to gossip, but not to exposure in the press. But Eleanor was also an extremely responsible person. When the play opened at the Eureka Theatre, I had her stay in bed with Hick rather than get up to phone her office to cancel her appointments for the day. I yearned for the First Lady to be so drowned in lesbian lust that she ignored her obligations completely. Yet I knew this was false to Eleanor Roosevelt's character. So for the second production, I grudgingly rewrote the scene to include her phone call to her office.

Revelations From Research

My research in the FDR Library in Hyde Park is the only time I've ever delved into original documents. I discovered two very important aspects of this story that hadn't been revealed in my reading of other people's books.

First, Eleanor's later letters proved there was a constant intimacy between the two women, lasting 30 years. As she lay dying, Eleanor dictated her final letter to Hick: "I'm still horribly weak. But as soon as

I'm able to hold the phone I'll call you." After Eleanor died, her secretary sent Hick a letter she found on Eleanor's desk: "Dearest Hick: I was glad to get your letter and I do hope the blood sugar leveled off a little bit lower and you don't have to take more insulin. I'll be back Monday. Love, ER."

Clearly, Eleanor worried about Hick's health and expected to talk to or see her soon after that Monday. But when Monday came, Eleanor was in the hospital. Even if we only had these two final letters, they would suffice to prove Eleanor's deep and lasting involvement with Hick.

Friendships between women have been trivialized forever. Like most of womens' activities, they're deemed unimportant. Yet Hick and Eleanor's friendship of 30 years was a strong thread in the fabric of both their lives. So *HICK: A Love Story* was written not just to honor their lesbian affair but to also honor their friendship.

My second discovery through reading original documents was the fact that many people loved Lorena Hickok—not just Eleanor Roosevelt. I read playful, adoring letters from Marion Harron, a beautiful young judge and Hick's one love relationship after Eleanor. I read the announcement of Hick's retirement party from her job as publicity director for the New York World's Fair—on a paper covered with dozens of signatures of all who would attend. I read one of the speeches given at that party, mourning Hick's departure. I read many of the letters from Hollywood starlet-turned-Congresswoman Helen Gahagan Douglas, reminiscing about their late-night talks and lamenting Hick's absence for a few weeks. In my opinion, an ex-starlet member of Congress can choose whoever she wants for a friend in Washington D.C. Mrs. Douglas chose Lorena Hickok.

One would think a badly dressed overweight masculine woman would have been a pariah in the 1930s and 1940s. But all the evidence points to the opposite. Hick must have had some powerful charisma. I decided that, not possessing such charisma, I'd better look as good as possible onstage. Otherwise, how could the audience possibly imagine the magnificent Eleanor falling in love with me? I freed myself from trying to reproduce Hick's dumpy look, and had a rather nifty three-piece suit made to order.

The Importance Of Hick

Lorena Hickok grasped the power of Eleanor Roosevelt before Eleanor saw it herself. Without knowing Eleanor personally, Hick insisted to her editor that it was worth assigning a reporter to cover this candidate's wife. It's difficult for us today to understand what a strange idea that was in 1932.

Hick telegrammed her boss from the campaign train: "Mrs. R has enormous dignity. She's a PERSON!" As a lesbian, Hick was uniquely open to recognizing the vibrant personhood of another woman. At a moment when Eleanor Roosevelt despaired of her future as First Lady, Lorena Hickok not only gave her emotional support and physical love, she also taught her to use the media to express her political passions. It was Hick's idea that Eleanor should have a weekly press conference for women reporters only. It was Hick's idea that Eleanor should write a daily column. In the beginning, Hick edited all of Eleanor's articles, teaching the First Lady to express herself succinctly and powerfully. Eleanor looked up to Hick as someone who had overcome obstacles that Eleanor could not even imagine.

Hick was instrumental in helping Eleanor fulfill her destiny as a great activist for progressive causes. This destiny culminated in her acting as midwife to the birth of the Universal Declaration of Human Rights. This powerful document, ratified by the United Nations in 1948, still inspires us with its radical vision today.

Hick chose Eleanor over her calling as a reporter. That was not a wise decision in terms of Hick's well-being. But when I think of everything that Eleanor Roosevelt gave to the world, I'm grateful to Hick for her sacrifice. And I'm in awe of the great love and deep friendship between these two amazing women. This love story is an important part of our history as lesbians. The world needs to know it.

BIBLIOGRAPHY for HICK: A Love Story

Besides reading the books below, Terry spent a week in Hyde Park, NY, doing research in the FDR Library and interviewing people who knew Lorena Hickok.

The Life of Lorena Hickok, E. R.'s Friend
By Doris Faber

Empty Without You:
The Intimate Letters Of Eleanor Roosevelt And Lorena Hickok
Edited by Rodger Streitmatter

Eleanor Roosevelt: Reluctant First Lady
by Lorena A. Hickok

Eleanor Roosevelt, Vols. 1, 2 & 3
By Blanche Wiesen Cook

One Third of a Nation:
Lorena Hickok Reports on the Great Depression
By Lorena Hickok

America 1933
by Michael Golay

ABOUT TERRY BAUM

Terry Baum is an actress, director, teacher, filmmaker, political activist and a pioneer lesbian playwright. She has been creating theater since 1974 on issues ranging from gay rights and medical-ethical dilemmas to the eternal pursuit of love. Critics have compared her to Lily Tomlin, Norman Mailer, Godzilla, Bea Arthur and Woody Allen—but never in the same review.

Her plays have been published in three anthologies, produced all over the world and translated into many languages. As a solo performer of her own work, she has toured the U.S., Canada, Western Europe, Israel, South Africa, Cuba and Morocco.

Born in 1946 in Los Angeles to a middle-class Jewish family, she received a B.A. in Theater (Antioch College) and an M.A. in Theater (U.C. Santa Barbara). In 1974, she moved to San Francisco to found Lilith a Women's Theater Collective, which she led for five years. She came out as a lesbian in 1976. *Dos Lesbos*, her first play, opened in San Francisco in 1981.

Between 1986 and 1994, Baum lived mostly in Amsterdam. She toured Europe extensively as a solo performer and wrote two plays. One play explored a search for lesbian love in Holland (*One Fool*). The other one delved into the experience of Dutch Jews under Nazi Occupation (*Divide the Living Child*). From 1996 to 1999, she lived and produced her plays in New York City. Since 1999, she has stayed put in San Francisco.

Her short films has been shown at gay films festivals in San Francisco, Berlin and Milan. A Dutch version of *Immediate Family* was made for prime-time network television in Holland.

Baum is a passionate believer in democracy, working on campaigns and running for office twice. She was the Green candidate for U.S. Congress in 2004. When she ran for Mayor of San Francisco in 2011, she made a difference and had a good time.

Starting in 2010, she has been one-half of The Crackpot Crones, performing subversive feminist comedy and improvisation with Carolyn Myers throughout the U.S.—and in Mexico as Las Rucas Locas. In 2014, Baum and Myers became, once again, Lilith Theater in order to produce *HICK: A Love Story*. Since then, she has performed *HICK* around the country, introduced the concept of using postcards as a form of political action, and written a blog (www.terrybaum.blogspot.com).

ABOUT CAROLYN MYERS

Carolyn was inspired to produce her first play at age eight, when she looked down the sidewalk and saw 20 discarded Christmas trees, some still tinseled. She dragged them home to create a backyard set for *Hansel and Gretel*. In eighth grade she helped create a passionate, if misguided, all-caucasian version of *A Raisin in the Sun*. In her senior year in high school, she directed the first student-written play the school had ever produced, *Nastley Quick and the Revolt of the Paper People*. In her senior year in college, Terry Baum directed Carolyn's play, *Jimmy Sodacracker*, the first student-written work the university had ever produced.

From the first, Carolyn has specialized in producing original plays written with, or by, her friends. She has been blessed with three spectacular theatrical partnerships: Terry Baum in The Isla Vista Community Theater, Lilith Theater, and The Crackpot Crones; Dori Appel in Mixed Company Theater (Ashland, Oregon), and The Crater Cabaret; and Cil Stengel in Planned Parenthood's Teen Theaters (including Duct Tape Theater and Ophelia Rising), and The Hamazons (a glamorous improvisation troupe).

Carolyn has directed the premiere productions of over a dozen solo shows, and many high school plays. She has written for *Changing Bodies, Changing Lives*, a teen health manual, and The *We'Moon Calendar*. Her epic poem *She-Bop*, about her life and hard times seeking The Goddess, was made into an animated film. Directing *Hick: A Love Story*, and editing *One Dyke's Theater* have been exhilarating projects of which she is very proud!

Collage Design & Photo Credits

These credits are woefully incomplete for two reasons. First: Some work was done long ago and we both don't remember and have no record of who did it. Second: Many of the posters were commissioned by independent producers (some in other countries), and we never had the information. If you see your photo or design in *One Dyke's Theater* and it's not credited, please contact the playwright with the information.

DOS LESBOS (p. 2) Photo with dog and duck: Nina Loricco

TWO MONOLOGS (p. 52) Upper Design: Lily Hillwomyn; Left Design and Photo: Margo Tufo; Right Design: Godelieve Smelt

IMMEDIATE FAMILY (p. 68) Central and left photos: Cammie Toloui

ONE FOOL (p. 90) Central photo: Cammie Toloui; Background photo: Terry Baum; Poster on right: Lucille Moquette

TWO FOOLS (p. 116) Poster on right: Design by Tim Lewis, photo by Nina Lorrico

WAITING FOR THE PODIATRIST (p. 166) All photos by Liz Payne; Upper left design: Bill Selby; Upper right design: Mary Wings

BUBBIE & HER BUTCH (p. 204) Central photo: Liz Payne; Upper design: Melissa Walker; Moms poster Design by Melissa Walker, photo by Holly Wallace; Holidays poster: Design by Bill Selby, photo by Liz Payne; Valentine's poster: Design by Melissa Walker, photo by Liz Payne

BRIDE OF LESBOSTEIN (p. 222) Central and lower left photos: Liz Payne; Lower right photo: Holly Wallace; Upper & lower right design by Melissa Walker; Lower left design: Margo Tufo

HICK: A Love Story (p. 258) Design: Bill Selby; Photo: Lynn Fried

MORE PLAYS FROM EXIT PRESS

Woyzeck, Pelleas and Melisande, Ubu Roi: translated by Rob Melrose

"Rob Melrose is a kind of magician, and his theater, Cutting Ball, is one of the most exciting and integrity-filled enterprises going in the sometimes-shabby field of the American theater. These translations, lucid and sharp, are a beautiful testimony to the value of Rob's achievement." — Oskar Eustis

Three Plays by Mark Jackson

"Playwright/director Mark Jackson has made his name as a first-class theatrical provocateur. Gutsy showmanship, brainy literary instincts and laser-sharp satire mark his canon." — San Jose Mercury News This collection of plays by Mark Jackson includes three plays based on incredible historic events: *God's Plot*, *Mary Stuart*, and *Salomania*.

Working For the Mouse by Trevor Allen

Ever wonder what really goes on at the Happiest Place on Earth? Trevor Allen answers this while recounting his tales of backstage debauchery, militant managers and his quirky coworkers in this unique coming-of-age tale that blows pixie dust in your eyes while offering a glimpse behind the ears of the Magic Kingdom. With four other plays.

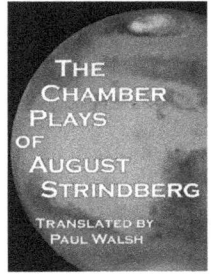

The Chamber Plays of August Strindberg translated by Paul Walsh

The Ghost Sonata, *The Pelican*, *The Black Glove*, *Storm*, and *Burned House*. Yale professor Paul Walsh provides modern translations while keeping Strindberg's "curiosity and his strangeness as specific and opaque as they are in the Swedish."

EXIT Press is the publishing division of EXIT Theatre, a San Francisco theater company founded in 1983. EXIT Press is distributed by Small Press Distribution of Berkeley, California.

www.exitpress.org

www.ingramcontent.com/pod-product-compliance
Lightning Source LLC
Chambersburg PA
CBHW050547160426
43199CB00015B/2572